THE ACHIEVEMENT OF
GREECE

LONDON: HUMPHREY MILFORD

OXFORD UNIVERSITY PRESS

THE ACHIEVEMENT OF GREECE

A CHAPTER IN HUMAN EXPERIENCE

BY

WILLIAM CHASE GREENE, Ph.D.

ASSISTANT PROFESSOR OF GREEK AND LATIN
IN HARVARD UNIVERSITY

πάθει μάθος

CAMBRIDGE

HARVARD UNIVERSITY PRESS

1924

PRINTED AT THE HARVARD UNIVERSITY PRESS

CAMBRIDGE, MASS., U. S. A.

TO

MY WIFE

PREFACE

TWO convictions underlie this book. The first is that true education means not merely the accumulation of information, but rather the gradual approach to a personal attitude and way of living. Such an approach, to be sure, must proceed from a body of sound experience that we may classify as information; but in the process we find ourselves dealing with it always in a more masterful fashion. Beginning, as it were, like humble errand-boys and peddlers, we learn to fling away the pack that once seemed so precious, as we discover new burdens and a new quest; and without ever quite losing sight of our earlier home or giving up a certain affection and loyalty toward it, we turn to the road as sportsmen and adventurers, or even, it may be, as crusaders and pilgrims marching toward a far country. The only danger in the transformation is that of a too sudden change, which may deprive us of all continuity and sense of direction. Even the explorer will not throw away his map and compass, eager though he may be to press on beyond the frontiers marked by his predecessors.

The second conviction underlying this book, accordingly, is the one more fully set forth in the first and in the last chapters: that no chart of human experience will speed the adventurer on his way so surely as that which records the achievement, in success and in failure, of the ancient Greeks. It will not take the place of his own experience; but it will save him many a false start, and will show him many a fair prospect that he will be glad to explore for himself.

Several of the following chapters have been presented, either in substance or in something like their present form, to various audiences, or have formed the basis of discussions with individuals. From all these persons, — from the boys at Groton School, from my students in Harvard University, in Radcliffe College, and in the Harvard Summer School, — as well as from my former teachers in Harvard University and in Oxford University, I have learned much. I am especially indebted for helpful criticisms to my colleagues Professor Clifford H. Moore and Professor Charles B. Gulick, who have read this volume in manuscript, and to Professor R. K. Hack, who, with Professor A. E. Phoutrides, of Yale University, has read it in proof. My father, Professor Herbert E. Greene, of Johns Hopkins University, not only has helped me with the proofs, but during an ocean voyage, now twenty years ago, gave me my first lessons in Greek, and awakened my interest in the achievement of Greece.

W. C. G.

CAMBRIDGE, MASSACHUSETTS
July, 1923

CONTENTS

x CONTENTS

THE ACHIEVEMENT OF GREECE

CHAPTER I

INTRODUCTION: ANCIENT GREECE AND
THE MODERN WORLD

FOR the study of things Greek there are several bad reasons and many good ones. About one hundred years ago, Dean Gaisford ended a Christmas sermon at Oxford with these words: "Nor can I do better, in conclusion, than impress upon you the study of Greek literature, which not only elevates above the vulgar herd, but leads not infrequently to positions of considerable emolument." In our time the argument sometimes turns a complete circle. "Why study Greek?" is the question. "In order to read certain books," comes the answer. "But why read these books?" "Because they are written in Greek." Sometimes, on the other hand, we are told that the study of Greek is to be avoided because it is not of any practical use. This remark seems to imply that there are other subjects of study which are of practical use. But as a matter of fact anything is of practical use only if it is used; and the most obviously practical subjects, — physics or medicine or economics, — are often the least used by those who praise them. Some things moreover, — tennis-rackets, and theatre-tickets, and keys, — though extremely useful for special purposes, are utterly useless for anything else; but muscles and eyes and social tact are everywhere useful. If the study of things Greek is of value, it is not because of its utility in special emergencies but because of a larger utility.

Men's motives in the most important things in life, such as the choice of an occupation or of a wife, are generally

3

complex. Yet the grounds for our interest in the ancient Greeks are surprisingly simple. We are interested in them because we find their experience of life singularly varied and profound, and at many points like our own. We find that in trying to understand their life we have probed most of the phases of our own life. A good deal of life is always spent in gaining what we call "experience"; this is different from what we mean when we speak of having "experiences." The difference may be made clear by a homely illustration. If I fall down stairs six times, and do not learn thereby how to avoid falling again, I have six distinct experiences, but I gain no experience. Life is too short, however, for us to gain all the experience that we need by first-hand and sometimes painful experiment: the most practical expedient is to borrow largely from the experience of others, both living and dead. And if we go beyond the experience of our contemporaries to the experience of the past, we find a larger field, in which issues are often more distinctly sifted than they seem to be to-day; from it we can return more confidently to the perplexities of modern life.

For life is a perplexing series of questions. The necessity of work and its effect on us, and the burdens of wealth and of poverty are always with us. Shall we trust, as the lower animals seem to trust, to natural impulses, or is man a different kind of animal, and is self-control as important as self-expression? Can we trust our senses and believe that the stream of change is everything, or must we suppose that something permanent persists through change, that there is unity as well as multiplicity? Do we want our poets and artists to be personal or impersonal, preservers of conventions or pioneers and iconoclasts? Does might make right? And if might does not make right, what does make it? What is the right of the state to govern the individual? Is any form of government, autocracy or democracy, necessarily best? What right has a small nation to exist? What is worth working for, and what, if anything, is worth fighting for? What is it in a man's life or in his country's that makes him willing to sacrifice even life itself to it, and to feel that the loss of life itself need then cause no regret? Is it the hope of personal glory, or of personal immortality, or of the survival of something else that man holds dear? Is this life, with its motley of good and evil, the result of blind forces, or the theatre of struggling wills, or the expression of a divine purpose? How can a good God will that there shall be suffering and evil? And are all questions to be answered by an appeal to authority, or to reason, or to intuition?

Stated in this baldly abstract form, these questions sound not only perplexing but perhaps also unattractive. We meet them, however, in forms both more concrete and less easy to cope with; we have definite choices to make, yet we are not sure just what the issue is. If we could find our problems embodied in human experience as concrete as ours, but with the issues more clearly defined, our choices would often be easier. It happens that the ancient Greeks within some few hundred years passed through an amazing variety of experiences that raised most of the human problems that men have ever had to meet; and in many of them, consciously or unconsciously, they also achieved experience. It would be too much to claim for them, as some rash friends of the Classics sometimes seem to claim, that the Greeks were supernaturally gifted in every way, and that we can take them as models for direct imitation. In some matters the ancient Greeks were ignorant or immoral; and they varied among themselves and at different periods. We gain nothing by indiscriminate eulogy of them. Nevertheless, in many fields they did learn so much that they are our spiritual ancestors; and it is worth while to follow in their foot-steps in order to see how their experiences led to experience. Some fields they made so much their own that we still use Greek words to designate them.[1] Even where they failed, — and their failures are often more apparent to us than they were to the Greeks themselves, — we can learn much; for failure is not infrequently more significant than success.

Most of us are less easily moved by discussions of abstract qualities than by living personalities. Here again the ex-perience of the Greeks appeals to us because it consists so largely of the acts and the points of view of intensely real individuals of whom we have vivid records. Achilles and Pheidias and Socrates are singularly tangible personalities, whose careers and characters are hardly less real to us than are those of many of our contemporaries. In fact, they are nearer to our own world of thought and expeﬁience than are most of the figures of the Middle Ages or even of much more recent times. They are good companions, good all-round men, who have to deal with many kinds of problems at once; they are generally sane, right-minded, lovers both of the practical and of the beautiful. They are not *unco guid*, and indeed we must always be ready to find them relapsing into selfishness, superstition, and cruelty; for theirs was a world still in the making. And so, we may add, is ours; persecu-tion for witchcraft is a matter of only yesterday, and we still have lynching, exploitation of some kinds of labor, patent medicines, irresponsible journalism, grotesque religious sects, and wars more devastating than ever. No one pre-tends that a knowledge of Attic drama or of Plato will

---

[1] For example: athletics, poetry, drama, epic, lyric, music, geography, physics, geometry, biology (a coinage of the nineteenth century), mechanics, astronomy, politics, democracy, economics, philosophy, ethics, metaphysics, theology.

directly solve all our problems: but it will go far to help us find our bearings. Good baseball players have been found to make good aviators; there is something in the process of understanding fundamental human experience that can be applied to any environment.

Such companionship with the Greeks is not altogether easy. We may see the country in which they lived, and some of their temples and theatres and statues; many of these things speak for themselves. We may read the narrative of some of their achievements as soldiers and statesmen. But for a more intimate companionship with them we need a common language. Much Greek literature can be more or less adequately translated into English; much cannot. The ancient Greek can speak modern English only haltingly; to speak with him we must, if possible, learn his language. But even a fair knowledge of the language is only a preliminary. Many a journalist who speaks the same language as the personage whom he interviews brings away an erroneous conception of him; he does not seize upon the relevant and significant remarks, and he fails to interpret correctly what he hears. For the same reason it is possible, even for one who knows the Greek language, to read extensively in Greek literature without any real understanding of it. He fails to see what is relevant, and what is negligible; he does not distinguish between what is a mere series of experiences and what is experience of lasting value; he cannot see the wood for the trees.

Real understanding of the Greeks, then, is a matter of interpretation. The present book cannot hope to give a complete and detailed account of their experience, still less of all their manifold experiences. It seeks rather to select certain significant phases of their experience, and to suggest the direction in which they point. Generalities without details are not convincing; details without context are bewildering. This book aspires to be neither a handbook of facts nor an abstract philosophy; it aims to be both more and less than either of these. For those who wish to learn more of the various matters here treated, lists of reading are provided. Any one who reads many of them will realize how much I am indebted to various works on these lists; and readers who are not already somewhat familiar with Greek civilization will find their reading of this book more profitable if they constantly supplement it with reading from these lists. Yet, though this book does not aim at giving a systematic and detailed account of the facts involved in the experience of the Greeks, it does seek constantly to support its statements by concrete illustrations, and, especially in dealing with the thought of the Greeks, its method is historical as well as critical. In a word, it aims to fall accurately between two stools; it attempts to give such exposition and interpretation of facts and problems as may stimulate the reader, who has to face many of the same problems, to make his own analysis and criticism.

Any interpretation of Greek experience runs the risk of betraying the bias of its author. It is easier to state facts than to deal judicially with the achievements of a race. I can hardly hope to avoid making judgments that others will not approve; but I prefer to challenge disagreement rather than merely to register harmless information. Many of the excellent books that discuss the Greeks seem to me somewhat defective in their method of approach. Some of them, like the average student of Greek literature, appear to find only a sequence of loosely related persons and events and ideas. They are aware of the trees, but not of the wood. Others, in their eagerness to find the unity of a picture in what they see, are inclined to beg questions and to assume that there was a single and definite Greek character or point of view; they are therefore reduced to the expedient of ignoring historical developments, and of treating as exceptional any tendency or figure, — even a Plato, — that does not fit into the picture. The true course, I am convinced, is to look for the unity, not of a picture, but of a growth that absorbs elements from different sources, and that is never complete and ready to be tied up in a neat bundle.

The present study is an attempt to see the experience of the Greeks, not as a bas-relief, but as sculpture in the round, or even as a fragment of drama; and that is its only claim to originality. We are mistaken if we seek to confine the experience of the Greeks to a formula; we must recognize its conflicting elements, and reckon with the *bon vivant* as well as the ascetic, the mystic as well as the rationalist, the average man in the back row of Aristophanes' audience no less than Plato, and Cleon no less than Pericles. That does not mean that all these elements are of equal significance and deserve equal attention, either for the Greeks or for us; or, on the other hand, that any of them are wholly bad or wholly without significance; but there they are, and we must make of them what we can. And the result is neither a compromise nor an Hegelian synthesis, but a recognition of tendencies among which we, like the Greeks, must at any rate find a *modus vivendi*. The Greeks, it is true, did at times strike a characteristic though precarious balance between conflicting tendencies; and it will be our concern in part to determine how far this balance was the result of sheer luck and how far it was their deliberate achievement, and how far it is possible or desirable for us to strike a similar balance. In the interest of fairness, however, we shall be content to find that some facts and stubborn tendencies simply will not fit into any nicely-balanced system of things; these are the loose ends of experience that the Greeks found troublesome and that we have not always been able to tie up neatly.

The scheme of this book is simple. We begin with the background of our drama, the country of Greece, and notice some of the features that influenced the course of its action. Then the actors enter, and we watch them as they pass rapidly from one phase of their development to another throughout history. Next, in succeeding chapters, we examine more closely their experience in certain activities. We investigate the effects of their daily lives; the character of their art and letters; their social and political adventures and ideals; and their attempts, by myth and religion, by science and philosophy, to explain man's larger environment, and his place in the universe.

The experience of the Greeks is for us in one sense a record of past achievement, and has the finality and repose of all things that lie in the past. The record is so nobly expressed that we are often the more tempted to pause in the sheer delight of passive contemplation. Greek poetry and sculpture and other activities seem to have a timeless value quite different from the no less remarkable discoveries in science that are now out of date and of only historical value. Unlike scientific statements, artistic experiences can be approached by no short cut or summary, but must be lived over again. But most of the issues that the Greeks first raised are not yet closed; we and our successors still have to deal with them. In this sense the ancient Greeks are not men of the past, but our contemporaries, and we have to determine our relation to them. Here the objective is not so much contemplation as action. Accordingly, this book ends with an attempt to discover the meaning of humanism. We must resist the temptation to be over-dogmatic; for too narrow a formula will stultify any conception of progress and new experience; yet we must be on our guard, too, against a notion of humanism so hazy that it loses all sense of direction. Not, then, by passive contemplation alone, or by servile imitation, and surely not by blind experiment, we may make our progress more sure-footed. History does not automatically repeat itself; but men who understand the experience of the past can better choose their course for the future.

CHAPTER II

THE BACKGROUND OF GREEK LIFE: GEOGRAPHY

WE are so much in the habit of thinking of the antiquity of the Greeks that we are apt to imagine them much further removed from us than we should. We call their history "ancient history," though it extends to the present moment; we sometimes call their language a "dead language," though it is spoken to-day, in no greatly altered form, by millions of Greeks. But if we are not yet convinced by these facts of the nearness of the Greeks, and are still inclined to think of them as a mythical people who live for us chiefly between the covers of books (mostly grammars and dictionaries, at that), there is no answer so convincing as a visit to Greek lands. For, although the great actors in the drama that we are to watch have left the stage to their interesting yet less brilliant descendants, and can be seen only by the eye of the imagination, the stage itself has hardly changed at all. Mountain and plain and sea are the same that Homer and Pericles knew. And the great influence that they have always had on the life of the Greeks makes it the more important for us to realize as vividly as we can what the country of Greece is like.

In spite of its small area, no country in the world has more variety than Greece; perhaps no country is more beautiful. Here the palm and the pine, the South and the North, join hands. The traveller passes, within a few miles, from the wild and sombre grandeur of the mountains of Epirus and Ætolia, a land of savage gorges and deep defiles, of forest and

12

cloudy sky, to the smiling vineyards of Elis, whose hillsides
are sprinkled with scarlet anemone and with narcissus and
daisy, where the almond tree is in flower before the blue iris
and the spiky asphodel and the crocus have left the fields.
In the valley of Sparta he finds oranges ripening and the
silvery gray of the olive trees shimmering in a soft wind; a
few miles above he sees the crest of Taygetus gleaming with
snow. Over the gulf of Corinth, a sheet more deeply blue
than lapis lazuli, tower the peaks of Parnassus and Helicon,
also snow-topped, with the narrow valley and ravine of
Delphi at their feet.

Unless the traveller has been warned, he will be surprised
to find most of Arcadia not the land of idyllic peace and
elegant shepherdesses that the poets have described, but
a bleak plateau, surrounded by rugged cliffs and a wilder-
ness of mountains. In the plain of Attica he will find himself in a different world: a plain bounded on one side by the
sea, on the others by mountains, the long bare outlines of
which are doubly distinct in the clear Attic atmosphere.
Greece is full of color; but there is no color in Greece to
rival the tints of the mountains of Attica, — Pentelicus, the
source of the marble of the Parthenon, Hymettus, whose
wild thyme affords a justly famous honey, and Parnes, —
and of its smaller crags, Lycabettus and the Athenian Acropolis. Russet and brownish purple and golden, they take on
a pink or a rosy flush at sunset, and by moonlight their
forms are intense blue. From the heights of Cape Sunium,
the eye wanders from one marble island to another stud-
ding the Ægean Sea. In the neighborhood of Athens one
can still walk among olive groves that mark the site of
Plato's Academy.

Indeed, one of the great charms of Greece is the survival
of buildings and other landmarks that tell of the successive

strata of human history. Now it is the cyclopean walls
of a prehistoric citadel that attract the eye; now it is the
massive golden columns of a temple. In the folds of a
mountain pass one comes upon a mediæval monastery,
flanked by tall cypresses; and one even finds monasteries
clinging to the perpendicular walls of precipices, or perched
on lofty pinnacles of rock that are accessible only by
ladders and rope-slung baskets. Here and there are the
castles of Frankish barons and Venetian princes; and the
minarets of a mosque tell of the Turkish occupation. Well-
built schools and hospitals bear witness even in the remote
islands to the new Greece that is growing up after centuries
of foreign domination. And the people of modern Greece
are a lively and intelligent nation in whom many types
are mingled. In the course of a walk in the outskirts of
Athens one may meet a village priest, with his long, black
beard and his long, black hair tied in a knot under his
tall, round hat; schoolboys wearing on their caps a button
with the owl of Athene, the emblem of wisdom; soldiers clad
in the petticoat costume of the Albanian race; shepherds
with their shaggy, undyed cloaks, carrying crook and gun;
and peasants driving their goats to market.

If we could borrow the wings of Hermes, the great traveller among the gods, and soar over the mainland of Greece,
we should at once be struck by the extraordinary ruggedness
of the coast-line.[1] Not only the great fiords of the Corinthian and the Saronic gulfs, which all but completely sever
the Peloponnese from the rest of Greece, but innumerable
smaller gulfs and bays indent the coast; and in every direction, but especially off to the eastward, appear countless

---

[1] The outline of the Peloponnese has been variously compared to a mul-
berry leaf and to the webbed foot of a duck; but neither of the comparisons is
really adequate.

islands. So it need hardly surprise us that, although the whole of Greece proper, of which perhaps more than half can be seen from the lofty crag above Corinth, contains an area rather smaller than that of the state of Pennsylvania, its coast-line is almost as long as the whole Atlantic seaboard of the United States, from Maine to Florida. No part of the country, therefore, is more than a few miles from the sea. Almost as striking as the length of the coast-line is the aggressiveness of the mountain-ranges, which cover about four fifths of the country. Toward the west they drop steeply to the Adriatic Sea, affording few footholds for the homes of men; but they slope more gently from the northwest toward the southeast, with more numerous plains and harbors. Thus Greece "turns her back on Europe," and invites relations with the East. Even to-day the mountains are a considerable barrier to intercourse; each valley and coastal plain tends to be a self-contained unit, and to find its associations not so much with the plains across the mountains as with those on neighboring islands. Greece, therefore, is not so much a part of Europe as a part of the rim of the Mediterranean Sea; and as such it partakes of the Mediterranean character in climate and vegetation and way of living.

The mountains of the Greek world seem to have been thrown up in a cataclysm comparatively recently in the history of the earth's surface, as geologists argue from their jagged outlines, which appear with incomparable distinctness in the clear atmosphere of Greece. Rising abruptly from the sea, they remind one of mountains that tower above the lakes of Switzerland, often being capped with snow late in the summer. The plain of Thessaly appears to be the bed of a former lake that has subsided, probably at the time that the trident of Poseidon rent Mt. Pelion from Mt. Ossa, ac-

cording to the legend. Many of the islands of the Ægean
Sea, too, mark continuations of the mountain-ranges of the
mainland, which have subsided; and some of the narrow
straits are only submerged river-valleys. The island of San-
torin (the ancient Thera) is only the rim of a volcano that
has nearly disappeared.

Greek mountains consist mostly of marble and other
forms of limestone, and their summits are almost always
bare.[1] Some, to be sure, are higher than the line at which
trees are found in the Alps; but even the lower ranges are
usually bare. Many of these were once wooded, but have
lost their forests in the course of centuries; the trees have
been swept away by fires, or cut down wantonly by the
Greeks and the Turks, and the mountain-ranging goats have
nibbled up what was left by the hand of man. During the
greater part of the year the air is so dry that vegetation cannot find in the mountains the moisture that it needs. Even
on the lower slopes the forests have been greatly denuded in
the search for timber and fuel and resin, so that few forests
exist to-day except in northwestern Greece. Even the ship-
builders of ancient Greece had to bring timber from the
Black Sea. Still, there are woods of evergreens and of smaller
leafy trees; the oak, the plane, and the chestnut are common,
and even among the rocks there are sparse growths of bushes,
— scrub-oak and juniper and oleander.

As in all the Mediterranean countries, the climate is temperate. Sudden changes of weather are rare; the difference
is between the dry and the rainy season, and spring is short.
In Attica there are about three hundred sunny days in the
year; snow falls perhaps half-a-dozen times. However hot
the day may be, there is generally a sea breeze in the early
morning and a land breeze in the evening. Where almost all

[1] Such islands as Paros and Naxos are almost wholly of white marble.

the rain falls within a few months, it naturally falls with the force of a torrent; and that is one of the reasons for the absence of real rivers in Greece, as well as for the deforestation. There are no rivers that can be navigated by anything larger than a small boat; most of them are torrents in winter, and dry ravines or rocky gullies in summer, with nothing more than a trickle of water, and hard to cross in any season. Greek streams, too, have an odd way of disappearing underground, sometimes to reappear farther down, sometimes to lose themselves permanently.[1]

Between the mountains and the plains are the pasture-lands, where shepherds and goatherds tend their flocks. The sheep and the goats do not enjoy the luxury of grassy meadows, for the plough claims every foot of land that can possibly be cultivated; so they range the foot-hills or even the higher slopes, and forage among the prickly bushes till the winter snows drive them down to the lowlands. Since there are no walls or hedges to confine the flocks, the herdsmen and their dogs lead an active life.

In the flat valleys between the mountains, as at Sparta, and in the alluvial plains bordering the sea, as at Athens and Argos, are the farmlands. Almost every inch of this precious land is under cultivation; for of the total area of Greece barely one fifth is fit for the plough, yet has to support the people. Though Greece as a whole is rocky and barren, this land is very fertile. In earlier days each valley or plain, walled in on all sides by mountain or sea, was self-contained and self-supporting, till the population grew and trade overseas supplemented the crops. Somewhere on a spur of the mountain-side, or even on a rocky hill in the midst of the plain, the farmers had a citadel or acropolis to which they

[1] Hence such myths as that of the flight of the nymph Arethusa in Greece and her reappearance in her spring in Sicily.

could retreat in case of invasion; and they always tended, as they do to-day, to live together sociably in villages, rather than in scattered homesteads.

The Mediterranean climate is friendly to the farmer. Grain (chiefly wheat and barley), wine, and olives are the staple products. The grain was eaten by the older Greeks as bread or as porridge; the wine was always drunk mixed with water. Meat and fish had no large place in their menu. The olive tree was one of the most treasured possessions of the Greeks; it was given to Athens, they believed, by Athene herself, and grew in even the most rugged regions, but was usually planted in trim rows. It is no wonder that the tree was prized; for its fruit and oil gave the Greeks all that they had in the way of butter, of soap, and of illumination. Though the cultivation of the olive requires no great toil except in the picking, it was some years before young trees came to bear; and the damage caused by the destruction of them in warfare could not easily be replaced. Of other trees, the older Greeks had figs in abundance, apples, pears, and pomegranates; but oranges, lemons, and peaches, which now flourish in Greece, were introduced later. Since the Middle Ages, the small grape which we call the currant has been cultivated; many vineyards are planted with it along the Gulf of Corinth, from which indeed the currant takes its name. It is now one of the chief exports of Greece. Only in very recent years have modern methods of farming been introduced into Greece, especially in Bœotia. The iron plough was unknown half a century ago; and there are still peasants who know only the wooden forked stick that was used in Homer's day. Even plains so rich as those of Thessaly suffer from lack of irrigation and drainage, and from malaria and the former depredations of Turks and brigands.

The coast of Greece is nearly everywhere rocky; there are in few places what we should call a beach. For this reason a storm was for the Greek mariner a serious matter; and he never sailed, if he could help it, in winter. The prevailing wind in summer (the "Etesian" wind) is northerly; most of the harbors in Greece therefore face to the south.[1] An anchorage was, however, not necessary in ancient times, for the absence of tides in the Mediterranean made it quite easy for sailors to haul their boats up on the shore when they were in port and to launch them again for the voyage. But if there are no tides, there are strong currents; for the Mediterranean is almost entirely land-locked, and being more shallow than the Atlantic, receives a constant flow of water through the straits of Gibraltar, as well as through the Dardanelles. These currents often baffled the sailor who was bound for the western coast of Italy or for the Black Sea; so that, rather than risk the dangers of Scylla and Charybdis (the straits between Italy and Sicily) and the narrows of the Dardanelles, the ship-master often preferred to land his cargo and carry it along the coast. More than one town, as we shall see, waxed fat by charging toll for the portage. Pirates were another source of danger. The Greek sailor, therefore, having no accurate charts, tended to navigate only the familiar coasts of his own seas, clinging to the shore, or cruising from island to island.

That the geography of Greece has always had a great influence on the life of its inhabitants is a truism. Some historians, to be sure, have tried to explain history almost wholly in terms of geography — climate, mountain-ranges,

---

[1] Since the mouths of the few rivers were usually obstructed by silt, we find harbors more often near them than at them; a trade-route might follow the river-valley, but would be by land.

trade-routes, and the like. But that is too much like explaining the action of a drama chiefly by the scenery and leaving out of consideration the characters. We shall try to recognize what the Greeks did by free choice and under the influence of their national and individual tempers; but it is worth while to keep constantly in mind the background against which they are seen, the mould in which their actions are cast. Often we shall find that a detail of geography — the form of a battlefield, or the occurrence of a storm — influenced history almost accidentally. But other elements are so permanent that we are justified in considering them almost as parts of the Greeks themselves.

Herodotus, an experienced traveller, remarks that of all countries Greece enjoys by far the best-tempered climate. Aristotle has a similar judgment; the dwellers in the colder regions of Europe, he says, are energetic, but deficient in intelligence and artistic skill, whereas the Asiatics are intelligent and artistic, but lack energy; the Greeks, however, occupying geographically an intermediate position, partake of both qualities, and are equally energetic and intelligent. An impartial judge might well agree with this opinion; for Greece is so endowed by her climate as to render activity necessary and reflection not impossible. The barrenness of much of the land, moreover, means that only persistent, though not incessant, toil is the price at which a living can be won. Even the hardest toil, however, could not feed a growing population on the produce of the small plains of Greece; agriculture had to be supplemented by warfare and by industry and foreign trade, and finally by colonization, by which Greek civilization was destined to be spread abroad.

Wars for the control of trade-routes were sure to follow. The seas that surround Greece, with their islands and numerous harbors, invite the sailor. We shall not be surprised to find a more adventurous spirit and a more lively imagination among the sailing peoples of Greece than among their inland cousins. Yet such is the compactness of Greece that all its inhabitants were familiar with varied kinds of life: mountain, plain, and sea, with all their multitudinous interests, entered into their ways of thinking. Versatility was the natural result. On the other hand, the barriers of mountain and sea, which tended to keep the Greeks in small compartments, and the hills that seemed intended by nature to become walled citadels, encouraged the preservation of small units, — the "city-states," — with all the intense provincialism of civic pride, which only slowly gave way to national cohesion; and even when something like Hellenism was felt, it did not interfere with the individuality of the Athenian or the Argive. The city-state — like the school or the club or the local guild — might err by excess of devotion to its own little circle of ideas; but it had the merit of developing without undue interference whatever individual excellences the Greeks had. Various arts and sciences and political forms sprang up and reached maturity in small communities before they were fused in the larger world of Greece.

And, finally, the beauty of the Greek lands sank deeply into the minds of their inhabitants, and taught them to think in terms of beauty. If they were not given to sentimentalizing about nature, there is ample evidence of their susceptibility to its appeal. Nor is it altogether fanciful to suppose that the clearly defined outlines of the Greek landscape, seen through the transparent atmosphere of Greece, had something to do with the simplicity and definiteness of Greek architecture and sculpture; it is even possible that they are in part responsible for the clearly defined images in which the Greeks conceived their gods, and for their avoidance in their political and philosophical speculation of all that is vague and subject to no logical bounds.

These are a few of the matters that must occur to any one who thinks of the land of Greece as the background of a human drama. We must now watch the entry of the actors and the unfolding of the drama itself.

CHAPTER III

MEN IN THE MAKING: THE GREEKS IN HISTORY

1. THE FORERUNNERS OF THE GREEKS

W E live to-day in many ways at second hand. Though the child learns at first by experimenting with his hands, his later education trains him more and more to avail himself of the experience of others; he makes his experiments by proxy. In this there is doubtless an element of loss, if the child loses the ability to act and think for himself. But there is a corresponding gain, because he can build on the foundation of past experience. Originality does not have to begin at the beginning. The kitten doubtless thinks no other kitten ever tried to catch its own tail; and the kitten never learns that the thing cannot be done. And for primitive races to-day there is little garnered experience for the individual to appropriate and to surpass.

For us in the twentieth century, with our tools and facilities for transportation, with the possibility of storing things for future needs and of exchanging them economically for other things, above all, with the knowledge given us by written records about other times and other parts of the earth, it takes a vigorous imagination to realize the life of primitive men who have none of these advantages. Yet the first men had no more property than they could carry on their backs, no more food than the next meal, no more information about the region beyond the hills or the sea than they could get by hearsay or by hard travel. Life was more than a struggle; it was a game of chance in which the dice were loaded; for neither the forces of nature nor other men, except those of the same blood, were constantly friendly. The waste of human life must have been enormous; the single life counted for almost nothing.

Even to-day the forces of nature have been imperfectly mastered; a shipwreck or a famine is a reminder of our close dependence on the soil and the winds. The earliest races of which we know are governed largely by their need of finding areas in which they can wring a living from nature by hunting, grazing, or farming, and of keeping other races, if they can, from using these areas. If they cannot hold their fields and pastures, they must move on, with what chattels they can carry, to new territories, or they will be enslaved or exterminated.

Such was the story of the earliest inhabitants of the countries to the east and to the south of the Mediterranean; the fertile river-valleys of the Euphrates and the Nile harbored tribes in constant flux and in constant conflict. And in much the same way the Balkan Peninsula and the islands of the Ægean Sea became the home of successive hordes of invaders; each horde clung to the strips of vegetation that would feed man or beast, until in their turn they were pushed further by new invaders. Those invaders whom we call Greeks found the Ægean world already in the possession of an older, and in some ways a more civilized, population. Who they were, and how they reached this region, written history has not told us; but the spade of the archæologist has within recent years let us see how they lived. These small dark men had made their home in this part of the world as early as the late Stone Age, and were still there at the end of the Bronze Age, a period of some three thousand years. Though they built citadels in Greece and the Cyclades and even in the Troad, and carried on a friendly commerce with Egypt and the western Mediter-

ranean, it was in Crete that their civilization was oldest and
flourished most. So it is not unfair to Mycenæ and to Troy
if we call this age, after the legendary lord Minos of Crete,
the Minoan Age. The discovery of Minoan objects in Egypt
and of Egyptian objects in Crete has enabled the archæologists to date this age within general limits. The first great
palace at Cnossos, already the heir of centuries of civilization, must have been built about 2200 B.C.; the last palace
was destroyed about 1400, and the Minoan Age came to an
end not long after.

We cannot but admire even the earliest of the works of
art that have come down to us from these precursors of the
Greeks; the very pottery of the late Stone Age has a sturdy
vigor in its zig-zag patterns. Some time after the use of
bronze was discovered, the Cretans learned to adorn their
wares with fanciful curves and with colors. At times they
imitated metal utensils with their pottery; at other times
they painted animals and scenes from human life. They
even developed a very beautiful faïence, and moulded in it
the figure of a nature goddess, and made terra-cotta images
of bulls and antelopes. They turned to the sea for patterns,
and painted its life — flying fish, and sea-weeds, and shells,
and the octopus. For it was to the sea that they owed their
prosperity; and the kings of Crete must have had willing
subjects and powerful navies, to build such luxurious and
intricate palaces and to defend them, without fortifications,
though they were so near the sea.

From the terraced ruins, with their ample halls and stairs,
from the frescoed walls and the reliefs, and from the huge
jars and the well-constructed plumbing, we can form a vivid
idea of the life of the age, even though the picture-writings
and the linear writings that have been found mean as yet
almost nothing to us. We see an active, artistic people,

chiefly employed in agriculture and handicrafts and sailing
for trade. We see their men, dressed in a loin-cloth and high
boots, or armed with a leather cap and a flexible shield bent
like a figure 8, and equipped with sword and spear; and we
are familiar with their women's costume, not unlike that of
Italian peasants, with its full skirt and tight bodice. We
have some idea of the religious notions of these people: at
first they worshipped the fertility of nature, using as emblems only pillars and double axes; later they made images
of the goddess Mother attended by doves or holding snakes.
From this it seems that their worship included the heavens
as well as the earth; and they appear also to have offered
sacrifice to the dead. The shrines were always in the palace;
apparently religion was under the control of the king, who
may have been chief priest as well. Typical of his political
power are the great throne at Cnossos and the lists of treas-
ures, if such they be; all point to a despotism.

During the latter part of the Minoan period, strongholds
grew up in other parts of the Ægean world, often built on
hillocks at a slightly greater distance from the sea, and
better fortified, since they could not rely for protection on a
navy. Sometimes they were founded, as it appears, at
points dominating trade-routes; so Mycenæ, "rich in gold,"
may have levied toll on the travellers through the mountain
pass from the Corinthian Gulf into the Argolid plain; and
the inhabitants of the successive towns of Troy, built just
opposite that part of the Dardanelles where winds and currents held back the sailor and forced a portage, may have
harried the trade that passed through, exacting tribute or
customs — tariff profiteers in their day.[1] At any rate, the
"Cyclopean" wall of Mycenæ, the lintel of its gate surmounted by a panel showing in relief a pillar guarded by two

[1] Cf. G. Murray, *Rise of the Greek Epic*, pp. 55–61.

lions, its "bee-hive" tombs, and its wealth of gold masks and ornaments, shows many traits in common with the civilization of Minoan Crete — more, to be sure, in its ritualistic emblems and its method of burial and in the scenes depicted on its vases and daggers than in its architecture. If the strong fortifications and the arched galleries of compact Tiryns and the great walls and bastions of the sixth city of Troy have little in common with the broad-spread palaces of Cnossos, still the mosaics and frescoes of Tiryns and the beautiful golden cups found at Vaphio, near Sparta, show that the life was not different.

2. The Coming of the Greeks: The Heroic Age

For centuries this life continued; then suddenly it came to an end. Cnossos was destroyed about 1400, the better fortified citadels of the Ægean world perhaps a century or two later, and civilization seems to have been set back for several hundred years. What caused the eclipse, we do not know in detail; but we shall not be far wrong if we attribute it to the first of the great waves of invasion that swept down from the north. Various branches of the race later to be known as the Greeks, forced by other tribes still farther north, pressed down into the mainland of Greece and across the Ægean. Perhaps there was first a period of peaceful penetration, during which the newcomers got a foothold; then there was warfare. The peoples of the Minoan world, dark, artistic, worshippers of a nature goddess, subjects of a despot, sailors at heart, fell before the onslaught of these fair northerners, horse-tamers and wielders of iron swords, carrying round shields, men who worshipped the gods of the sky, and who had already learned something of social organization and fair play. Though it was long before the

newcomers learned to write or to adorn the necessities of life
or to sail extensively, they were soon able to subdue the old
inhabitants, who now lost their independent existence.
Sometimes, no doubt, they were exterminated or driven out
of the Ægean area; more often they remained as serfs, and
the two races were fused, as the English and the Normans
were fused after the Conquest. Perhaps the older inhabitants are those whom the later Greeks, in their puzzled state
of mind, called Pelasgians; or possibly the Pelasgians represent an intermediate people. We must allow, too, for a certain amount of approximation of the newcomers to the older
inhabitants, caused by the very conditions of living imposed
by the Mediterranean world; only those of the blood of the
invaders who were physically fit to live in this region long
survived.[1] In cases where, as at Sparta, the invaders refused
to mingle with their predecessors, the result was in the end
not fortunate, for it meant a divided house. It may be that
Attica had least Greek blood of all the Greek states, and
merely learned the Greek language from its conquerors;
Herodotus said the Athenians were "not Greek but Pelasgians," and the Athenians themselves always boasted that
they were not immigrants but children of the soil.

Though the invaders stamped out the civilization that
they found, they lived with it so long that they were not altogether unaffected by it. They never forgot that heroes
before them had cleared the world of lions and other beasts.
With the worship of sky-gods they incorporated the worship
of an earth-goddess, in various forms. As they built permanent settlements, they made use in their incipient art of
motives caught from their conquered subjects — designs
from vases, and the rudiments of the Doric temple developed
in part from the Mycenæan palace. The myths, also, pre-

[1] Cf. J. L. Myres, *Greek Lands and the Greek People*, pp. 19–23.

serve in many forms the reconciliation of the religions; the gigantomachy typifies the struggle; the dethronement of Cronos by Zeus and the conversion of Minos, perhaps once a god, into a king, embody the results.

Why the Ægean civilization succumbed so easily and so completely to the newcomers is a matter of conjecture. The very perfection of the material well-being enjoyed by the lords of Cnossos may have been a source of weakness, if it measured a decay in hardihood and vitality; and the despotic character of the government and the unequal distribution of wealth may have made the common people ready for a revolution. The Russian Revolution of 1917 would be a partial parallel. It may be, too, that the settlements were weakened by the departure as colonists of many of the most enterprising men.

From the region north of the Balkan Peninsula, then, the Greek tribes were forced down into the Ægean world. In a succession of great waves they filtered through the mountain passes and the valleys, lingering till new waves of invasion forced them still farther south and east, and finally some of them sailed from island to island of the Ægean and passed over to the coasts of Asia Minor, leaving settlements on the islands. For centuries the tide flowed into Greece. Though the details are obscure, it appears that the first great wave brought the "Achæans" [1] into the greater part of the mainland of Greece. Next, again under pressure from the north, they sent bands of adventurers across to the islands and the northwest coast of Asia Minor, to which the name of "Æolia," belonging to their fellows the Æolians, was accidentally given. During these migrations the Achæans

---

[1] A general name including many tribes — such as the Achæans, the Æolians, the Hellenes, the Danaoi, and those who later settled in Asia Minor and were there called Ionians.

came into conflict with the Ægean inhabitants of the Troad, whose leaders, at least, were not Orientals but northern invaders not unlike themselves. They did not forget, as we shall see, their weary years of conflict with the defenders of Troy. Other settlements in the central part of the west coast of Asia Minor were called by the general name of Ionia, because they were founded by a different branch of the "Achæans," who had settled in Attica and the islands. Before the conflict of the Greeks with the inhabitants of Troyland had ended, the Dorians, not mere colonists but a nomadic tribe, began to filter through many parts of the Greek mainland, and passed eventually even to the southwest coast of Asia Minor; they left communities in central Greece, dominated sacred Delphi, and controlled Corinth and Laconia. Full of race-consciousness, they seldom mingled with their predecessors, and remained to the end practical, conservative, and, with rare exceptions, uninspired.

The life of the "Achæan" adventurers during these centuries was full of martial exploits.[1] Border forays innumerable, expeditions to distant lands, and memories of "old, unhappy, far-off things, and battles long ago" with the older dwellers in Greece filled their minds. The prowess of individual heroes became the subject of ballads, sung in the halls of lords in northern Greece. When they crossed to Lesbos and then to Troyland, the Achæan and Æolian singers already knew many a tale of the deeds of famous men, perhaps among them that of the wrath of the tribal hero, Achilles, against another chieftain, Agamemnon, who

[1] For a vivid and imaginative reconstruction of the emigration by sea, cf. G. Murray, *Rise of the Greek Epic*, pp. 72–75. A fine poem, expressing the spirit of this period, is R. M. Heath's "Achilles" (Newdigate Prize Poem, Oxford, 1911).

had taken his captive from him. Other tales grew up of the deeds of "Achæan" heroes in the land of Troy and of their unhappy return. For centuries the sagas were sung in the courts of the "Achæan" lords and at the Ionian festivals. Then a great artist, who used the Ionian speech, conceived the notion of uniting in a long poem many lays and of setting forth the struggles of the "Achæans" with the men of Troy and their allies. Somewhat indifferent to considerations of historical accuracy,[1] he transferred to Asia Minor many an incident which long tradition had brought from the Achæan mainland; he used the wrath of Achilles as a motive to give unity to the poem; he carelessly introduced not a few customs of his own age; and he did his best to adapt the language of the older Æolian singers to his own Ionian tongue and to the rapid hexameter of the Ionians. The man we need not fear to call Homer; the poem is the "Iliad."[2] Whether it is a folk epic or a literary epic is an idle question; it is both a folk epic and a literary epic. And though in one sense the unity of the poem is due, as I have said, to the choice of a single phase of the Trojan War, in a larger sense it achieves its unity by reflecting in concentrated form all that the Greeks were or thought they were in the age of the heroes. Whether Helen ever lived or not, matters very little; what does matter is that the Greeks could now believe in her. If she was not actual, she was real. Achilles might be a fable; the bitterness, the brief glory, and the broken-hearted chivalry of Achilles was no myth when thousands of Greeks accepted it as the noblest thing they knew. These things to

[1] For a mediæval analogy, see "The Saracen Siege of Paris," by W. W. Comfort, N. Y. *Nation*, Jan. 11, 1919.

[2] It is impossible here to go into the "Homeric question." A sane discussion may be found in J. W. Mackail's address, "How Homer came into Hellas," followed by an exchange of remarks between him and G. Murray. (*Proceedings of the English Classical Association*, Vol. VI, 1909, pp. 5–19.)

them spelled the meaning of their past; and if their understanding of the past was not at all points true, at least it was for many hundred years the guide of their actions.

Not many years after the "Iliad" was composed, the "Odyssey" took form. For our purposes, it is not of great importance whether it comes from the same author as the "Iliad" or is the product of another. It brings before us, as it brought before the Greeks, the same world of wonders and of beauty, the same conception of human destiny that is the burden of the "Iliad." The two poems may have survived in oral tradition for several centuries before they were written down.[1] Because of disagreements about the real words of Homer, an edition of the poems was published at Athens in the sixth century under the instructions of the Peisistratidæ.[2] Homer was now a book, and shared the fate of books. Lecturers explained him, critics attacked or defended him, schoolboys studied him, rhapsodes recited him, and cities claimed him.[3]

There is always a temptation to see in any great work of art more than its author intended — more indeed than it can possibly be or mean. So, for example, we are apt to read between the lines of Shakspere a philosophy that the poet would probably disown; and the mysterious smile of Mona

[1] The schoolboy Niceratus was forced by his father to memorize the whole of Homer, as we learn from Xenophon; and though modern peoples have weakened their memories by their dependence on writings, Lord Macaulay knew by heart a large part of "Paradise Lost."

[2] The evidence for this statement is late; and it can no longer be held that the text was changed in the interest of Athens. See J. A. Scott, *The Unity of Homer*, pp. 46–72; and D. B. Monro, ed. *Odyssey*, pp. 402 ff.

[3] The rivalry implied in the Greek hexameter lines that told of this claim is hardly conveyed by the often quoted English version:

"Seven wealthy towns contend for Homer dead,
Through which the living Homer begged his bread."

Lisa has been the pretext for interpretation, romance, and rhapsody. But it is also true that great artists frequently paint and build and write better than they know; the Gothic cathedral is in a sense the epitome of centuries of civilization. Probably nothing was further from the purpose of the poet whom we call Homer than to compose a handbook of history or of archæology, a treatise on religion, or a model for future poets; his object was doubtless merely to tell a tale. Yet the "Iliad" and the "Odyssey" do unconsciously bridge a gap in history, and answer many questions of the archæologist; they did provide the Greeks for centuries with something like a Bible; and they have been imitated, in details or in larger aspects, by countless later poets. The reason is not obscure; the poet by a happy accident composed his poems at just that moment in the history of the Greeks when they were emerging from helplessness into self-mastery and self-consciousness, from a nomadic life into settled life, from brutal superstition into reverence and reflection; he was still near enough to the hard facts of life not to lose his grip on them, yet he was just far enough from them to see them with the outlines somewhat softened. Facing the dim past with its conflicting legends, he told what he knew without moralizing and without sentimentalizing. And if he was, with Hesiod, responsible for the orderly development of the primitive notions of the Greeks about the gods, as Herodotus says, his achievement was one of harmonizing, not of invention.

It is no wonder, therefore, that the Greeks looked upon Homer as their guide in all matters. The old inhabitants of the Ægean world, with all their material prosperity, may have had their local legends; but it is doubtful whether they had anything that could, like the poems of Homer, gather together their experiences in such a form that men could think deeply about them. With the Homeric poems it was different; the stories of Achilles and of Odysseus, recited by the rhapsodes throughout the Greek world, not only were stirring tales, but prompted action. Even in the time of Pericles a Pheidias moulded a Zeus in the likeness of him whom Homer had sung; down to the time of Alexander, men strove to be like Achilles, as the Jews tried to be like David; and schoolboys, hoping to become generals, studied the exploits of the Achæans before Troy. But the study was becoming more and more "literary," a subject for the critics and the scholiasts; for the Greeks had passed through new experiences. The ideas of Homer about the gods were doubtless in advance of his time, or they would not have swayed men's minds for so many years. But the age of reason could point at many moral flaws in Homer's gods and heroes; a Xenophanes could ridicule the "Bible of the Greeks" with criticism, and a Plato must expurgate it. It was of no avail for the defenders of Homer to allegorize their poet and to turn his gods into moral qualities; Homer must stand as a poet or not at all. And as a poet he held his own; in politics, in religion and ethics, in practical affairs, he was surpassed; but he held his own as a teller of stirring tales in swift and musical verse, and as the poet who had told what life and death and joy and sorrow had meant to men who had lived intensely. More than this he had never pretended to do.

3. THE GROWTH OF GREECE

Though the Homeric poems cannot be read as history, they do give us something like evidence about many phases of life during the centuries that saw the coming of the Greeks into Greece and their struggles in Asia Minor. After their voice is stilled, there is silence for several centuries, and

hardly a single witness tells us just what happened. By the
time that records again tell us anything, the Greeks are
settled in Greece, and their life is very different from that of
the Homeric warriors. The gap in our knowledge is bridged
in many ways. The Greeks themselves in later times bridged
it by poetry and myth, and with elaborate genealogies tried
to connect themselves with their god-descended ancestors;
partly unconsciously they used these myths to draw nearer
to each other, though national feeling was imperfectly realized before a national peril brought the Greeks together.
The gaps in our knowledge are further bridged by later
legends and tales preserved by the historians and the dramatists. This dark age [1] veils many changes; the results
appear when clear history begins in the seventh century.
Yet Hesiod, who wrote probably not later than 750 B.C.,
serves in a sense as a stepping-stone. He looks back, in the
"Theogony," to the world of gods and heroes of which
Homer wrote; but, unlike Homer, his interest is also, as we
find in the "Works and Days," in common men and their
toils, and even in the individual common man; and the lyric
poets deal chiefly with the affairs of the individual and of
the moment. Of the five ages concerning which Hesiod
writes, the golden and the silver are gone, and the bronze
age, too; the age of the heroes is a thing of the past, and
Hesiod himself lives in the age of iron, when justice has fled
the earth, and men must toil for a living. Not till some centuries later did the Greeks learn to see the golden age in the
future, and not till still later did Christianity try to find it
potentially in the present. In Hesiod's time the plain fact
was that life *was* hard, especially for those who enjoyed no
privileged station.

[1] It might be called the second "dark age" of Greek history; the first lay
between the Ægean civilization and the age of Homer's heroes.

Yet privileges were being questioned, and we can see in historical times the last stages of a devolution of power that first made away with kings, next tolerated aristocratic governments for a time, then let clever tyrants pose as the people's champions, and finally did away with them in favor of some more truly democratic form of government. The sequence was by no means universally carried out; Sparta preserved to the end the semblance of a monarchy, though actually controlled by an aristocratic clique. But where the sequence was uninterrupted, each of the forms of government in its turn accomplished invaluable work. It was the merit of the kings that they succeeded in welding together the rural tribes and villages into city-states, the most characteristic expression of Greek political development. The aristocracies provided a larger fund of talent on which the state could draw, and often neutralized the possibilities of mismanagement. When they had forfeited the confidence of the people, the tyrants (by whom the Greeks meant merely unconstitutional monarchs, who might be either good or bad) stabilized government, and in order to maintain their popularity built splendid public works and were lavish patrons of artists and poets. Like Louis XI of France and Henry VII of England, the tyrants found that the readiest way of strengthening the monarchy was to weaken the aristocracy; unconsciously they were at the same time removing the obstacles for a democracy that was soon to clamor for the overthrow of tyrants. An easy way of removing political opponents as well as of increasing trade and finding an outlet for the population was to encourage enterprising men of a troublesome nature to found colonies. The first wave of Greek colonial expansion had spent itself in the Ægean; now the Greeks sent colonists into the Black Sea and dotted with settlements the shores of the Mediterranean even as far as

the Pillars of Heracles. Only gradually did they learn that
"peaceful penetration" and "spheres of influence" are apt
to prove to be the seeds of future wars. Next, the rise of
democratic governments solved some old problems and
raised new ones. Whether a Draco was codifying the laws
or a Solon was removing economic injustices, the goal was
always the same — the liberating of the individual through
his orderly use of a share in the state. However crude the
method, the aim itself was an enormous advance over the
lawless marauding and the arbitrary wills of Homer's heroes,
though the idea of justice toward foreigners had hardly yet
appeared.

Nevertheless, though the barbarian was entitled to scanty
consideration, a Greek of the seventh century no longer regarded his own tribe as the vessel of all that was good, or
thought that a war with his neighbors beyond the mountains
or on the next island was to be fought without some sort of
pretext. Several things had brought about this result. The
poets who had sung of the old heroes and who had contrived to mingle the family trees of many noble houses had
led the various states to think of their common stock; above
all, Homer had reminded them of their joint undertaking
against the common enemy in Troyland — a legend, as we
have seen, that may have had but a slender basis of fact, at
least so far as the unity of the Greeks is concerned. As Homer
had spoken of all the Greeks under the name of one of the
divisions, the Achæans, or the Hellenes, these later Greeks
accepted the name of Hellenes, much as England to-day is
named for but one of several tribes that conquered the island.
It is easy to forget differences in the pride of ancient achievements; how many Americans to-day, whose fathers were
born in Italy or Poland, sing without conscious irony of the
"Land where my fathers died, Land of the Pilgrims' pride"?

Still more powerful in the growth of national feeling was the force of the Olympian religion which the Achæans had brought with them and grafted upon the older nature-worship and ancestor-worship of the Ægean inhabitants. The Zeus of the Dorians and the Zeus of the Athenians might be different; but all could and did unite at Olympia in the games held in honor of Zeus, and they suspended wars while the games lasted. Incidentally, the games promoted trade and gave the heralds an opportunity to proclaim treaties; not least of all, they gathered poets and sculptors who vied with each other in celebrating the god and his athletic worshippers. Apollo, too, the manly god of the Dorians, whose oracle at Delphi drew pious questioners from countries even beyond the borders of Greece and sent out colonists to distant lands, united cities for the protection of his temple; and other Amphictyonies, or bands of dwellers near a shrine, brought men together in a common interest. So history and geography and law found a shelter and a champion.

During these centuries since the days of Achilles, then, the Greeks had done far more than spread their settlements through the Ægean world and through much of the Pontus and the Mediterranean. They had discovered the difference between themselves and foreigners. Others might still rival their material civilization, or might even, like the Phœnicians, teach them to write. But others had not learned, as they had learned, by hard experience, that a man or a people survives by freedom tempered by discipline, and that between the extremes of tyranny and license there is a healthy compromise. They had learned, too, taught by a lucky instinct and by a saving reason, to avoid the grosser forms of cruelty and vice. Content with moderate prosperity, and indeed forced by the conditions of a country that made toil the price of existence, they had to live largely by their wits.

Especially among the Ionians, of course, the arts found a home; and they were already beginning to speculate on ultimate things, first in the spirit of poetry, then in a scientific spirit. It is in this profound sense that these centuries witnessed a growth of the Greeks, a growth more intellectual and spiritual than physical. There was never a moment in the history of the ancient Greeks when there was not a danger of some old superstition or prejudice cropping up and jeopardizing the slowly-won heritage of generations; but the Greeks always felt the gulf that divided them from the barbarians. Already by the end of the sixth century the Ionians of Asia Minor and the Greeks of Sicily were coming into conflict with the Persians and the Carthaginians. One may doubt whether, in the great age soon to follow, the Greeks could so triumphantly have held their own against despotism in the east and in the west, if they had not so clearly seen that the life they had won by discipline and suffering was one for which they might gladly stake everything.[1]

4. THE GREAT AGE

During the sixth century, the Greeks of Asia Minor had been separated from Persia by a buffer state, the kingdom of Lydia. But when this state had fallen before the Persian arms, nothing prevented the Ionian Greeks from being absorbed by the rapidly-growing power of Persia. For Persia had already conquered all the territory of the old eastern empires, and it was only a question of time before she would in the natural course of events swallow up any land in Europe that seemed worth conquering; in fact, she had already made invasions into Thrace. Descended from stock not very remote from the ancestors of the Greeks, the Per-

[1] Cf. J. A. K. Thomson, *Greeks and Barbarians*, Macmillan, 1921.

sians were naturally an able and even an enlightened people; but they had been corrupted by the races that they had subdued, and the Persian Empire was now a typical oriental despotism, in which everything was subordinated to the end of mechanical efficiency. To be a part of such a machine was not a destiny that the Greeks could be expected to endure.

In Ionia, the cities revolted. Of course the revolt was unsuccessful; but the old capital of Lydia, Sardis, was burned. Nor was it only the Greeks of Asia Minor that were involved. The Spartans, to be sure, true to their home-keeping, cautious traditions, had refused to have anything to do with such a harebrained expedition; but Athens, always ready for adventure, had helped to singe the beard of the Great King of Persia. Herodotus, the historian of the Persian wars, never failing to see the romantic and the dramatic side of a story, tells us that the Great King had a slave remind him daily to "remember the Athenians." Like the assassination at Sarajevo in 1914, the burning of Sardis, in itself only an incident, served to precipitate a great war that was already on the verge of breaking out. Yet one may doubt whether a generation earlier the Greeks would have fought successfully; for the tyrants were apt to acquiesce in the collapse of the Greek cities before Persian invasion, and only the new democracies had the desire or the spirit to resist. Time or luck was playing on the side of the Greeks and of western civilization; we may take it as a warning against following those historians who try to explain too much in terms of mountain-ranges and trade-routes. Human nature has a good deal to do with human destiny; and chance is not to be ignored. Herodotus, to be sure, saw the gods and fate in everything. The Persians, through their insolent pride and the very greatness of their ambition, made themselves the mark for the jealousy of the gods; pride went before the fall. That was the burden of the drama of Æschylus that celebrated the Greek victory.

The chief events of the wars may be briefly told. The first expedition of the Persians to punish the European Greeks was frustrated by a storm. The second attempt was gloriously overcome at Marathon. Here again time favored the Greeks, for if the walls of Athens had not been destroyed by the tyrants, Miltiades could not have carried the proposal to fight at Marathon rather than risk a siege. But the victory belongs to the tactics of the commanders and to the spirit of the free Athenian warriors, aided by hardly any other Greeks. So Athens was saved from destruction and from the restoration of her exiled tyrant, Hippias, who had been befriended by the Persians; but she only postponed the greater trial of another invasion. The spiritual effect of the victory, however, can hardly be over-estimated; she was exalted, and she never forgot the day. What might a Greek not hope to do?

During the next few years, while the Persian king was busy in Egypt, Athens was at war with her neighbor, the island town of Ægina. By good fortune, the silver mines of Laurium were discovered at this time; and Themistocles, most astute of statesmen, persuaded the Athenians to forego the present enjoyment of the treasure and to build a navy for the Æginetan war. But the real naval enemy, as Themistocles foresaw, was Persia. Ten years after Marathon came the last Persian invasion, this time with an enormous army and fleet, even if the fabulous figures given by Herodotus are to be discounted. Athens generously yielded her just claims to leadership in favor of Sparta, nominally the head of Greek military unity by reason of her leadership of the Peloponnesian League. The Persian forces entered Greece from the north, army and navy keeping abreast. The

Greeks abandoned as impracticable the Vale of Tempe, their first line of defense. To Thermopylæ the Spartans sent only an advance guard, keeping most of their warriors at the Isthmus of Corinth, which they proposed to defend. The guard at Thermopylæ, like the Belgians at Liége and Namur, stemmed the tide of invasion, but only temporarily, since the passes had been forced elsewhere. Meanwhile the Persian fleet had suffered great losses through storms. The Athenians took to their ships again, leaving Athens to be burned. Even now it was only the threat of the Athenians to leave Greece altogether and to found a colony in the west that prevailed on the Spartans not to retire to the Isthmus; the Spartans did not wish to see half the Greek fleet sail away. So Themistocles by double intrigue forced the Greeks and the Persians to fight at Salamis; and there, before the eyes of the Great King, the Persian fleet was overwhelmed in the narrow straits. With his navy defeated, he had no choice but to retire, in order to defend Ionia and his lines of communication. The undefeated Persian army was left to subdue Greece. Athens, her city lost, her country ravaged, was invited to make easy terms with the invader and betray the rest of Greece. To her lasting glory, she defiantly refused. But the Persian army, like the German army after the first battle of the Marne, now stood on the defensive. Sparta at last was persuaded to move, and largely by her own energy won the battle of Platæa. And so the tide of invasion was rolled back. The battle of Mycale, fought a few days later, overthrew the Persian control of the coast of Ionia; the Athenians then followed up the victory by further action in Asia Minor, while the Spartans, with characteristic provinciality, sailed home.

The eastern Greeks had hoped to win for the wars against the Persians the aid of the Greeks of Sicily, whose resources were at least as great as their own. But the western Greeks were engaged in a great struggle with the Carthaginians, whose attack was doubtless timed to coincide with that of the Great King, so that the Greeks of neither part of the world might help their kinsmen. Legend told that it was on the very day of Salamis that the Syracusans at Himera defeated the Carthaginians. In the west, as in the east, the Greeks could now build without serious hindrance their splendid cities and live as freemen.

One might have supposed that the Greeks would learn, through their tense coöperation in the Persian Wars and through the spiritual rebirth that the struggle had brought about, to act as a nation. Such a supposition, however, would hardly reckon enough with the strong local feeling of the several states, to whom the city not only was all-sufficient in time of peace, but was the unit that most thoroughly aroused their imaginations. What cohesion was possible was to come from a league of city-states; but Sparta forfeited any claim to the leadership that might have been hers as head of the Peloponnesian League. Though no state had given braver soldiers than Sparta, she had not merely once but constantly shown her lack of leadership and of every intellectual quality of leadership. Her repeated absence from the field of battle because of superstitious observances, — a festival, an eclipse, or a phase of the moon, — always seemed curiously to fit with her own narrow, selfish policy, till she did at last to a certain extent redeem her good name. Above all, Sparta was not a naval power, and the future of Greece lay on the sea.

All that Sparta was not, Athens was. The brilliant naval policy of Themistocles, the resolution of the Athenians to fight even without a city, and the quick assumption of the Greek cause in Ionia marked the city of Athens as the leader of Greek freedom. Against the will of Sparta, and by trickery, Athens rebuilt her walls, thus asserting her sovereignty. For some years the fleets of the Athenians and of their island and coastland allies cruised about Asia Minor and neighboring shores, successfully attacking the Persian forces. They acted as members of the Confederacy of Delos, a voluntary association of cities leagued against the common foe. The burden of warfare was supported partly by contributions of ships and their crews, but more commonly, especially as the years passed, by contributions of money. Athens, with her large fleet, naturally dominated the other states, and was not unwilling to accept money instead of ships, for the result was in fact simply an addition to her own fleet. The seas were well patrolled, and the cost of belonging to the Confederacy was far less than the tribute formerly levied by Persia; for a time, therefore, all the members were content. Cimon, the Athenian admiral, did all that he could to stimulate a friendly feeling toward Sparta, so that all the resources of the Greeks might be united in throwing the Persians entirely out of the Greek world. Unfortunately, he was snubbed by the Spartans. By this time the war with Persia was beginning to lag, and the Athenian democracy under new leaders adopted a hostile attitude toward Sparta, and devoted all its attention to the consolidation of its own strength. Twenty-five years after the Persians were expelled from Greece the treasury of the Delian Confederacy was transferred to Athens, and the Athenian Empire came into existence. Indeed, as the need for protection against Persia grew less, some of the allies of Athens had already begun to resent the lion's share of power that was falling to her, and she had to put down numerous rebellions. The question constantly arose whether in view of the original pact the allies were subject to Athens or whether they were still independent and might withdraw at pleasure, a question that Athens regularly settled by *force majeure*. The question was not unlike that of the secessionists at the outbreak of the American Civil War; but the Greek states outside Athens were not, as were the southern states of America, politically on the same footing with the rest of the federation, even though their welfare was in the main carefully guarded. A confederacy of equal states did no violence to Greek feeling; but membership in an empire in which they were at best the poor relations was not the privilege that the citizens of the metropolis hoped to make it.

The only justification for the Athenian Empire is its achievements. Built on a basis of subject and tributary populations, supported in part by the manual labor of slaves (in the main well treated), the Athenian Empire was now within its own limits as completely democratic as an English university or a well-bred club; to the outsider it seemed exclusive and perhaps arrogant, to its members it was an impartial and kindly mother. During the fifty years between the Persian wars and the great Peloponnesian War the men of Athens, whose citizenship was carefully restricted, developed a type of average citizen whose political experience and sagacity, whose contact with life in varied occupations, and whose capacity for appreciating beauty and reason has been surpassed by the average of no other race or time.[1] And if the average seems to us to be often irresponsible, ingenious rather than candid, fickle, impressed too easily at times by irrelevant things, let us not forget that these same fifty years saw the clear-sighted statesmanship of the Olympian Pericles, the dramas of three of the greatest tragic writers of the world and of perhaps its greatest comic poet,

[1] Cf. the opinion of Galton, quoted by A. E. Zimmern, *The Greek Commonwealth*, p. 362, n. 1.

the youth of the first critical historian, the masterpieces of architects and sculptors who exhausted the possibilities of certain kinds of art, and the obstinate inquiries of Socrates, the most influential personality in the history of philosophy.

Why this sudden blossoming of the Greek genius should have taken place within so short a time is a question that we cannot avoid asking. No answer will be complete; but any answer must take into account at least several influences, and above all their happy union at the right moment. One must reckon with the native ability of the old Ægean inhabitants of Attica, now fused with the lordly Greek invaders; the centre of influence has been shifted from the mountain-dwellers to the inhabitants of the plain and the coast, whose industry and foreign trade have developed quick wits; the overthrow of Persia has intoxicated the imaginations of the people, while the Athenian Empire has tumbled like a windfall into their laps, making them the administrators of hundreds of cities, necessarily concerned every day with the problems of war and peace; the deliverance from peril has become the occasion for a religious thank-offering in the form of the temples and statues of the Acropolis. Finally, this free, critical, enlightened people furnishes a public for the dramatists, who can still draw on the legendary past for material, but who can reshape it for the expression of the experience through which they and their fellow-citizens are passing, even for the expression of their misgivings or for their criticism of contemporary events, since personality is respected, and intolerance is rare. But, after all, explanations of the age of Pericles are as unsatisfactory as explanations of the Elizabethan age or of the Romantic movement; they explain too little, or they explain too much.

The extraordinary military energy of the Athenians at this time is reflected in an inscribed stone giving the names of those members of one Attic tribe who fell in the year 459–8, fighting in Cyprus, Egypt, Phœnicia, Ægina, Megara, and the Peloponnese. After reverses in Bœotia, Pericles wisely opposed any attempts to extend the land empire of Athens, and even reduced the imperial tribute; but her power on the seas extended her trade from Italy to the Black Sea, and built up manufactures of many kinds. An attempt to hold a Panhellenic Congress at Athens failed. For a generation, Pericles, nominally only a general regularly reëlected, dominated the Empire by his personal influence as "leader of the people," holding this new position outside, though not contrary to, the constitution. His imperial policies were opposed by Thucydides, the son of Milesias (not the historian), who, like some other oligarchs, took the part of the cities of the Empire, which chafed at the sovereignty of Athens. Thucydides was exiled; but the problem remained; was not an empire controlled by a democracy an anomaly? Is not the British Empire, governed by what is really a democratic country, an anomaly? Yes; but it is so, because of the growth of generations: England has become democratic since the foundations of her Empire were laid, and she is studying methods of extending democratic principles to the management of the Empire. The growth of the Athenian Empire, from the entirely democratic Delian Confederacy, was in the other direction, toward autocracy; and each time that a member of the empire attempted to throw off the yoke, the retribution showed more clearly by its severity the nature of the yoke, especially if Athens was at the time occupied with another war. It is sometimes easier to lift a load than to drop it, as Athens learned in her Empire, and as England has discovered in the case of Ireland.

It was not to be expected that the rest of Greece would view without anxiety the rapid rise of the new Empire; if mutual suspicion and conflicting commercial interests make wars inevitable, it was inevitable that war should arise between Athens and her neighbors. Already she had fought with several of them; but the conflict was indecisive, and the peace that followed was but an armed truce. Especially the Corinthians, as the second commercial and naval power of Greece, were jealous. The immediate occasion of the war was the interference of Athens with Corinthian interests in the north and the west; Athens the more readily accepted an opportunity for interfering because she was persuaded that by precipitating the inevitable war she would fight with more allies on her side. Corinth appealed for aid to Sparta, the head of the Peloponnesian League. Athens immediately set up an economic boycott against Megara, an important member of the League. The diplomatic charges that went back and forth between Sparta and Athens, though futile and trivial, are none the less instructive; for Sparta, the narrow-minded oligarchy, with her provincial tradition, was calling on democratic Athens, lately the champion of Greece against the tyrant Persian, to restore the independence of the Hellenes. The appeal was not wholly insincere; and the situation has a curiously modern flavor to us who live in a day when "a place in the sun," "the freedom of the seas," "economic warfare," and "the rights of small nations" are commonplaces. The tragedy was that before means of international understanding and coöperation could arise, — and the means are not yet perfected, — even so enlightened a state as Athens was a danger to the rest of Greece.

It is no part of our purpose to trace here in detail the military history of the war; but the general aspects of the campaigns are not hard to follow. Given a naval power confronted by a land power, one can predict that the chief scene of warfare will be in the coastland possessions of the land power and in the territories of the mainland held by the naval power. A fight between a dog and a crocodile must take place either on the beach or in shallow water. And so it was. Athens ravaged the outlying lands of the Peloponnesian states, and they retaliated by invading Attica. Pericles, who had already decided that Athens must not extend her land empire any further (as Augustus and other heirs to ready-made empires also decided, when it was too late), wisely followed the policy of Themistocles in the Persian Wars; Attica was abandoned, except the city of Athens and a narrow strip extending to the port of Peiræus, and the impatient farmers had to see their land raided year after year. He hoped, not unreasonably, that the Peloponnesian states could be exhausted by a war of attrition. But for the plague and the blunders of the Athenian leaders who followed Pericles, his policy would probably have succeeded. On several distinct occasions the Athenians could have had peace on favorable terms; but the opportunity was rejected by the jingo politicians whose constituents clamored for the unconditional surrender of the Spartans. Imperialism of the type championed by Pericles has no little attractiveness; there is not much to praise in the vulgar imperialism of Cleon. Meanwhile the other members of the Empire were constantly restless under the burdens of the war. The tribute was nearly doubled in 425; and Cleon, in recognition of the increased cost of living at Athens, increased considerably the pay of jurymen, who comprised a large proportion of the population. The war was becoming unpopular on both sides. Yet the inconclusive peace of Nicias, declared ten years after the war began, and named for a respectable, superstitious, and mediocre Athenian general, marked hardly more than a pause in the hostilities; for any terms that left the grievances of many of the Peloponnesians without a remedy could not last. The new war saw Athens make a great thrust at the power of her enemies in Sicily, a thrust that might well have succeeded if the control had not been first hopelessly divided and finally given to the inopportune Nicias, so that every advantage was thrown away, and the flower of the Athenian youth died in captivity at Syracuse. Meanwhile the clever Alcibiades, never a friend of the Athenian democracy, and now alienated by the distrust of his fellow-citizens, had induced the Spartans to fortify the stronghold of Decelea, near Athens. The loss of the mines at Laurium was soon reflected in the institution of taxes, now shared by Athens as well as her Empire, instead of the old tribute. Sparta, acting on the invitation of the old allies of Athens, now built a fleet, in order to strike Athens in her most vulnerable point, her control of the sea; and she won the support of the old foe of Greece, the Persian Empire. The power of Athens was beginning to crumble. She might still win naval victories; but her cause was lost. Something curiously like the internal conditions and the foreign relations of Germany in 1918 was at work: the Kaiser hitherto in the saddle had been the Athenian democracy; but oligarchs at Athens were ready to sacrifice the constitution of the democracy, provided that they could secure peace and a stable government; the adventurer Alcibiades meanwhile sent word that Persia would treat only with a reformed Athens, that is, with an oligarchy. This meant, probably, that Alcibiades despaired of regaining any foothold in an Athenian democracy; for Persia proved unwilling to treat with Athens at all. Oligarchy carried the day at Athens none the less, though the fleet repudiated it and claimed to represent the real Athens. The revolution was not altogether successful, and was followed by several counter-revolutions, which had the effect of moderating the extreme oligarchical tendency, and finally of restoring the democracy. But under the apparent reconciliation lay discord. There is even reason to suspect that there were many Athenians who welcomed the terrible naval defeat at Ægospotami (possibly the result of treachery), as there were doubtless Germans who rejoiced on November 11, 1918; for it seemed the only hope of saving an exhausted country. Athens, though her fleet was gone, refused to surrender, but hunger soon made resistance hopeless. Sparta generously opposed the desire of her allies to destroy Athens, and was content with compelling Athens to give up her Empire, her fleet, and her walls. A new oligarchy at Athens engaged in proscriptions and plunder; and civil war raged for many months, till peace was again restored only by Spartan intervention. Commissioners revived the democratic constitution, and after a generation of constant warfare Athens was again at peace.

Far more important than the military events of the Peloponnesian War is the light that the war threw on human nature; indeed it may fairly be asked whether the chief importance of the war is not the fact that it was chronicled by Thucydides, a master in the understanding of motives and issues and in the analysis of ideals. No doubt the war arose from commercial rivalries; but as it continued it became, as Thucydides saw, increasingly a contest between two types of civilization, between Ionians and democracies on the one hand, and Dorians and oligarchies on the other hand. Exceptions to the alignment occur, and we must not use the word "democracy" in a purely laudatory sense. The reader of Thucydides feels, moreover, a deepening appreciation of the bitterness of the struggle, as he learns of the ruthless massacres that were more and more frequent, of the desolating effects on human nature of revolutions, of the coarser moral fibre that is shown in the later years of the war. When the struggle began, Athens might well have seemed likely to win an easy victory. Many things kept the victory from her: such accidents as the plague and the death of Pericles; the emergence at Sparta of two very able commanders, Brasidas and Lysander; the weight of Persian influence thrown into the scales against Athens. But Athens was her own worst enemy. She lost the war principally by her overweening pride in her foreign and imperial relations, by her political disagreement at home, and above all by a corruption of *morale*. The Athens of Ægospotami was not the Athens of Salamis. Thucydides, unlike Herodotus, is a truly critical historian, not often given to the devices of epic and dramatic machinery; yet behind his tragic narrative of facts there stalks, barely veiled, the figure of Retribution. When he wrote the imaginary dialogue in which the Athenians cynically tell the Melians that might makes right, he is merely giving the state of mind of the Athenians at that time. It was left to Xenophon to take up the story and tell what a panic befell the Athenians when they heard of their defeat at Ægospotami, and thought of the extermination of the Melians; to their guilty consciences pride had indeed been the forerunner of a downfall. For Thucydides, and for us, the fall had already come when Athens had stooped to persecute the Melians. And though Thucydides was adhering strictly to the facts when he traced the effects on men of the wars that he knew, his utterances are true of War.

5. THE SPREAD OF GREEK CULTURE

The Great Age of Greece had seen the Hellenes for a time forget their differences and triumphantly hurl back the barbarian invader; carried on by a wave of self-confidence, Athens had created a world of order and beauty. But she had gone too far, and the rest of Greece had been forced in self-defense to unite in crushing her. So the century had ended in disillusionment and a sense of at least partial failure. The next century was to decide whether the Greek states had understood their sad experience.

The two generations that followed the Peloponnesian War were full of struggles. Though the issues are complicated, the explanation is painfully simple; the struggles are all attempts to secure supremacy by means of a balance of power. Each state in turn, as soon as it seemed to be outstripping the others, undertook to raise up obstacles against its chief rival. When its power was abused beyond the endurance of the rest of Greece, a temporary coalition arose and overthrew the tyrannical power. Then the balance of power shifted, new alliances were made, and the struggle began again. Occasionally a wise man lifted up his voice against this waste of energy and life, and tried to bring about a Panhellenic union against the real enemy, the Great King of Persia, who profited by the dissensions among the Greeks, and whose satraps shrewdly played them against each other; but even Isocrates was unheeded.

We have already seen the tyrant Athens dethroned by a coalition of Greek states; at the end of the War, Sparta proclaimed Greece free. Sparta's actions belied the proclamation. She found herself the heir to the Athenian Empire, and had the folly to keep it. Absolutely unfitted by temperament, by training, and by political and financial institutions to deal with imperial problems, the Spartans tried by setting up military despotisms in the several cities to hold together the Empire. Of course the Spartan rule was unpopular, especially since the original need for the Empire, as a safeguard against Persia, seemed to have gone. The Spartan control of Asia Minor was actually held by the assistance of Persia. The sympathy of the Persian government was largely forfeited, however, by the part that Greek and especially Spartan mercenary soldiers took in the unsuccessful rebellion of Prince Cyrus against his brother, King Artaxerxes. The Anabasis, though only an episode in Greek history, marks the turning of the tide against Persia; the great Persian army was unable to defeat the small and isolated Greek force, which retreated in an orderly march through unknown country to Greek cities. Though the Spartan King Agesilaus was now encouraged to invade Persian territories with some success, the destruction of the Spartan fleet by a Persian navy under Athenian command called him back to Greece. But the conquest of Persia no longer seemed an impossible dream, and boys now living were to see as old men the triumphs of Alexander of Macedon.

Sparta's unpopularity was not confined to the maritime Empire that had been won from Athens. Her late allies of the Peloponnesian War were reaping no advantage from the victory, and all Greece resented Spartan aggressions not only in the Peloponnese but in northern Greece. A league of states, including Thebes and Athens, by several costly battles drove the Spartans back into the Peloponnese. The Persians, now angry at the Spartans for their conduct in Asia, actually assisted in the fortification of Athens; and within a short time Athens was building up again a maritime Empire, this time on a purely defensive basis. But all factions were ready for peace. Peace came, but in a very ignominious manner. Athens had in a somewhat accidental way lost the Persian favor; Sparta succeeded by pledging the Ionian cities to Persia in prevailing upon the Great King to arrange a peace on a basis of autonomy for all the European Greek cities. It was a confession of weakness that Greeks could invite a Persian to arbitrate a Greek dispute.

The "King's Peace" lasted only a few years. Sparta began again to interfere impudently with the affairs of other states; above all, she broke up federations of cities wherever they were beginning to appear, for though they lacked the constructive political ability of the Romans, the Spartans understood at least the principle, "Divide et impera." By the insolence of the Spartans the Athenians were stung into successful naval warfare, and made an alliance with their old enemies the Thebans, who defended Bœotia against Spartan invasions and built up a Bœotian Confederacy. The prosperity of the Thebans indeed aroused the jealousy of the Athenians, who proceeded to make peace again with the Spartans.

Nominally all Greek states were now independent. Sparta went out of her way to stir up trouble, by objecting to the Theban leadership of Bœotia. Thebes was now strong enough to retaliate, and had a really brilliant general in Epaminondas, the inventor of massed infantry attacks; as the result of the battle of Leuctra, which crippled the Spartan army, Thebes was able to pass from the defense of her own territory to the invasion of Laconia, and from the leadership of Bœotia to the leadership of Greece. Sparta was now much depopulated both by wars and by the fact that the small land-holders were yielding to the temptation to sell their land; hitherto not only the possession of money but the sale of land had been forbidden. Thebes encouraged democratic movements among the neighbors of Sparta, and created a powerful federation in Arcadia and towns elsewhere, in order to keep Sparta disabled. It was the "Rake's Progress" again, with Thebes in the title-rôle. Athens soon became apprehensive, and was driven into the arms of Sparta; the arrogance of the Thebans in the Peloponnese led to strained relations and a rupture with Arcadia; and their interference in northern Greece clashed with Athenian aspirations. The inevitable Battle of the Nations came at Mantineia in Arcadia, where the tactics of Leuctra were repeated and overcame the armies of Sparta and Athens and many other cities. The victory proved fatal, for Epaminondas was killed; and the Theban leadership, being merely military, barely outlived its great general.

The balance of power as a political expedient was thoroughly discredited; jealousy, even when organized and aided by fair-sounding rhetoric, was proved to be no safeguard against ambition. Moreover, in their zeal for liberty and individuality, the Greeks seemed to have exaggerated the value of the form of government and organization to which they were accustomed. The city-state was indeed of a convenient size for giving its citizens a life developed on all sides and for exciting civic pride; but the advantages were fast being outweighed by very obvious shortcomings when the intensity of rivalry bled away the lives of the flower of the citizens and stirred up factions and fruitless revolutions and made the Greeks a prey to Persian diplomacy. The time was ripe for any one who could unite the Greeks in a national state. Though several minor federations were afoot, it is doubtful whether anything less than conquest and force could have succeeded in holding the Greeks together for more than a few years. They were fortunate in being conquered by Philip of Macedon, who, though considered by them to be more than half a barbarian, claimed to be more than half a Greek. The civilization of his Empire and of Alexander's was Greek in all but some of its external features.

The fall of the Athenian Empire and the sad experiences of the next two generations were not altogether a loss. As the intense devotion to a single city gave way to more tolerant views, men saw life less through the eyes of convention and more for themselves. Athens, in particular, was frequented by strangers who were eager to discuss with her teachers and thinkers all sorts of subjects, from rhetoric to socialism. An age of criticism is an age of prose; the poetry of these years was inferior to that of the Great Age, but philosophy, oratory, and political theory burst into flower. Never were men more curious to think things out and to know all that could be known; seldom have more interesting personalities met. Men were becoming more cosmopolitan; art was used less for the service of the gods and more for the pleasure of men, and it became accordingly interested in individual men and women and their daily life.

The fortunes of the eastern Greeks after the Persian Wars were in many ways like those of the Greeks of Sicily, who had defeated Carthage. For a time Syracuse and Acragas, not without rivalry, grew strong and beautiful and learned to know the qualities of tyranny and democracy. Syracuse was hardly less crippled by the ill-fated Sicilian expedition of Athens than was Athens herself; and as Persia profited by the bitter disputes of the old Greece for leadership, Carthage saw her opportunity and overran much of Sicily before the Syracusans could recover their power. An earlier attempt to unite the Sicilians in a world of their own, under the protection of something like a Monroe Doctrine ("Sicily for the Sicilians"), had failed; but Dionysius of Syracuse succeeded in uniting most of Sicily under his military leadership. He posed as the champion of the Greeks against the Carthaginians, but was shrewd enough not to let the Greeks defeat their enemies so thoroughly that they could dispense with him; he built up an empire that reached into Italy and the shores of the Adriatic, and maintained a brilliant court. For a time his was the most powerful state in Europe, and it might seem as if Greece was at last to become a nation. But where Philip and Alexander succeeded, Dionysius failed; his rule was only a military despotism which crumbled when his successors proved less able than himself. The philosopher Plato, an unwilling guest at Syracuse, could not establish his ideal state, since it required a longer education of human nature than an impatient young ruler could be expected to complete. The tyranny of Syracuse fell before Timoleon of Corinth, who modestly retired when he had driven back a new Carthaginian invasion, and when democracies had been safely established in the Greek cities.

The unity that the western Greeks failed to achieve was soon to be won in the older Greece; but it was not the Greeks themselves who were to succeed in winning it. The older Greeks, with all their brilliancy and energy, had wasted their substance and their lives in bitter rivalries, and their powers were now sadly depleted; the spirit was eager, but populations and resources were now scanty. The strong states were now not the proud cities of Athens and Argos, but the *nouveau riche* Rhodes and the semi-barbarian inhabitants of Caria, of Thessaly, and of Macedon. As in many modern countries the centres of economic and political and intellectual life shift from the old strongholds to new provinces, if a more vigorous life has arisen elsewhere, so the outposts of Greece, where Greeks and barbarians were mingled, now showed astonishing vitality. In some cases the new powers were soon eclipsed; Caria is now known chiefly for the huge Mausoleum in which its greatest sovereign, King Mausolus, was buried. It was Macedon that two men, father and son, were destined to make the conqueror of Greece and the champion of Greek culture throughout the greater part of the ancient world.

Till the fourth century, the Macedonians had remained a backward, half-civilized race, governed by kings who remind one of the Homeric warrior-kings, and who spent most of their time in fighting their northern neighbors. Yet they were becoming Hellenized; Philip II always showed a real respect for Greek culture, even engaging for his son Alexander the most learned tutor that Greece could boast, the philosopher Aristotle. Philip's genius was of two kinds, military and practical. He borrowed from the Thebans, among whom he had spent his boyhood as a hostage, the phalanx of closely-locked spearmen; he added to it a formidable cavalry and something like artillery; above all, his soldiers were professional soldiers. But his army would not alone have carried victory if he had not been a master of shrewd and cynical diplomacy. He played city against city, ally against ally; he bribed, threatened, persuaded, or compelled, as the situation demanded. And wherever his ambitions were turned, he usually found a substantial party willing to help him. He broke his word as readily as he gave it. His power crept from the hill country to the sea, absorbed gold mines and fortresses, and found an easy pretext for interposing itself in the quarrels of the older states of central Greece. We need not wonder that the older states were alarmed, or that amateur soldiers and impoverished treasuries fell before the professional armies and the golden arguments of Philip.

At Athens, as elsewhere, there were two parties. Demosthenes, who could not realize that the day of little city-states was over, launched his fiery oratory against the foreign aggressor, and berated his fellow-citizens for their inactivity and their military unpreparedness. His was a lost cause. He trusted to the equivalent of a Monroe Doctrine, supported by arms, rather than to a Greek military coalition under the auspices of an upstart Macedonian; events proved his oratory to be greater than his statesmanship.

Yet he was a true patriot, and it does not appear that the political opponents of Demosthenes were any more wise; for their policy would have let matters slide, and Philip would have marched rough-shod over Greece. Only the aged Isocrates, always the consistent prophet of Panhellenism, saw that the triumph of Philip was the only salvation for Greece, and might indeed be the beginning of the triumph of Greece over the East. Of the truth of this fact the Athenians were not yet convinced; it was not till Philip had actually crushed the opposition of the Greeks in the battle of Chæronea, and had amazed them by the mildness of his terms, that the real nature of Philip's Hellenism became apparent.

King though he was, and to Greek ears the name of king was now almost as hateful as it was to Roman ears, Philip did not intend to be despotic toward the Greek states. For the preservation of order, he placed garrisons at strategic points; but he interfered little with local affairs, and except that wars within Greece were prevented, civic interests were as keenly pursued as ever. By a congress of Greeks at Corinth Macedon was declared the head of Greece; and Philip presently announced that he was going to renew the war against Persia in behalf of Greece, and thus presented himself as a champion, rather than as an oppressor. Greek dissension was ended, but Greek unity was hardly yet achieved; Philip's plans were cut short by his assassination, and Alexander, only twenty years old, came to the throne.

The young king seemed destined by fate to carry victory. In form like a god, generous, bold to a fault, he was said never to have declined a battle and never to have lost a battle. In dealing with his fellows he had the art of being all things to all men, and showed his respect in turn for Greek culture, Egyptian religion, and Persian institutions and character; his ideas grew as his Empire grew.

When he came to the throne, he was at once compelled to subdue revolts in Greece and the Balkan interior; a few rapid campaigns that reached the Danube showed that Alexander was not to be trifled with. Then, as the elected champion of the Greeks, he began again the historic war of the West against the East, playing the rôle of a new Achilles. Asia Minor fell after a few battles; but he resisted the temptation to carry the war into the east till he had guarded his rear by the conquest of Syria and Egypt, and had left the new city of Alexandria as a bulwark of Greek civilization at the mouth of the Nile. Then in Mesopotamia he avenged the Persian invasions of Greece by conquering the gentle Darius and making himself the heir of the Persian Empire. Not content with this, he pressed on into the east, through incredible dangers, always putting himself in the van of his army, till he reached the northwestern territories of India. He would have gone still further, had not the murmurs of his war-weary veterans forced him to return to Babylon, which now became his capital. A mortal fever ended his career on the eve of his departure for a new campaign in Arabia.

Any account of Alexander's life is apt to deal chiefly with his spectacular military feats and his explorations in the east. Indeed, less is known of his political activities; yet these are what did most to mould the course of history. Beginning as a champion of Greece, determined to conquer Persia, he deliberately became an Oriental monarch and tried to fuse the West with the East. Greek and barbarian were to be under one lord, and were to fight mingled in one army. Persian administrators often replaced his Macedonians, who were sometimes resentful of the new policy; but the great Empire was leavened by many new Greek cities, usually named for Alexander, which were founded at strategic points. The king himself, following the custom of his

Persian predecessors, married several beautiful eastern princesses, and encouraged his Macedonians to take Persian wives. So his policy of toleration and adaptation produced a new type of civilization that was neither Greek nor barbarian, but a mixture of the two. Greece was the gainer by new sources of wealth and science, the East by contact with the quick minds of the Greeks. So vast a territory could not remain a single empire under any monarch less able than Alexander; but a certain unity of culture remained. Greek was spoken from the Danube to India, and in the following centuries no city in the world was more Greek than the Egyptian city of Alexandria. On the crumbling remains of this Empire the Romans were to build their eastern power; and through this Greek-speaking world Christianity was to spread. The work of Alexander, then, in a word, was not to change the quality of Greek civilization, but to extend its influence geographically throughout the world. Isocrates had said that Athens had caused the word "Greek" to apply no longer to a national division but to an attitude of mind; it is doubtful whether this penetration could have occurred so rapidly without the expansion of the Greek world forced by the spears of Alexander's armies.

The old Greek states were not yet ready, to be sure, to acquiesce in the magnificent plans of Alexander; during his eastern campaigns several minor insurrections among the Greeks had to be put down by his Macedonian lieutenants. Meanwhile even his old tutor, Aristotle, whose encyclopædic mind was engaged in reducing to orderly thought all that the world then knew, was convinced that not empires but small city-states held the greatest promise of political development, and that Greeks were by nature superior to barbarians. Only a slow growth could bring the fruition of Alexander's work. Already, however, the loss of opportunity for political activity caused by the Macedonian conquest had turned men's minds into other activities, — art, and philosophy, and commerce, — and the Greeks were fast becoming no longer citizens of their provincial towns but citizens of the world.

The vast Empire of Alexander fell apart soon after his death. After fifty years of intrigues and civil wars of succession, three smaller empires and a number of smaller kingdoms and states emerged. Macedonia, including Greece, was ruled by a dynasty of warlike kings; the rich provinces of Asia fell to the Seleucid kings, and Egypt was governed for several centuries by the Ptolemies. Within these realms the Greeks lived their comparatively uneventful lives, moderately well protected from barbarian invasion and not unduly oppressed by taxation. Indeed the Hellenistic Age — the age when Greek political life mattered less than Greek culture — was marked by great material prosperity, as well as by great poverty. Temples and theatres and libraries and lighthouses were built by wealthy benefactors; art and letters and philosophy flourished, but in a new spirit. For the days of originality and dominant personalities gave place to an age of imitation and respect for authority. Literature was now apt to be the concern of scholarly pedants; science tended, after a time, to lose its spirit of free inquiry. The new Comedy of Manners occupied itself with the manipulation of conventional plots and characters; romance was born anew, and busied itself with the trivial and the bizarre. Life was far from dull; but it ran for the most part in prescribed channels. A poet like Theocritus, though writing with no little charm, confined his art to a somewhat slight genre, the pastoral; and the most beautiful sculpture of the Hellenistic Age wins our admiration more by its grace and physical perfection than by any noble appeal to the imagination; it creates men, and gods in the likeness of men, rather than gods, and men in the likeness of gods. Yet for these very reasons the Hellenistic Age, preoccupied with daily life and dealing with it in human terms, has a peculiar appeal for modern men.

Political life was not altogether dead in Greece; indeed, a new experiment in coöperation was being made. Two leagues of cities grew up in western Greece, led respectively by Ætolia and Achæa. By the diplomacy of Aratus, the Achæan League won the control of most of Greece, though Athens and Sparta held aloof. Sparta under a reformed government succeeded in defeating the League, till it called in the aid of Macedonia and crushed Sparta. The price of this jealousy was that the League again became the vassal of Macedonia. But the real danger was to come from the west. Already Pyrrhus, the king of Epirus, had been forced to return to his kingdom after fruitless victories in Italy and Sicily; and Syracuse had fallen first to the Carthaginians and then to the Romans. Rome was launched on her career of conquest. Philip V of Macedonia became an ally of Hannibal during his invasion of Italy, and drew the enmity of Rome upon himself; and the Ætolian League, now at war with the Achæan League, invoked the aid of Rome. The battle of Cynoscephalæ saw the triumph of the Roman legions over Macedon and her subject states. Macedonia and Greece became a Roman province; two subsequent revolts of the Greeks were suppressed, and in 146 B.C. the destruction of Corinth marked the end of Greek liberty. Within a century much of the rest of Alexander's Empire in Asia and Egypt was brought under the rule of Rome.

6. GREECE IN THE MELTING POT

For some two thousand years Greece was under the dominion of alien powers. In destroying Corinth the Romans not only signalized the fall of the Greeks from independence but got rid of a great commercial rival. Under Roman rule the Greeks fared sometimes well, sometimes badly; for governors and traders and capitalists varied in their eagerness to exploit the country. On the whole, the Greeks were not treated much worse than troublesome subjects are generally treated by their conquerors; and after some years in which federations and intercourse and political activity were suppressed, a certain amount of local self-government was again tolerated. Greece suffered grievously as the battle-ground of wars between Rome and Mithradates and of Roman civil wars; but by way of compensation she was to a certain extent defended from various northern invaders. Heavy taxation was somewhat mitigated by splendid benefactions of wealthy individuals, in the form of public buildings.

Even more than in the Empire of Alexander, Greeks had to regard themselves as only hangers-on in a large state. A few men amassed large fortunes in trade and in grazing; and pauperism also grew. Men of superior intellectual abilities had to live contemplative, rather than active lives. Athens became again a university town, the resort of foreign students, and all Greece, living on its glorious past, was visited by countless tourists, to whom Pausanias played the *rôle* of Baedeker. The first Roman conquerors of Greece had not only carried off to Italy many works of art but had taken Greek prisoners of war as slaves, the more educated of whom became teachers and librarians and secretaries and chaplains. The Romans of this time, to be sure, practical men of affairs, could hardly understand or appreciate the Greeks;

and few Greeks could, like the captive Polybius, enter sympathetically into the conception of Rome's mission in history. But a few generations later the material conquest of Greece by Rome was all but eclipsed by the spiritual conquest of Rome by Greece; Roman poets and men of letters, artists and builders borrowed and imitated Greek ideas and formulas, and even the public that could not appreciate the refinements of Greek life was carried away in a mania for a superficial Hellenism. If Greek art or French literature is too subtle for foreigners, they can at least enjoy Greek dances and French cooking. And so the less the Greeks counted in the political world, the more they served to educate the world in the varied experience of their fathers. How thoroughly educated even the common people must have been we can judge from the very profound and subtle nature of the Epistles of St. Paul, which were sent to average citizens of Greek and Roman cities. But all eyes were turned to the golden past, and essayists and biographers like Plutarch and Dio Chrysostom found most of their themes in retrospect. Such an antiquarianism and such a divorce between thought and action is evidence of a sapped vitality. The Greeks in their most vigorous days had always found themes in the legendary past, but had always used them to express either contemporary or else eternal experience.

The Emperor Constantine made Byzantium, now named for himself, the capital of the Roman Empire. When the Empire was divided, this city remained the capital of the eastern half; and for more than seven hundred years after the western Empire had collapsed, the Byzantine Empire, with varying fortunes, endured, throwing back the invasions of Goths and Visigoths, of Persians, Saracens, and Slavs. In this Empire Greece was an obscure and subordinate part. Culture was at a low ebb; the philosophical schools were closed by imperial decree in 529 A.D., and Roman institutions were so far imposed on the Greeks that they adopted the name of Rhomaioi (a name which till recently clung to their language). Balkan invaders pushed into northern Greece, and the coasts were harried by Normans from Sicily. The warriors of the Fourth Crusade, at the beginning of the thirteenth century, turned aside to capture Constantinople, and a so-called Latin kingdom was established, though only for a short time. Frankish lords now overran Greece, and set up a Frankish dukedom at Athens. Other parts of Greece were seized by the Venetians; and travellers to-day may see carved over the gates of several Greek towns the Lion of St. Mark. But the most dangerous invaders were the Turks of the Ottoman Empire, whose forays began a hundred years before their capture of Constantinople in 1453. Constantinople became a Turkish capital; Greece came under the Turkish yoke, after the Venetians had been driven out, and remained a Turkish province till a hundred years ago. The migrations of Greek scholars and Greek manuscripts to western Europe and the increased knowledge of ancient Greek culture, already begun, was greatly hastened by the Turkish conquest. Florence and Rome were full of students of Plato and Homer. Western Europe, which for a thousand years had known Greek civilization for the most part only dimly and indirectly, now saw it face to face; and the literatures and the thought of every country were moulded to a large extent by Greek ideas.

Greece itself, however, fared badly during this period. No foreign rule had been so oppressive as that of the Turks, exacting masters, who required even a tribute of children for recruiting their armies, but who did not give protection against pirates and brigands. It was during a partially successful attempt of the Venetians to recover Athens that the

Turkish gunpowder magazine in the Parthenon, then a mosque, was exploded by a bomb fired by a German officer in the service of the Venetians. The eighteenth century saw a certain revival of prosperity, especially in commerce; but many of the most enterprising Greeks had emigrated. Sporadic revolts and a new growth of national feeling were the prelude of the War of Independence, in which the Greeks, aided by adventurers and Philhellenes from Russia, France, and England, won their freedom by 1827. Athens eventually became the capital of a united Greece. A German prince who was placed on the throne proved unsatisfactory; a Danish prince and his descendants found more favor. Agriculture and mining and shipping again began to thrive. Most of the political activity of the next fifty years was concerned with questions of frontiers. In the hope of adding Crete to the kingdom, Greece prematurely risked and lost a war with Turkey, in 1897; in the Balkan Wars, fifteen years later, Greek arms were more successful and won back considerable territory. A pro-German court kept Greece at least legally neutral in the Great War till 1917, when King Constantine, who had acted unconstitutionally and had carried on intrigues with Germany, was expelled; under the leadership of Eleutherios Venizelos, her premier, she then gave loyal support to the Allies, and was rewarded during the peace negotiations by the return to Greek sovereignty or control of large amounts of territory to which she had historic claims. Unfortunately, Constantine's second son, who had succeeded him, died in 1920; and the Greek electorate, with amazing ingratitude toward Venizelos, whose greatness and patriotism they were unable to understand (thanks chiefly to the intrigues of the royalist party), recalled Constantine. He forfeited the support of the Allies, yet continued the war with Turkey. But the autumn of

1922 saw the defeat of Greece in Asia Minor; Constantine was compelled for the second time to flee from Greece. The political and the territorial adjustments are still (1923) very uncertain.

Nearly two thousand years of rule by foreign powers have seriously depleted the human and material resources of the Greeks. In every century emigration drained Greece of many of the best citizens, and those that remained sometimes mingled their blood with that of the invaders. Greece was always a poor country, from which a living could be wrung only by constant toil; and her scanty resources have been wasted by the Turks. But a certain amount of prosperity has returned. Though the Greeks are a mixed race, they are now imbued with a thoroughly national spirit, and are keen students, both in the University of Athens and in the common schools, of the history and art and literature of ancient Greece. In fact there is a fervent party that favors a conscious attempt to make the language of modern Greece even more like that of Demosthenes than it now is; and Demosthenes would have little difficulty in understanding the modern language as it is written in the newspapers.[1] Indeed, it is even possible that Greece is now hampered, like many countries that have an ancient and a beautiful history, by an excessive veneration for her past. The secret of the old Greeks in their best days was their marvellous faculty of keeping what was vital in their inheritance, yet of adapting their inheritance to new needs. If the modern Greeks can win in their day the success that they deserve, it will be by keeping a middle course between mere antiquarianism and mere innovation.

[1] In 1901 occurred the "Gospel riots," caused by an attempt to introduce a modernized version of the Gospels.

CHAPTER IV

DAILY LIFE

1. POVERTY

IN the attempt to win a broad view of the successive achievements of the Greek race, we may lose sight, if we are not careful, of the life of the ordinary citizens. Yet the world consists mainly of ordinary citizens, who by no means regard themselves merely as interesting illustrations of great movements. They are devoted chiefly to the engrossing business of gaining a living for themselves and their families by employing the forces of nature or by pitting their wits against their neighbors', and to putting aside some part of their goods for the enjoyment of leisure. We shall not understand the achievement of the Greek race if we do not try in some measure to enter into their daily life and see in what way their daily experiences contributed to the fund of human experience. Now it is possible for us to-day to realize with a good deal of detail how the Greeks of various epochs lived, — how they dressed, what they ate, what kinds of work they did, and how they spent their hard-earned leisure. We can watch Agamemnon rise from his bed and put on his tunic and kingly robe and bind on his shapely sandals, or arm himself with sword and cuirass and helmet for battle. We can follow the sea-faring Greeks in the launching and the managing of their ships with sails and oars; we can see the very jewels that were worn by the women and the toys with which their children played. In fact there are few sides of the life of the ancient Greeks with which we are not reasonably familiar, thanks to their writings and to the pictures with which they adorned their pottery and to the other objects turned up by the spade of the archæologist. Anything that has to do with human life has a certain interest; and almost everything that the Greeks have left shows the mark of their peculiar genius. Dressmakers of our day have often taken a hint from the grace and the simplicity of ancient Greek dress; artists not seldom find motives in the most modest household utensils of the Greeks. But it goes without saying that we shall not become better citizens of our own country by any attempt to copy in detail the environment of the Greeks. We have better ships, more deadly weapons, swifter means of communication, more enlightened methods of sanitation. What is to our purpose is to ask what lasting human experience the Greeks gathered from their daily contact with tools and games and each other; for these are things that change slowly and that never wholly change. There is no room here to attempt any account of the varied objects that the Greeks fashioned for themselves; fortunately there are many books that bring them vividly before us. But we must try to reach conclusions about certain great influences that shaped their daily lives and that seem to confront us hardly less.

In the first place, let us try to imagine the relation of the Greeks to material things, to all that we vaguely call property. The remains of Cnossos and Mycenæ suggest a civilization in which the first rude pressure of the struggle for existence against hunger and weather has already been partially repelled. Some, at least, of the population lived at ease; even plumbing, one of the last refinements of a modern age, was not wanting. But the majority of the population was destitute of comfort, even of real necessities; Mother Nature had not yet been persuaded to give a competence to the inhabitants of the Ægean; and the more a few masters were able to claim as their due, the less was left for the others. Luxury and destitution, hand in hand, fell, as they have many times fallen, before the more sturdy invaders. The Achæans and the Dorians led a hardy life; their kings shared the hardships of the common folk, and even the glamor that Homer throws over the incidents of every-day life cannot conceal from us the fact that the palace of Odysseus is only a big farm-house, his ships only big dories. The princess Nausicaa does the family washing. Life is hard, yet life is sweet; hunger stalks in the background, yet for the brave and the industrious bread and meat and wine won by the sweat of the brow, quietly on a hillside farm, or by violence in piratical warfare, need no artificial sauce. Was it otherwise several centuries later, when the Greeks had lived long in their compact towns, tilling and trading all the while? "Want has at all times been a fellow-dweller with us in our land, while valor is an ally whom we have gained by dint of wisdom and strict laws"; so spoke the Spartan king to the Persian king not long before the battle of Thermopylæ. He spoke no more than the truth. The country of Greece, as we have seen, though blessed with a wonderful climate, was a rocky and mountainous country from which a living could be won only by great toil and rigid economy. Without machinery or capital, the Greeks even of the fifth century led a hand-to-mouth life which might be terribly affected by a single poor harvest or a single defeat in war. When we subtract the things which we regard as necessities, yet which they never had, it is rather hard for us to imagine any remainder at all.[1] Even our camps in the back woods, even our poorest tenements take for granted many conveniences and comforts that an Athenian of the time of Pericles would have regarded as unhoped-for luxuries. And the fact

[1] Cf. A. E. Zimmern, *The Greek Commonwealth*, p. 209.

that in general they did not hope for them brought about far-reaching consequences. Enterprising as the Greeks were, they did not at this time expect to find happiness by the multiplication of material things; their Utopia consists not in rapid means of locomotion and communication, not in large houses or in books or in mechanical conveniences, not in a Prussian paternalism or in material well-being, but in the enjoyment of what Nature provides, and above all in the enjoyment of each other as human beings. Since modern inventions and methods of business were outside their world, their energies were liberated for essentially human relationships. The stockmarket is an impersonal thing; selling your wares face to face with the purchaser is a very personal thing. The Greek was not concerned with the problem of the national ownership of railroads: his mind wrestled instead with the problem of the rights and the duties of citizens and of the right use of art and literature, and played about the foibles of his fellow-men. Since no amount of work was likely to amass a great fortune, the incessant pressure of our ambition "to get on in the world" was absent; nervous break-downs were unknown. We may not think it an ideal life to have to do without modern comforts; but to their absence the Greeks owed a simple diet, a sturdy physique, a direct and natural view of the things they saw about them, and a great deal of healthy social life. The Athenians of the fifth century, unlike the sea-kings of Cnossos, had no drains in their houses, and they paid the penalty in the great plague; but they had a civilization, a world of ideas that are alive to-day, whereas the kings of Cnossos have left none of their thoughts behind them, and indeed it is doubtful whether their ideas would have much value to-day if they had been preserved. Civilization and contentment could exist, the world was now learning, in spite of poverty, provided that industry and leisure both were assured; it was "plain living and high thinking." So Solon observed to Crœsus, whose name is a by-word for wealth. And so Hesiod, the same poet who so strenuously preached the gospel of work, is also the author of the saying, "The half is better than the whole." To us, accustomed to hear that "half a loaf is better than no bread," Hesiod's remark seems paradoxical. But if we ponder it, we realize that things are good only to a certain point, and that if we try to increase the supply of them beyond that point we are by no means sure of having something better. So Hesiod's aphorism anticipated the praise of *sophrosyne* and the golden mean, and comes not from philosophical contemplation but from direct experience of the effect of property on happiness. Other peoples have been poor; but of early peoples only the Greeks seem instinctively to have put their finger on the fact that happiness is not quantitative but qualitative, and deliberately to have chosen the middle course.[1]

The homes of even the more distinguished citizens during the Great Age were only huts of sun-baked clay; but their owners merely slept at home, and sometimes entertained their friends at dinner there; most of their waking hours were spent out of doors, on the farm, and in the market-place, the law-courts, the assembly, the theatre, and the field of arms. Their private life was but a small part of their life;[2] Socrates had not a "home-keeping wit," for he was always wandering about Athens. The word "economics" by derivation should mean the management of a household;

[1] For hints as to the application of these ideas to modern conditions, see my "Contentment in Poverty," in *North American Review*, Nov., 1921.

[2] To a Greek a failure to take part in public affairs implied a mental deficiency, so that his word for "private citizen" is the ancestor of the English word "idiot."

but to the Athenian his city was his household, and its well-being was in his thoughts quite as much as was the hovel that he called his home, probably quite as much, we must add, as was that wife whom he regarded with affection but could not consider his intellectual equal. And if his house was squalid, his larger home, the city, grew daily in the beauty of its temples, walls, and theatres. What the individual lacked in his private life he found in the life of the state; and he was ready to endow the state with his worldly goods because he felt, as every member of an early society is apt to feel, that his farm and his right to trade and his security from attack came from the god whose temple he helped to build, and from the men banded together in his worship. Socialism in its primitive sense, — joint effort and joint ownership, — was not to him, as to us, a novel theory but an ancient fact. The public buildings were there to prove it; in his city the temple and the citadel towered above the cluster of private houses as the cathedral and the castle soar above a mediæval French town.[1]

The Greeks of the Great Age and of later ages gradually learned to build up industry and capital; but "business" in our sense of the word was only one of a number of things in which a man of affairs was interested; and he would probably prefer deliberately to remain poor rather than to acquire wealth by giving up the large amount of leisure which he considered his natural right.

---

[1] Even an old print of an American city may show the meeting-house and a few private houses as the land-marks; a Greek would be puzzled if he were shown a recent photograph of the same city and saw no church or residence above the sky-line, and learned that the towering edifices that caught his eye were office-buildings and factories.

2. WORK

The world has never seen a time when the majority of its inhabitants have not had to spend most of their time in work. The dwellers of the bleak north have generally had to work harder to wring a living from the earth than have the children of the tropics; and some individuals have by luck or by a shrewdness of their own found it possible to avoid their share of the work by letting others do more. But every human life has been supported by the performance of a certain amount of work, whatever the kind and by whomever it has been done. Nations and individuals have found that their destinies have depended a good deal on the kind of work that they have done and on the extent to which they have done it in person or by proxy.

The earliest Greeks were all hard workers by dint of necessity; those who were too lazy to help with the herds and the ploughing, or too timid to join in the hunting of wild animals or of their neighbors' flocks, naturally went hungry. There was no reserve of food stored up, no capital on which to live; the wolf was always very near the door. Such a life rewarded most the strongest muscles and the stoutest hearts; the idle and the weak went to the wall. As the contest with nature became a little less keen and hunger was a less urgent cause for plunder, wars and piracy became more a matter of sportsmanship, with recognized rules. Colonization relieved the pressure of the increasing population. Life was now not quite so strenuous; the farmer's lot was always hard, as Hesiod reminds us, yet almost every citizen had his little farm and loved it. He did not hope to become rich, and there were no large estates. Gradually some of the Greeks found that they had emerged from the struggle with a little property laid by for a rainy day; they continued to live simply, but some of their time could now safely be regarded as leisure. Meanwhile the farmer and the hunter found it worth his while to barter some of his produce for articles made by other men, rather than try himself to make everything that he used; the division of labor and the beginnings of an industrial age had arrived.

Industrialism is familiar to us; but to understand Greek industrialism of the fifth century we must think away the modern machinery, the class distinctions, and the vast scale of production that we take for granted. We must think of the potters and stone-cutters and metal-workers as working in little shops, often in their own homes, like the cobblers and blacksmiths in our country villages. Each workman was concerned with a number of processes, carrying his article usually from the raw material to the finished product. That meant, for one thing, that he regarded himself, and was regarded by others, as an artist, not as a laborer who repeated one of a series of processes in the manufacture. He had the chance to use all the skill that he could acquire in a lifetime; with this incentive he could, and generally did, find real pleasure in his work. Indeed, when Socrates wished an example of skill and real knowledge, he turned in scorn from the politicians and the poets to the craftsmen. There was no prejudice against manual labor; in fact what prejudice there was, unlike the modern one, was directed against monotonous clerical work and all confining, indoor work, as bad for the health. That is the exact opposite of the point of view of those men who to-day aspire to "white collar jobs." A craft or a trade was as dignified as a profession, and there was no distinction of names between them; the skilled and the unskilled laborers in any craft seem to have been paid about the same. Money, in fact, does not seem to have been the first consideration in the minds of these workmen; they

were really interested in their work, and forfeited the respect
of their fellow-citizens when they made their occupation
merely a means of making money, for the Greeks always
respected the amateur who was in love with his work, and
looked down on the professional who charged for his services.
The trade guilds were mainly social clubs for the preservation of the traditions of the trade, like scholarly and artistic
associations to-day, rather than institutions for collective
bargaining. As for the material products of such a system,
we need only look at a Greek temple or a group of Greek
vases to see the results of honest workmanship and the free
play of personality. The vases were made not for museums
but for every-day use; yet no two of the thousands that have
been preserved are just alike. It was not an economical way
of making pots and jugs, of course, to ask an artist to let his
fancy have free play, rather than to turn them out mechani-
cally by the hundred; and this is only one of countless evidences that the Greeks were willing to go without many
articles in order to have a few well-made and beautiful
things, and in general preferred quality to quantity.

Something like this method of industry survived through
the Middle Ages and had not entirely passed away when the
steam-engine brought in the Industrial Revolution. Machinery was hailed as "labor-saving," and therefore as a
blessing to humanity. But that is one of life's ironies. Machinery has, to be sure, enabled the manufacturer to dis-
charge some of his "hands," replacing them by mechanical
processes; it has enabled him to produce by the same outlay
of money a much larger amount of manufactures. It has
allowed a larger population to live in a given area. But except in the cases in which a manual laborer has himself been
able to substitute a mechanical operation for one done by
hand, the invention of machinery has usually not meant

that his hours have been shorter or his life easier. It has meant rather that the total production of the world has greatly increased, and with it the population; luxury, poverty, and the cost of living have increased. Mill was probably only a shade too pessimistic when he expressed his doubt whether "all the mechanical inventions yet made have lightened the day's toil of any human being." [1] What is of especial interest here is the effect both on the manufactured product and on the workman. Large scale production in many cases means economy; in many cases it means slipshod workmanship and monotonous mediocrity of design. For the workman it means a loss of interest in the work, since his share in it is limited to only one repeated operation, and he cannot feel that it matters much whether he does it really well or only just well enough to avoid losing his job.[2] His whole relation to his employer and to the public is expressed by his weekly wage; his whole interest is therefore in making the wage as large as possible and his working hours as short as possible; and it goes without saying that since he can seldom find any joy in his work the reaction in his leisure hours will be the greater, and what pleasure he can get will be wholly while off duty. Indeed, the whole principle of modern industry has been by the introduction of machinery at every possible point to dispense with skilled labor, and to divide the work into so many minute operations that a low grade of intelligence is all that is needed.[3] When the interest is concentrated on the multiplication of things and human

[1] J. S. Mill, *Principles of Political Economy*, ed. Ashley, 1909, p. 751.

[2] Some manual workers, to be sure, do still find real pleasure in their daily work, as even the form of their tools occasionally shows. Cf. A. E. Zimmern, "Progress in Industry," in *Progress and History*, ed. F. S. Marvin, p. 202.

[3] Cf. Carleton H. Parker, "The Technique of American Industry," in *Atlantic Monthly*, Jan., 1920.

beings are subordinated to this interest against their wills, human nature deteriorates.

All this may be admitted in a severely scientific spirit, without any animus against individual employers, who may be of excellent character and who merely submit to the system that machinery has created. Much has been done in the way of "welfare work" to make the lives of factory workers more tolerable; and workers themselves have tried, often successfully, by collective bargaining and by strikes to limit the terms on which labor can be obtained, so as to keep up their standard of living and insure for themselves a margin of leisure. Both these attempts, however, proceed on the assumption that the work is in itself a disagreeable thing to be avoided as far as possible, and that the life of a worker is pleasant, if at all, only because it brings high wages or because there is at times a release from toil which can be spent at the moving pictures.[1] Neither of these methods really hopes to make work interesting; yet work will doubtless always occupy most of the waking hours of most men. William Morris and John Ruskin and other gifted men in the nineteenth century held that there could be no real satisfaction for the worker and no beauty in the products of the industrial arts until by a renewal of the old system of handicraft each workman could feel that his initiative and his interest in the work really counted. There can be no doubt that in theory they were right; and many men of talent have shown that for them there is no happiness greater than in work well done. There are, however, stubborn people who

[1] Mr. Arthur Pound, in *The Iron Man in Industry*, shows that the increasing use of automatic machines is making workers largely tenders of machines; they need very little intelligence and almost no training. For such people, he suggests, not vocational training is needed but training for their leisure hours and for citizenship — thrift and the enjoyment of good games and other recreations.

will insist that it is all very well to have artistic, hand-made furniture or rugs rather than mediocre machine-made things, provided that you can afford to pay for them; but that it is not economical to do without machinery which can make things so much faster. They will even feel doubtful whether the Athenians of the Great Age would by preference have dispensed with machinery if they had known its advantages. And in particular they will accuse us of having taken an unfair example when we discussed the potters and the stone-cutters of Greece; was there no monotonous drudgery, no dirty work to be done in those days? Did the miners and sailors always enjoy their work and never look forward with pleasure to a holiday? And why have we said nothing about slavery?

It is only fair to admit that there has always been drudgery, and that it can never be wholly eliminated. The Greeks certainly knew this, and their slaves were employed to do much of the rough and monotonous work; many people have not the skill or the imagination to do any other kind. Some men, they held, are by nature fit only to be slaves. Even Aristotle thought so.[1] On the other hand, we have learned to discount the old statement that the great achievements of the Age of Pericles rested on a sordid basis of slavery. For we know that the household slaves were generally treated with at least as great kindness as were the domestic slaves of the American South before the Civil War; and slaves who showed real intelligence had a chance to take up trades or arts in which their skill counted. In these cases the slaves and the free workers were on an equal footing; slaves often received the same pay as freemen, for all were engaged in the same service of art. It was by no means unusual for a slave to save up his wages and buy his freedom. Those slaves, how-

[1] Cf. p. 210.

ever, who were fit neither for the household nor for the farm nor for the shop, — perhaps one in every four or five, — were sent to the heart-breaking labor of the mines. There, below ground, they toiled till they sickened and died. Death was indeed their only release. Without any interest in their work, they felt no loyalty toward their employers, and, unlike slaves of other kinds, tried, and, during the Peloponnesian War, tried successfully to escape. For this kind of slavery there can be no word of apology. Yet a similar system has been carried on by Europeans with equal severity on tropical plantations within the last generation.

The problem of industrialism in any age is to remember that things must at all costs be kept as the tools of men, and must not be allowed to gain the mastery over men. The Athenians of the fifth century succeeded, so far as they succeeded, in this matter by finding it possible to do without many of the things that we consider almost essential; since there are only twenty-four hours in the day, they preferred to spend their labor on a limited number of things, and to make them as well and as joyously as they could. They accepted poverty, bad sanitation, discomfort of all sorts; but they remained masters of themselves. The Athenians of the fifth century failed, so far as they failed, by aiming at so high a standard of artistic perfection in their national monuments that some unfortunate members of their society were doomed to involuntary toil so that the material foundations might be provided. The question for us is whether we are willing to prefer quality to quantity, to have fewer but better things, and whether machinery cannot be definitely governed in such a way as to do most of the monotonous and unhealthful work. Some work will always be uninteresting, and some workers will always lack ambition and imagination; and perhaps all that can be hoped for in such cases is that the conditions of work may be so regulated as to provide the leisure and the opportunities for enjoyment that cannot come from the work itself. And in every sort of work it is worth while to investigate to what extent the actual management and the profits of industry can be shared by the workers; their interest in good work and their conviction that men, not things or money, are the first consideration in industry, can in no other way be so surely won. This again is the application to large scale production of the experience of the older craftsmen of Greece.[1]

Of matters of finance, the Greeks were generally ignorant. Coined money replaced barter during the seventh century; but the use of credit, the very foundation of modern business, was understood by very few Greeks. Their business methods indeed strike us as almost childishly hand-to-mouth. The idea of storing up capital for development or for a rainy day hardly occurred to them; and any suddenly acquired wind-fall was apt to be squandered at once. A sort of prejudice kept the middlemen of all kinds within narrow limits, and a similar instinct prevented interference by the government in the fixing of prices, except in cases of great need. What seems to us more strange is the system of public finance. The Athenians of the fifth century relied chiefly on more or less voluntary contributions from wealthy and ambitious citizens for the equipment of the navy, the productions of the theatre, and other public institutions, and used taxation only as a last resort. Probably this is only another example of the instinct of the Greeks that made them trust the amateur and avoid the professional. Certainly there was a feeling on the part of wealthy Athenians that it was their pleasure as well as their duty to support the state;

[1] Profit-sharing was in fact not unknown to the Greeks. Cf. Xenophon *Œconomicus*, 9. 12.

and they gave more lavishly than they would have given under compulsion.

Late in the century, when the resources of an amateurish, hit-or-miss scheme had been exhausted, taxation and socialism, in the interest of a larger population, emerged. Meanwhile, however, Athens had attempted the precarious course of imperialism. It is possible to contemplate the Age of Pericles from either of two very different points of view. We may look, with Pericles, at the magnificence of Athens, and rejoice with him that men had been able to devote such wealth and toil to the things of the spirit. But from another vantage-ground we cannot help remembering that as the national ambition of Athens grew, free states, once her willing allies, were compelled against their will to contribute to the material foundations of her greatness. Her increasing population required an assured supply of food from other lands; and that meant a larger navy and an enforced system of food-control. There could now be no backward step; fear forced her to cling to her Empire, or even to attempt defense through offense. For many years she clung to the policy, defined by Themistocles and Pericles, that free trade made for peace and prosperity; and indeed industry and trade did flourish. Ambition grew apace. To meet the increasing liabilities of the state, Athens included in her assets the plunder of the Persian coast-lands, a fraction of the tribute of her own allies, and the treasure of the goddess Athene herself. The splendid buildings of the Acropolis and the Peiræus went up, swiftly yet with rigid economy; for they were paid for, at a cost of nearly $50,000,000, out of a war-chest which might at any moment be needed for war. And the Peloponnesian War, a war arising largely from commercial rivalries, came before the buildings were all completed. Of course this expenditure of money on temples and

statues and walls had been in the main economically unpro-
ductive; no one had ever supposed it to be productive of anything but spiritual satisfaction. And when her resources
were presently exhausted, Athens resorted to taxation and a
redoubled tribute, and, abandoning her free trade policy,
enforced an economic boycott against her commercial neighbors. Idealism and morale were gone; power alone was
prized. Slowly Athens, once the liberator of Greece, was
brought to her knees by less enlightened states. Her citizens,
originally subjected to toil for material things, and at last
liberated for a few glorious decades of mastery over material
things, had unwittingly become enslaved by their possessions. Few facts in human history have been more melancholy.

3. LEISURE

Because the Greeks were blessed with a moderate climate
and were content with a frugal manner of life, they were
comparatively free from the necessity of hurry. The occupations in which they spent their leisure hours are as characteristic of them as are their methods of work.[1]

In the first place, the Greeks ordinarily took a sane and
normal view of the value of health and bodily vigor. There
was not yet any notion that the flesh was to be subjected or
mortified; and we find their free time spent by day chiefly
in the open air, in exercise, their evenings generally in
modest feasting among friends. Youth is for them the joy-
ous time of life; hardly before Plato does old age come in for
any share of appreciation.[2] We have in the poets delightful

---

[1] On the difference that leisure made in the life of the Athenians, see John
Fiske, "Athenian and American Life," in *The Unseen World*, pp. 302–337.

[2] Cf. R. W. Livingstone, *The Greek Genius and its Meaning to Us*, pp.
124–133.

pictures of the joys of care-free hours on the farm, or of the
pleasures of the feast. Even the festivals of the gods, like
those of the Roman Catholic Church that is in one sense the
heir of the religion of the Greeks and the Romans, gave a
large scope for merry-making and for the use of the muscles
as well as of the mind and the spirit.

In fact, athletics was for the Greeks first of all a religious
institution; the runner ran, and the boxer pummelled his
opponent, primarily for the glory of God, and secondarily for
the honor of his city and for his own pleasure. The tragedy
of the death of Patroclus toward the end of the "Iliad" was
softened by the games that attended his funeral; in them his
surviving friends carried on the interests that would have
occupied him if he had lived, and thus gratified his spirit.[1]
From the funeral games, the athletic exhibition was transferred to the regular worship of the gods; and athletics never
quite lost its religious character. The prizes at the greatest
games consisted merely of wreaths from sacred trees; the
honor was therefore the greater. Victory was followed by
celebrations and gifts in the victor's native city; and his
deeds might bring forth a statue by Polycleitus or an ode by
Pindar. The games always included sacrifices and a religious
procession, and the competitors had to satisfy the officials
that they were not guilty of violating certain ceremonial
requirements. The result of this connection of athletics with
religion, so strange to us, was that the Greeks always had
happy associations with their religion, and that athletics was
for more than twelve hundred years conducted generally on
a high level of sportsmanship. The very word "asceticism,"
by which we are apt to mean the subjugation and mortification of the flesh in the service of the spirit, to the Greeks

---

[1] So, too, the *stele*, or gravestone, of later times, usually depicted the
ordinary occupations of the deceased.

meant from the first what we know as athletic "training," the harmonious development of the body and the avoidance of anything that could injure it. This development was not undertaken, to be sure, solely in the service of religion, but was required as the foundation of military service; any young man must be ready to fight at any moment, and must therefore be "in training." Gymnastic training accordingly ranked as one of the two parts of education, the other being "music," which included all the literary and artistic training that was devoted to the Muses. The interaction of the two was fortunate; athletics kept Greek art from being effeminate; and art refined athletics, preventing brutality and the striving for mere strength and the breaking of records at the expense of form and grace. Indeed physical training was often carried on to the accompaniment of the flute. The result appears in those statues of athletes of the fifth century which have never been surpassed for their harmony of manly strength and grace; probably they represent in part a tendency to idealize, but the models must have been found in the young athletes of Greece. At times, of course, the keenness of competition and the excessive attention paid to athletics caused the rise of a class of professional athletes, whose burly forms are familiar to us from the statues of the Roman period. Specialization, commercialization, and cheating were not unknown; and crowds of spectators, themselves far from athletic, used to get thrills by watching paid professionals exercise for them. Undoubtedly the standard of performance was raised by more scientific methods of training. We have heard of such conditions in our own day. But this was not in keeping with the spirit of the Greeks of the best days, who respected the amateur, and could thoroughly respect only the man whose body and mind were trained together. The success of this training is shown by the fact that some of the athletes of the sixth century kept in trim for eight or even nine Olympiads. In athletics, then, as in many other things, "Excess in nothing" was the ideal.

Athletics was not the only form of exercise: hunting of many kinds of animal was popular, and Xenophon thought it worth while, when he had retired to his country estate in Elis, to write a pamphlet on hunting. Military training and service in the field naturally took a large part of a young man's time during some thirty years of his life, and were regarded as only a natural occupation for every citizen, except slaves and the very poor. But military service was seldom thought of as a recreation, in the fifth century and later times, except by those restless spirits who despised the life of peace.

Religion, besides giving a great impetus to athletics, was the sponsor of the drama, which interested perhaps even a greater proportion of the Greeks. The whole population, probably including the women and even the children and slaves, used to frequent the dramatic festivals, to see enacted the stories of legendary heroes or to laugh at the weaknesses of their fellow-men. Whether tragedy sprang from the choruses sung in honor of the god Dionysus, or whether it grew from pantomime used in the worship of dead heroes, there can be no doubt that, like the "mysteries" and "moralities" of the Middle Ages, it was long held to be a form of religion, and only gradually came to stand on its own merits as an engrossing human interest. Even comedy traced its descent from the revels of the god Dionysus. Some of the various characteristics of Greek drama we shall discuss in another place; here it is enough to notice the spirit in which the spectators went to the theatre. At Athens there were two dramatic festivals every year, each lasting for several days. All the city turned out in a holiday mood and crowded the theatre almost at daybreak. Perhaps as many as seventeen thousand persons at once would sit all day in the theatre of Dionysus,[1] carved in the hillside under the brow of the Acropolis. In order to allow even the poorer inhabitants to attend the performances, the state in the time of Pericles instituted a "theoric" fund, from which free tickets and even spending money for the festival were provided. During the spring festival, many strangers from other parts of Greece came to Athens, and were allowed to be present at the theatre. It was a keen audience, far from *blasé* by much theatre-going, and extremely ready to express its enjoyment or its disapproval. It would clap or call for an encore, if pleased; if displeased, it would hiss and groan, or even pelt the actor from the stage with figs or stones, and call for the next play on the programme. And in spite of some of the elements in the audience whose taste was bad, and to whom inferior dramatists occasionally condescended, the judgment of the Attic audience seems to have been extraordinarily good. Though the plays were acted in the open air, and the actor was at a considerable distance from most of his audience, his acting and his reading of his lines were followed with the greatest vigilance; even a slight error brought a deluge of disapproval. Until a late period there was so little in the way of scenery that the spectators did not go to the theatre in the expectation of seeing sensational stage-settings; their interest was concentrated on the skill of the dramatist in handling his plot, on the poetry and the music and the acting. These things they noticed with the keener interest, for the plays were entered against each other in a contest, and the Greeks always dearly loved a contest. From the character of the plays that have come down to us and that we know to have won first or second prize,

[1] The present theatre on this site dates only from the fourth century.

and from what we know of their popularity when acted before an audience of ordinary citizens, we can only wonder at the extraordinary intelligence of the public that flocked to these performances. For the thought of the tragedies is often profound, the form is very subtle, and the language noble; while the humor of the comedies, though often coarse, is very highly finished. That such drama was thoroughly enjoyed, and that Sophocles should have been the favorite for half a century, argues an educated public. Yet the people of Athens and of the other towns of Greece were not great readers. In the fifth century the recitations of Homer, the daily meetings in the assemblies and courts and market-places, and the theatre itself supplied most of their ideas. This meant, however, that till toward the end of the fifth century there was not a separate class of educated book-worms or of *habitués* of the theatre out of touch with the rest of their fellow-men, any more than there was at this time a special class of athletes. Drama and athletics were both truly national, and gave a common education and common ideals to all men alike.

4. Versatility

When Solon visited Egypt, he was told by an Egyptian priest, "You Greeks are but children." Surprising as the remark may seem to us, who are apt to think of the maturity of the Greek mind and to regard the Greeks as in many things our masters, the Egyptian was not wrong. He was contrasting the youthfulness of the Greek race with the venerable civilization of Egypt. The Greeks were young in the sense that they were still experimenting in every walk of life, and their virtues, as well as their defects, were those of pioneers.

One of the striking things about the life of a pioneer is that he has to do many kinds of work. He has to be farmer and carpenter and soldier and judge all in one. That was true of the Greeks for many hundreds of years. Agamemnon was priest as well as king and general; Æschylus was soldier and poet; Pericles was general and statesman; Socrates was stone-cutter and philosopher. Even when the growth of industry brought about a division of labor, the average man was still concerned in so many other activities that he thought of himself by no means merely as a farmer or as a dealer in lamps or as a playwright. The same man would be found on different days building a ship, taking part in the annual procession to the Parthenon, sitting in the theatre at the "Birds" of Aristophanes, helping with his neighbors in the courts to decide as to the guilt of an absconding treasurer of state funds, voting in the assembly to declare war on Corinth, and the next day taking down his shield and spear to carry his vote into action. As an artisan he was not a drudge, like the modern factory worker; as a worshipper he was expressing only his gratitude to the protectress of his daily life; at the play he was laughing at the high-falutin notions of men whom he actually knew; though no politician, he felt that he had a right to see for himself whether his own interests were being guarded by his servants, the state officials, and whether he wished to fight with his commercial rivals fifty miles away; and naturally he would carry out his own vote in person. Of course all this was possible only because Greece was young and her towns were so small that their citizens could meet each other as individuals who knew each other; and something like this is found to-day in every pioneer region and in every small community.

Such a world is the natural home of experience and of ideas. Men are adventurous and are willing to try new things when they have to shift for themselves, and when they have not among them groups of professionals whose authority they must respect. They stand on their experience simply as human beings. No race has ever been more versatile than the Greeks; their native genius was many-sided, and the conditions of their life forced them to engage in many activities and to be ready to adapt themselves to new conditions. It was this characteristic that made the Athenians, who in versatility surpassed all the other Greeks, so formidable rivals of the more military Spartans: "Our trust," said Pericles, "is not in the devices of material equipment but in our own good spirits for battle. . . . They toil from early boyhood in a laborious pursuit after courage, while we, free to live and wander as we please, march out none the less to face the self-same dangers. . . . Our city as a whole is an education to Greece, and her members yield to none, man by man, for independence of spirit, many-sidedness of attainment, and complete self-reliance in limbs and brain." The ideal of Pericles was a complete contrast to that of Prussian efficiency; in fact, it was criticized by Plato, who preferred a more reasoned orderliness in all things. Was there any justification for his criticism?

It must be admitted that versatility has its dangers. The man of ability in many things may become a jack of all trades, good at none; the clever man of affairs, without moral scruples, may turn into an Alcibiades. There is a real need for specialization of some kinds, and the expert has his place. Amateur generalship and half-time business are not efficient. And the later Greeks won an evil name among the Romans for their fickle characters; they were clever, but had no depth of purpose. Plato even doubted whether the profession of an actor was good for a man, for it compelled him to enter into the spirit of many types of character;

and he traced much of the evil of his day to the aimlessness
of life that was fostered by democracy, which gave everything and every one an equal chance. We must recognize
that these criticisms are partly based on truth; but that need
not prevent us from seeing how great a benefit it has been,
for the Greeks and for us, that they lived so many-sided a
life, not confined to narrow paths of profession or business,
but acting first as men, and only secondarily as professionals.

The benefits of versatility are especially to be found, of
course, in those activities that deal with human interests and
that try to find in them what is valuable not merely for a
given time or for a given situation but for all times and
places. The dramatist who had fought at Marathon could
never become a mere closet poet; the Socrates who walked
about the streets and shops of Athens, talking with every one
he met, was not likely in his philosophy to lose sight of the
average man. The sculptor who had himself run races in his
youth was not in the way of becoming eccentric in his art.
In experience and in intellectual equipment the artists and
thinkers of Greece had at their command a contact with a
normal and varied life that has never been surpassed and
that has hardly been equalled by that of the artists and
thinkers of any other nation.[1] And that is doubtless one of
the reasons not only for their extraordinary range of subjects and ideas but for the solid basis of their experience in
human nature; it helps us to understand the "universality"
of Greek art and literature which we shall presently consider. There will be many characters and ideas that will
seem to us strange; but they will nearly always have their

---

[1] This fact was realized by those "Humanists" of Italy in the Renaissance
who tried to exhaust the possibilities of human experience. The result was
sometimes a Michelangelo or a Leonardo da Vinci.

roots in something that is fundamental in human experience. Even Euripides, when he most shocked his audience, was in reality applying to the typical experience of the Greeks the wider circle of ideas that new and even more fundamental experience was introducing. For reasons of economy, the Greek poets and artists restricted themselves, within their own art, to definite types; a dramatist wrote either tragedies or comedies, but not both; Pindar wrote odes to celebrate athletic victories; Pheidias made statues of the gods, Polycleitus chiefly statues of athletes. But we must not mistake this sort of specialization, which was self-imposed, for the kind of limitation that comes from scanty knowledge of life. In Pindar, narrow though his theme may appear, we find the glory of the athlete's victory, description, history, mythology, religion, and a sort of philosophy, all expressed in elaborate and musical verse of great splendor. And however profound the thought of the poets became, their firm foothold in the manifold experiences of their fellow-men kept them from becoming abstract at the expense of vividness; they never forgot that they were writing about men of flesh and blood, for men of flesh and blood. Even the gods whom they worshipped were never so far idealized as to cease to be the patrons of war or sea-faring, of the trades and the works of the mind; and the worship kept before the eyes of the Greeks a series of visible things, — temples and statues and processions and dramas, — which made the worshippers feel that the gods were after all not very different from experienced men.

The early settlers in America, like the ancient Greeks, were pioneers and men of several occupations. Blessed with a great country, the development of whose natural resources required initiative and adaptability, they learned how to turn readily from one kind of life to another. Yankee versatility and Yankee shrewdness have become a by-word. It is not unusual in our New England villages to find in one man an ex-sailor, small farmer, store-keeper, notary public, and post-master. Probably the West can boast of still more striking complexities. But to-day the pressure of modern industry, with the division of labor, makes such a combination more and more unusual. The typical man of to-day is a trained specialist in some one trade or profession; he may be described first of all as a brick-layer or as a physician, and only incidentally do we think of him as a member of other social groups,— a voter and tax-payer, a church member, a college graduate, a commuter, a possible soldier in case of war, a patron of the theatre, a player on an amateur base-ball team. The division of labor has certainly increased the efficiency of industry; but, as we have already noticed, it does not always mean an increase in happiness. What is more, society tends to split apart more and more into groups of kindred economic interests, so that men do not meet on the basis of common humanity but as friendly or as hostile members of certain organizations. The growth of cities has made a gap between city-dweller and countryman. City boys sometimes grow up without the bodily vigor and the first-hand knowledge of the natural world that comes from country life; and the country boy often has little knowledge of the world of human relationships. Many of our most influential artists and writers tend either to become a professional clan, developing their personal tastes and living a life that cuts them off from any close contact with the experiences of other men, or else to attempt so slavishly to reproduce superficially the taste and the notions of the "average" man that the public is in neither case the gainer. Printing-press and moving pictures, admirable in many ways, magnify these tendencies by giving them a larger audience.

Yet there are other influences that may keep us from becoming mere fractions of human beings. The very purpose of schools and colleges is to put at the command of their students a larger fund of experience than they can ever hope to gain from their ordinary environment. In school and college, moreover, a boy often gets his best chance to be in the country for part of the day or for some years of his life, and to live the healthy kind of life that the majority of men once lived. Education is often condemned as too bookish, and out of contact with "real life." The criticism is almost as old as education itself. When a better substitute has been found for books, they will no doubt be discarded; and we must not underestimate the value of the "Socratic method" of living discussion, as well as of independent investigation and experiment. But for lack of anything that has yet been found to take their place, a great part of education will have to be gained from the experience recorded in books. After all, good books, which we generally dignify by the name "literature," whether they deal with historical fact or with scientific fact, or with the realm of things that the poet calls into being, are simply convenient means of reaching the minds of other men and other times; they open windows for us. Books will not be the whole of education: Plato himself had a scornful distrust for books, those dead, unresponsive things which can never take the place of living speakers. And even the most eager student of the most profound book cannot get from it the same vivid experience of life that will be his if he lives through the experience himself. We must know how far to use books, and we must also live with men. Friends, especially friends who differ from us in age and in tastes, and travel, if it does not mean merely the most superficial sort of globe-trotting, help us to enlarge our horizon and to escape becoming provincial. The modern man, for better and for worse a specialist, needs also to cultivate interests outside his own work; a hobby or an avocation is sometimes the saving of the professional man. It is worth noticing that the men who are most happy try to use at least part of their leisure in some occupation that offers a complete change from their daily work; [1] the office-worker becomes an amateur gardener, the manual laborer learns to play a musical instrument. We Americans, to be sure, do not lack distractions; sometimes we suffer not so much from monotony as from the attempt to avoid monotony by picking up amusements that require nothing of us and that therefore can really do little for us. The ordinary musical comedy and the mechanical toy or the mechanical musical instrument are examples of this. There is something to be said both for the profit and for the pleasure that come from the toy that the boy has made for himself, and for the music that one produces, however imperfectly, by one's own fingers.

It goes without saying that a margin of leisure is necessary for a many-sided life. Holidays and occasional vacations are real necessities; for most of us they mean the only escape that we have from routine, the best chance to drop our specialties and become human beings. That is the opportunity for the man whose daily life is spent in the artificial and unhealthy atmosphere of the city to get into the country and to use his muscles again; that is the opportunity of the tired manual laborer to rest and to gain some contact with beauty and a larger environment, even if it is only by means of the moving pictures. Not without such releases can the strain and the concentration of modern life become tolerable.[2]

[1] For a somewhat similar reason, we who live in the city and have modern methods of heating our houses, actually prefer wood fires in an open fireplace. It is fortunate that our tastes are in some ways unreformed.

[2] The building of "garden cities," comparatively small industrial communities in the country, achieves a similar end.

Still another expedient has been suggested, but with a somewhat different purpose in view, by the philosopher William James. His object was to find some way of diverting into a useful channel all the energy and spirit of adventure that have hitherto been lavished in war. His proposal is that the young men of the country for a year or two of their lives be enrolled in a citizen army, whose work is to be the conquest of the forces of nature. They would build the roads and irrigate the deserts and cultivate the farms needed by the nation. Not only would they gain in physical strength and in discipline and in knowledge of the world, but their joining in this common task would make for national unity and for democracy.[1]

These are some of the forces that might make for a more well-rounded life to-day. The Greeks enjoyed such a life, partly accidentally and partly because they wished to live as they did. We shall not do well to imitate them in the details of their life; but we may well consider whether, in view of the experience of the Greeks, we could not order our lives, as individuals and as a nation, in such a way as to become more many-sided. Some things we cannot change; others we can change if we will. Fashion and habit are to a large extent our sovereigns; but the Great War saw changes in our ways of living,—economies and charities and enthusiasms,—which fashion and habit would till then have ridiculed.

The Greeks owed their many-sided life in part to circumstances, but even more to their own choice. Their country was poor; they accepted poverty and learned to enjoy what happiness could go with plain living. They had to work; but they chose to limit their wants to such things as they could supply without sacrificing quality to quantity or the work-

[1] William James, "A Moral Equivalent for War," in *Memories and Studies*, 1911.

man to the product. They found at last a margin of leisure, which they used in the development both of body and of mind. And by a lucky instinct they tended to resist any specialization that prevented them from remaining in their lives and in their art anything less than well-rounded men. Above all, they were in the main successful in making themselves the masters of their surroundings and their material possessions, without letting things dominate them. On the west pediment of the Parthenon they placed the statues of Poseidon and Athene in rivalry for the chief worship of the Athenians. For many years of the fifth century it seemed as if the Athenians had chosen Poseidon, and were going to found their greatness on the material wealth that sea-power gave them. We know how disastrously the attempt failed. The goddess Athene, patron of the arts and the things of the spirit, was their ultimate choice; and their lasting gifts to the world have been not material but spiritual.

CHAPTER V

THE FINDING OF BEAUTY

1. ART AND LIFE

ALTHOUGH few things in the experience of the Greeks were more characteristic of them than their art, we could make no greater mistake than to think of their art as something apart from their ordinary life. The simple fact is that half unconsciously, half by steadfast and austere determination they learned to do certain things, which must in any case be done, in a superlatively satisfying manner. A story was to be told; they found that the restriction of dactylic verse or the conventions of the drama gave it heightened intensity. There was a water jar to be made, or a coin to be struck, or a home for the statue of a god to be built; no long period of experiment taught the Greeks what proportions and what use of decoration gave the most pleasing effect. And so it was no accident that the same adjective, *kalos*, was used of what is noble and effective and pleasing in any kind of activity, whether it was a brave act on the field of battle or a well-proportioned human body. This truth has sometimes been expressed by the saying that the Greeks made no difference between the beautiful and the good; that their æsthetics and their ethics were one. They admired with all their hearts a finely conceived act or a harmonious form, without stopping to ask whether it was an outward physical charm or an inward fitness and harmony that commended it. Good conduct was not wholly a matter of good taste, nor was art judged wholly by its moral effect; nevertheless public respect was given to no character that was

100

boorish and unattractive, and no work of art could find
favor if it violated the national ideals of human excellence.
Music, they thought, affected character, and character
could be depicted in music. Plato's denunciation of certain
tendencies in Greek literature and art arose from the growing severance between art and philosophy in his own time;
the denunciation is not typical of earlier Greek thought, nor,
as Plato believed, is there any inherent incompatibility between art and philosophy (which for this purpose means
only the idealized view of life).

Greek art was therefore not a matter of particular *objets
d'art*, of extraneous ornaments added to the usual occupations of men as a relief from sordid business or domestic
drudgery. The Greeks were not often collectors of the
bizarre. Curios always have an attraction for the sophisticated taste that is already sated by the appeals of a normal
environment; but the Greeks generally cared less to be
sophisticated than to be wise, and found an escape from the
limitations of their lives not in eccentric but in heroic art.
Their art, then, was not the concern of a special class of artists and writers out of sympathy with the life and the interests of ordinary men. There were no cliques of artists
who carried on a special and esoteric cult; Greek art was
truly national. And however deeply interested the artist
was in the technique of his art, his eye was first of all on his
subject-matter; for it was that which first attracted his fel-
low-countrymen. The Greeks demanded statues of the gods;
the sculptors undertook to express in their works the traditional conceptions of the gods, and a Pheidias would bring
forth a Zeus even more majestic than the ordinary image of
the god. We must not forget, in our interest in the technique
of Greek art, that the Greek artist would have forfeited the
approval of his public if he had given all his attention to

technique or had made his art the vehicle of personal whims that were not within the comprehension of the average citizen. Art existed neither for art's sake, nor, on the other hand, for the service of a code of morals; art was a part of life.

We cannot easily keep in mind the great extent to which the art of the Greeks came from their daily lives and addressed itself to the general public; for we have many different publics, and our art is often regarded as something superficial, to be enjoyed only by those who have the inclination and the wealth to buy it. There are those who "go in for" art and those who do not, we say; and we do not expect them to meet on a common ground except as "economic men" or as voters. We do not all read the same newspapers, see the same buildings, hear the same music, or feel that the same things are beautiful or ugly. Perhaps there is no reason why we should. But the artist whose work is to be of large and of lasting significance must in some way address himself to the common interests of humanity. Greek art did this; and that is one of the reasons for its vitality. Homer may have been a court minstrel or a singer at a religious festival; but his appeal was not merely to the courtly group or to a religious sect. For centuries the Homeric poems were recited at public gatherings and were memorized by schoolboys. Greek drama, as we have seen, was patronized by the whole nation; like the drama of Shakspere, it had something for everybody. The most ignorant member of the audience, who was incapable of appreciating the profundity of a chorus or of a soliloquy, could at least enjoy the stirring plot of the play. The "Œdipus Tyrannus," like "Hamlet," is a good detective story, and appeals to those who like blood and thunder, as well as to more subtle minds. Greek architecture and sculpture served the national religion; even lyric poetry was for a long time chiefly choral. History was given forth at religious and athletic gatherings; even philosophy descended for many fruitful years from the skies to the market-place, and permeated the life of Athens. The same public that fought in the Persian wars and voted in the assembly and competed at the Olympic games was the audience of the poets and the patron of the architects and sculptors; it is no wonder that Greek art was vigorous and kept a wholesome contact with national ideals.[1] If Greek art ever did depart from this norm, it was because it catered to only a part of the public or attempted to force the peculiarities of the artist on the public. In spite of the splendor of Pindar, one can hardly help feeling that his eulogy of the athletic ideal has been bought by the reactionary nobles of Sicily, and that it does not compare worthily with the spirit and the interests of the Marathon-fighter Æschylus. At times we feel that Euripides strained to win by sensational means the ear of the modernists in the theatre; and his drama was at times tainted with decadence and theatrical posturing. Yet even so his drama reflected the change in popular sentiment and ideals that the Sophists had helped to accomplish.

Like many things which are religious in origin or in spirit, Greek art tended to be conservative. The general plan of a temple was seldom changed; certain types of sculpture persisted for centuries; the principles and many of the details of drama were, comparatively speaking, fixed. Other forces, too, made for conservatism. But the fact that art was restricted in its subject-matter and in some of its conventions, and was nevertheless the sphere of keen competition, put the artists on their mettle to discover new methods of treating their material. The more strict the rules of a game, the more resourceful its players become. In athletics this leads to ex-

---

[1] Cf. J. A. Symonds, *Studies in the Greek Poets*, vol. ii, pp. 11–15.

tremely skilful technique and sometimes to professionalism; in art, too, it often leads to such emphasis on the technique that the subject-matter is regarded as of little or no importance. It is then that we hear of "art for art's sake," and that artists and writers rebel against what seem to them artificial restrictions and conventions. We are accustomed to think of Greek literature and art as formally excellent, and we may even think that the Greeks concerned themselves first with form and technique, neglecting content or subject-matter. This is a mistake. It was not till a comparatively late period that the Greeks attached more importance to the "how" than to the "what"; during the best years of Greek art and literature, there was a happy condition in which the matter and the manner were partners.

No formula, of course, can explain why the Greeks were able within so short a time to produce so much that is beautiful, however helpful it may be to analyze certain principles that they seem to have followed.[1] No formula can explain personality or genius; and the genius of a race is even more difficult to define than is that of an individual. We have to begin with the obvious fact that the Greeks were extraordinarily sensitive to certain kinds of beauty.[2] They lived close to nature, and were keen observers of the varied life of mountain and valley and sea. The same zest and love of description appears in the figures of animals and flowers on the early vases and in Homer's rapid descriptions of a forest fire or a hungry lion. These things are interesting for their own sakes, and a life that includes them has a tang of downright reality. For Homer there is no detail of everyday existence, no bit of wild nature or of man's occupations, too trivial to arrest his attention or too homely to be sung by

[1] Cf. p. 46.
[2] Cf. Livingstone, *op. cit.*, p. 35.

him. But this does not mean that all things were for the Greeks of equal interest. Keen lovers as they were of the beauty of the sea and of the changing pageantry of the seasons, these things were for them only of secondary importance and served only as a setting for their chief interest, which was man. Often as Homer and his successors dealt, for example, with the sea, it was chiefly not for its own sake, but as background for the human drama; and descriptions of the world of nature occur most often in the form of metaphors and similes.[1] In fact, all the strange events of nature, the daily course of the sun, the thunder, the death in winter and the resurrection in summer of the trees and flowers, were explained by being turned into human forms; Apollo and Zeus and Demeter took the place of less familiar beings.

The Greeks therefore did not leave us landscape paintings; but they did interest themselves in the beauty of the human form, in the deeds and the emotions and the thoughts of men. In all this a fortunate instinct kept them from excesses. The men whom they depicted were seldom, in the first place, like the monsters with which oriental and Celtic art have made us familiar, animal-men or hobgoblins; nor were the gods whom they imagined mere shadowy abstractions, as the gods of the Romans sometimes were. On the other hand, the Greeks were seldom content to take for their subjects men just as they happened to be. The accidental, the insignificant, and the ugly must be sloughed off and ignored; the typical and the beautiful were their concern. This does not mean that they were interested very much in the superficially pretty. What has been called an "athletic leanness" characterizes most Greek art and literature; and their beauty comes from the perfect adaptation of resources

---

[1] I have traced the relation of these interests from a single aspect in "The Sea in the Greek Poets," in *North American Review*, March, 1914.

to ends that we associate with sane athletic training. In Greek poetry, therefore, we sometimes miss the riot of adjectives and the high-pitched emotional key that are common in modern verse; and the Greek statue does not seem concerned to catch our eye and excite it by a theatrical appeal, like the average magazine cover of to-day. But this very economy and restraint of the Greeks enabled them, when the occasion offered itself, to rise to the emotional intensity of the "Agamemnon," or to place in the midst of a group of statues so commanding a figure as the Apollo of Olympia.

We may think, for convenience, of the art of the Greeks as consisting of two stages; these are not absolutely distinct, and the various arts attained their full stature in different periods. We may call these stages the discovery of beauty and the creation of beauty. In the earlier stage, the Greeks lived much in the world of the senses, and strove merely to describe or to depict first the natural world and then the forms and the acts of men. Things existed in their own right, and the sensitive eye and imagination discovered what was beautiful in them. This is the primitive notion of art; and it is not very different from the view of some of our contemporaries, realists or naturalists, who feel that the whole function of art is to record in colors or in words as exactly as possible the "facts" of which they are aware. Of course it takes no profound analysis to show that in even the most superficial record the artist is bound, consciously or unconsciously, to select from among the countless impressions that come to him. This selection, as it becomes more and more conscious, amounts to creation; and the Greeks passed at a very early era from the discovery to the creation of beauty. The sculptor suddenly realized that by altering the pose of the figure before him a new power or charm could be gained; that the drapery which he had represented merely because he had seen it could be manipulated so as to contribute to a chosen effect. The architect who had inherited the general scheme of the temple found by experiment that certain proportions and relations in the structural members of the building produced a satisfying result. The poet who had told his story as it had been told to him conceived the idea of altering the plot or of changing the nature of some of his characters. Perhaps he even used the story as the vehicle for expressing his ideas on political or social or religious themes. And doubtless all the time, as he wrote down what he chose of legends about men and gods, he more or less consciously idealized his material; he wrote not merely about the tribal hero Achilles or the Titan Prometheus, but he attributed to them all the experience that men had or might have; he expressed, as we say, the universal by means of the particular. And generally he succeeded in resisting the danger of becoming didactic; his story carries us along by its own power.

Greek art and literature, then, arose amid the ordinary activities of life, and was the gradually perfected performance of things that must in any case be done. The artist and the writer discovered, however, that much depended on his command of the technique of his craft; and he spared no labor to evolve such artistic types or conventions, even such limitations, as would ensure in each kind of work the greatest effectiveness which the material was capable of producing. But he was so deeply interested in the matter and in the thought that, except sometimes in later art and literature, form was regarded merely as the fitting vehicle for the substance.

2. DIRECTNESS AND IDEALISM

Two qualities in the art of the Greeks distinguish it from much of the art of later ages: the first we may perhaps best define by saying that the Greeks drew constantly on the evidence of the senses, and that they told directly, without interpretation, what the objective world presented to them. They let facts speak for themselves. Read at random a page of Homer, and notice how much of it is the simple record of the visible acts of men or of the sensible forms and events of the natural world; look at the Parthenon marbles or at a vase-painting, and observe how much of the concern of the artist has been simply to make us see the beauty of clearly-defined and well-grouped human forms. Greek art, then, in its directness of method means careful observation and faithful record; it does not allow the artist to get between his subject-matter and his audience, or even to let his shadow fall across his work. On the other hand, the Greek artist did not hold himself in a purely receptive mood, and record in words or in marble each and every impression that came to his eyes and ears; the task would obviously have been impossible, even if it had been attempted. The Greek, like every true artist, had to choose among the impressions that came to him, and to subordinate the parts to the whole. These are the two striking qualities in his art and literature; he selected his material with a large purpose in view; yet whatever facts he did select and record, he allowed to speak for themselves.

The world of nature, with its multifarious forms and activities, was treated in this way. Homer gives us a few striking characteristics of a scene, lets us see them clearly, and without further comment passes on to his next subject. He wishes to put before us the image of the noisily thronging

Greek army going to battle. "As the many flocks of winged birds, geese or cranes or long-necked swans, in the Asian meadows about the streams of Caÿster fly here and there, rejoicing in their pinions, and with noisy cries keep settling forward, and the meadow resounds, so from their ships and huts the many tribes of the Greeks kept pouring forth upon the Scamandrian plain, and the ground rang terribly under the feet of them and their horses. And they stood in the flowery meadows of Scamander, countless as the leaves and flowers that bud in spring." Alcman describes night: "Sleeping are the crests and the chasms of the mountains, the headlands and the ravines, and all the creeping things the dark earth rears, the mountain-ranging beasts and the bees, and the monsters in the depths of the purple sea; sleeping, too, are the flocks of wide-winged birds." And there Alcman stops, without adding, as his paraphraser Goethe adds, a couple of lines that make the peace of nature a symbol of human emotion.[1] The same poet writes of the gull, "that flies over the blossom of the swell in the halcyon's company, with a careless heart, the sea-purple bird of spring"; and he resists the temptation, if he feels it, to sentimentalize the gull, as Mrs. Browning did.[2] Flowers appear countless times in Greek poetry; but it is almost always the outward aspect and the associations of flowers that are introduced, and only a few late Greek writers make them symbolic of woman, as the mediæval writers constantly did.

Nature was to the Greeks, after all, of only secondary interest; their first concern was with man. Here again we are

[1] Cf. F. G. and A. C. E. Allinson, "External Nature in Greek Poetry," reprinted in L. Cooper, *The Greek Genius and its Influence*, pp. 34–46; and my *The Sea in the Greek Poets*.

[2] Cf. R. W. Livingstone, *op. cit.*, pp. 75 ff. I have found his chapter on "The Note of Directness" very stimulating; I think it may have suggested my use of the term "directness" in this chapter.

struck by the directness with which they treated their subject. In sculpture, of course, it is to be expected that direct
representation, firm outline, definite and clear-cut masses
will be achieved; it is more likely that the obvious and external characteristics of an object will be brought before us
in a statue than that we shall see in it the more inward qualities of its model. The tendency of the Greeks to work
directly made them, to our mind, better sculptors than
painters; the few landscapes and painted portraits from their
hands that have survived fail to give the atmosphere and the
insight into human character that we expect to gain from
paintings. To this objection the Greek would perhaps answer that sculpture and painting are by nature external and
deal with externals; that the young athlete and the goddess
are the fit subjects of sculpture, and that the mental anguish
of Prometheus or of Hamlet are the fit subjects of poetry.
A Greek artist would probably not have chosen such a subject as did Rodin in "Le Penseur." All that is vague and
undefined or that is the concern of the spirit, rather than of
the senses, their instinct tended to avoid in the plastic
arts; the young men of the Parthenon frieze are nobly-
formed young men, and nothing more; their faces do not try
to show religious ecstasy or any other emotion. The "Laocoon" group does indeed show deep, even terrible, feeling.
But we cannot regard this group as so fine a masterpiece as
the works of the Great Age; and we are inclined to agree
with Lessing and his followers in holding that the subject of
the "Laocoon" is more fit for poetry, an art dealing with
associations and with events in time, than for one of the
spatial arts.[1] The "Hermes" of Praxiteles relies for its
effect wholly on its grace of pose and line. One of the secrets
of the superiority of the best Greek sculpture to most of
modern sculpture lies in the fact that it did not try to accom-

[1] Cf. Lessing's *Laocoon*, tr. Frothingham, pp. 91 ff.

plish more than lay within its powers; unlike romantic art, it did not lose its hold on what is within its grasp in the attempt to reach the vague phantoms of the imagination.

Even in literature, however, the Greeks tended to deal with man as directly and externally as possible. Epic poetry was necessarily concerned with events, rather than with psychological analysis; compared with even the average modern novel, Homer is straightforward almost to the point of *naïveté*. But the events that he narrates are so chosen and so told as to make analysis superfluous; it is what Achilles does, rather than what is said about him, that makes his "wrath" so potent a *motif* in the "Iliad." In the drama, effects were often very cleverly, even subtly, drawn; but in a large theatre in the open air the most telling effect was bound to be one of action. The plot came first; poetry and the multifarious appeals of the theatre were contributory. Homer does not try to describe, item by item, the beauties of Helen; he merely recounts the effect that they produced on the elderly Trojans: "It is no cause for blame," they say, "that the Trojans and the well-greaved Achæans for such a woman a long time suffered woes; for in her countenance she appears terribly like the immortal goddesses." What is more surprising, Homer can sound even the deep emotions of the heart by the simple statement of external fact. Briseis, the captive of Achilles, is taken from him: "the woman departed unwillingly," is all that Homer says. The Pompeian painting of the scene shows Briseis brushing a tear from her eye; how a modern writer would yield to the temptation to sentimentalize the scene, it is interesting to conjecture.[1]

---

[1] As a matter of fact, the story was later strangely twisted. Chaucer makes of the fortunes of Cressida (a character growing out of a confusion between Briseis and Chryseis) "an elaborate psychological novel " (G. L. Kittredge, *Chaucer and His Poetry*, p. 112). In Shakspere, the tone is cynical, and Cressida has wholly degenerated.

When Helen speculated on the reasons that withheld her brothers from battle before the walls of Troy, not thinking of the real reason, their previous death, a plain statement of fact, without exploitation of the irony of the case, is enough for Homer's purpose: "So she spoke, but them the life-giving earth already held, far away in Lacedæmon, in their dear fatherland." But these instances, it may be objected, are only incidental; Homer here restricts himself to these few words of fact, in order not to wander from the main theme. Let us therefore hear the words of Andromache just after she has learned of the death of her husband, Hector; here is a theme worthy of as full treatment, of as emotional treatment, as any that we could imagine, for Andromache is a devoted wife, and her husband is one of the chief person-ages of the "Iliad." She faints; and when she returns to her senses she laments the untimely death of that husband who was intended for her by fate; she had better never have been born. "But now thou dost go to the house of Hades under the hidden places of the earth, and me thou dost leave a terrible sorrow, a widow in thy halls. And there is still our son, a mere child, whom we brought forth, thou and I hap-less; nor wilt thou be a comfort to him, now that thou hast died, nor he to thee. For even if he escape the war of the Achæans, that brings many tears, ever there will be toil and sorrow for him in after time; for others will despoil him of his plow-land. Yea, the day that makes a child an orphan be-reaves him altogether of comrades, and he is cast down, and his cheeks are wet with tears. And in need the child goes to his father's companions, pulling one by the cloak, and an-other by the tunic; and one of them is touched with pity, and holds a cup to the boy's lips for a little time, and moistens his lips, but does not moisten his throat. And one whose par-ents are living thrusts him from the feast, beating him and upbraiding him; 'Away with thee! thy father hath no seat at our table.' And tearful our child will go back to his widowed mother, he, Astyanax, who formerly would eat nothing but marrow and the rich fat of lambs, sitting on his father's knees; and when sleep came and he ceased from his frolicking, he would slumber in his bed, in the arms of his nurse, in a soft couch, filling his heart with good cheer. But now, bereft of his father, he shall suffer many things, Astyanax, 'lord of the city,' as the Trojans call him, for thou alone wert wont to defend for them its gates and long walls. And now beside the curved ships, far from thy parents, the worms will quickly devour thy naked body, when the dogs have had their fill; fine raiment and beautiful, wrought by the hands of women, lie in thy halls; but verily all these I will burn with blazing fire, not that they may give pleasure to thee, since thou shalt not lie in them, but that they may be a glory in the eyes of the Trojan men and the Trojan women." How little of Andromache's personal emotion is expressed, except in concrete images! It is the loss of Hector as a defender that is foremost in her mind, and that is expressed in the most vivid and definite way. It is the relation that Hector himself had expressed when he left her for an earlier battle: he had evoked a picture of his enslaved widow, plying the loom and carrying water in far-away Greece, and Hector would not be there to save her. The obvious facts of the separation are what the poet puts before us; there is nothing mystical or spiritual about the relation. Yet who can say that the story is not moving?

Even in the personal lyric of the Greeks, with its lack of reserve, we do not find, till a late period, anything but the obvious phases of love, sorrow, and happiness. As the drama, true to its name,[1] deals primarily with action, the

---

[1] *Drama* means a thing done.

lyric is more apt to share the definite imagery of drama and of narrative poetry than to lose itself in reflection and abstract language. Perhaps love is the emotion that we are most apt to lift out of its earthly plane and to spiritualize; how differently the Greek poet treated it we may discover by reading a poem of Sappho, addressed to a young girl. "He seems to me to be the peer of the gods who sits opposite thee and listens near at hand to thy sweet voice and thy lovely laughter, that makes my heart flutter in my breast; when I look upon thee for but a little time, my voice fails, and my tongue is broken, and a subtle fire runs straightway stealthily through my body; my eyes have no sight, and my ears ring; sweat pours down me; and a trembling seizes the whole of me; I am paler than grass, and I am all but dead; I seem distraught." Emotional intensity can go no farther than this; yet it is all on the physical plane; indeed, the poem was once cited by a Greek physician as a record of the symptoms of the disease, love.[1]

In all these matters the Greeks were keeping their eyes fixed on the world of the senses, and recording what they saw. But surely there were some things which could not be seen, but which were none the less real and interesting — causes, hopes, motives, and all the furniture of the mind. What did the Greek do with them? As far as was possible, he put them on a level with the objects of sense, and then dealt with them directly. In other words, he personified the emotions and the processes of the mind. The gods and the heroes were much more than forces of nature, however closely they were bound to nature; Apollo and Athene came to enter into the intellectual life of the Greeks, as well as into their physical life. Achilles in his anger debates whether to kill Agamemnon; while his hand is drawing his sword from

[1] Cf. R. W. Livingstone, *op. cit.*, pp. 74–96.

the scabbard, Athene comes down from heaven at the behest of Hera, seen only by Achilles. She rebukes him, and bids him refrain from violence of deed; he admits the justice of her words: "I must needs obey the word of you twain, goddess, angry at heart though I am; for so it is better. Whoever obeys the gods, him especially they hearken to." His hand, which has been all the time on the hilt of his sword, now thrusts it back into the scabbard, and Athene returns to Olympus. In ordinary speech, we may say that Achilles hesitates between two courses, and that his better judgment prevails. Rather than make such a flat statement, Homer throws the conflict into a picturesque and dramatic form. A later age might rationalize the episode, and get from it a valid psychological account; or a later poet might turn the gods and goddesses, as Ovid did, into merely human beings, whose superior qualities lent themselves to comic or pathetic plots. But in the age of Homer and of the great lyric and dramatic poets of Greece the myth was the natural device for filling gaps in the understanding; there was no effort of the imagination, for it was easier to imagine than to reason. And even in the drama, in which deep problems of human life are raised and debated, the problems arise immediately from the action, and their solution is carried out in action. Prometheus suffers before our eyes; vengeance and retribution move visibly from one member to another of the House of Pelops.

If an artist or a writer fixes his attention very closely on the things that he is trying to express, he has not much opportunity to make a display of his own personality. No literature and no art is more impersonal than those of the Greeks generally were. It is not merely that their artists worked in certain conventions, or that their poets wrote in certain literary types, without always caring to claim au-

thorship by signing their works; it is not even that their
great sculptors were sometimes little more than directors of
schools of workmen, a Pheidias only *primus inter pares*, and
their writers members, as it were, of a guild. What is more
to the point, is that their interest was first of all in what we
may call the objective world of facts, and that personal, sub-
jective reactions and preoccupations came later. In any art,
the matter, the artist, and the spectator or auditor form a
triad. It is possible for any one of the three to take more
than its rightful place: if the matter alone is considered, the
result may be bald, uninteresting, lacking in proportion; if
the artist thrusts himself too much into the foreground, we
may get mannerism, personal whim, unreality; if the spectator's claims are too urgently pressed, the art will be specious and rhetorical. Too great attention to the matter
gives us the naturalism or the realism of a Zola; the exploitation of the artist gives us at best the whims of a Lamb or a
Hazlitt, at worst the eccentricity of a Baudelaire or a Wilde;
the excessive cultivation of the public results in journalism.
The Greeks realized, of course, that the interests of the public and the genius of the artist must govern the selection of
material from all the chaos of life; but if they emphasized
one element in the triad of art at the expense of the other
two, it was apt to be the matter. The artist was willing to
subordinate himself to the story or the theme that he was
treating; and the public was so much interested in the objective facts that it did not expect to have its passing fancies
made the criterion of the artist's appeal. The Greek was not
so much interested in what Homer thought of Achilles as in
what Achilles himself did and thought; and Homer rarely
speaks in his own person except to tell the story. The result
is no less a clearly conceived outlook on life. The other poets
and artists are on the whole not much less reticent than

Homer. In all this the conservatism of arts that spring from religion no doubt played a part; the artist was content to be an almost anonymous servant of a god. The day of literary reputations came only slowly; copyright and a feeling against plagiarism did not exist. It was in the theatre that competition caused the poet most consciously to pit himself against rival poets; even here, however, the poet put forward personal idiosyncrasies only at his own peril.[1]

Of course the amount of individualism in Greek art and literature varied somewhat according to the race of the artist. With the Dorians we associate conservatism in politics and manners; we think of the severity of the Doric order of architecture, the sturdiness of Apollo, the patron of the Dorians, the athletic figures of the Argive sculptors, and the self-forgetting choral ode which belongs, in the main, to the Dorians. With the Æolians and the Ionians, on the other hand, we associate luxurious living and adventurousness of thought; the human interest of Herodotus and the sentimental elegies of Mimnermus reflect their pliant spirit, the delicacy of the Ionic column their outward life. Among the Athenians, who, though perhaps partly of Ionian stock, appropriated whatever of other civilization they admired, we find the best of both the Dorian and the Ionian; the drama preserves certain traits of the choral lyric, which was a form of poetry cultivated more by the Dorians than by the Ionians, but also gives scope for new ideas; the Parthenon, with its Doric columns, has a frieze that is characteristic of Ionic temples; and Attic philosophy combines the physical speculation of the Ionians and the mathematical inquiries of

---

[1] We know that the judges at dramatic contests were occasionally corrupted; but they were then moved by personal considerations, such as fear of the wealthy and influential man who had acted as "producer," rather than by low standards of art. Cf. A. E. Haigh, *The Attic Theatre*, 3d. ed. (1907), pp. 34 ff.

the Dorians with Athenian humanism. Generalization, however, is dangerous: the "Works and Days" of Hesiod, who lived in a Dorian environment, is more personal in tone than the Ionic epic of Homer; many "Dorian" poets are Dorian by adoption, and are merely expressing the ideas of their patrons; and conventional artistic types appear everywhere before the artist wins any degree of free play for his ideas.

The modern world, though willing to admit that the Greeks saw clearly and in their art aimed at fidelity to fact, may sometimes miss in Greek art and literature something to which we are accustomed. The Greeks were direct; yes, but does not this directness at times means baldness, hardness, lack of sympathy? Does it not fail to give us color and atmosphere and emotional moods, of revery, or of melancholy, or of elation? Is it not worth while to blur the outlines of things, to lose them in a splendid mist, to see the poetry of half-truths and of the imperfect? "The Grecian gluts me with its perfectness," wrote Lowell, glorifying the Gothic architecture of Chartres. Shall we agree with him? [1] And was not the Greek perhaps too austere in regarding his audience so little? Is not the audience a leading partner in the triad of art, and rhetoric essential for adapting the matter to those who are to receive it? Let us try to answer this last question first.

Certainly adaptation to end is a large part of the artist's task; and that is the office of a true rhetoric. But adaptation may easily become an end in itself; and then true rhetoric gives place to false. Not the sane and normal audience, but the eddies of public opinion become the criterion, and we have journalism. Or, again, both the matter in hand and the

[1] For an eloquent but not wholly convincing statement of this attitude toward the Greek view, see Renan's *Prière sur l'Acropole*.

audience are forgotten, and the swelling phrase or the hollow gesture takes the place of truth. Nothing is so unreal as theatrical rhetoric that has lost its contact with the facts on which art ultimately rests. And much of the world's literature consists of rhetorical commonplaces, *topoi*, as the Greeks called them, polished but empty declamations. The pretty conceits of the Alexandrian poets and their Roman imitators, like the conceits and the extravagances of some of the Elizabethan and the Jacobean poets, ring hollow; they may please us for the moment, but they give small lasting satisfaction. The rhetorical pathos of much of Latin epic and drama and of many of the Romantic poets is at times tawdry fustian, compared with the austere statement of Homer and Sophocles. The power of brevity and simplicity and complete adaptation of words to subject and to occasion is always felt, whether it is in the "Funeral Oration" of Pericles or in its modern counterpart, the Gettysburg Address of Lincoln.

But what of real sentiment and color and mystery? Did the Greeks gain by their limitations? Did they simplify life too much, and reckon too little with the infinite and the imponderable? I think we must admit that there are reaches of human experience into which they seldom entered; they paused on the threshhold of the vague and undefined, and passed into it unwillingly. Not that they could not feel, with our Romantic poets, the lure of the remote and the strange; from Homer to the last poets of the Alexandrian Age there was magic of adventure and magic of the human mind.[1] But the Greek preferred to place his magic quite definitely and concretely where he could watch it; and he

[1] Cf. J. A. K. Thomson, "Classical and Romantic," in *Greeks and Barbarians;* and S. H. Butcher, "The Dawn of Romanticism in Greek Poetry," in *Some Aspects of the Greek Genius.*

did not feel the need of overstating it. There was enough cause for wonder and enough beauty in the multitude of things that were about him everywhere, without his often inventing new wonders or telling us all that they meant to him. A primrose was not merely a yellow primrose to him, and nothing more; but he could feel something more without rhapsodizing. In his emotions he did not "slop over"; in his words he left much to the imagination.[1]

There is much in common, therefore, between Greek poetry and the aims of the modern "Imagist" poets. These poets hold, among other beliefs, that poetry should "employ always the exact word, not the nearly exact, nor the merely decorative word"; it should "present an image . . . should render particulars exactly and not deal in vague generalities, however magnificent and sonorous. . . . The cosmic poet . . . seems . . . to shirk the real difficulties of his art." They "strive to produce poetry that is hard and clear, never blurred nor indefinite." [2] With most of this a Greek would almost instinctively agree, nor would it be hard to quote passages from Æschylus that are admirable examples of the theory of these "Imagists." In one respect, nevertheless, there is a wide divergence of aim. Æschylus, like the "Imagists," does "render particulars exactly," without feeling it necessary to pump the proper emotions for us; but these particulars are details in a larger picture, parts in an organic whole. The modern "Imagists," believing that "concentration is of the very essence of poetry," are apt to lavish their skilful technique on detached scenes and episodes which do not, severally or collectively, give a large satisfaction; they are interested in rendering faithfully certain kinds of matter, seen through their own personalities,

---

[1] Cf. R. W. Livingstone, *op. cit.*, pp. 40–42, 96–108.
[2] *Some Imagist Poets: an Anthology*, 1915. Preface, pp. vi and vii.

forgetting that men in general are apt to ask that art shall bear a close relation to life as a whole. It is not the "cosmic poet" like Æschylus, treating details faithfully but subordinating them to a scheme in which human destiny is the theme, who shirks the real difficulties of his art; it is the poet who limits his art to the fragmentary.

It was because the poets of his own time seemed so content to remain among the particulars of the sensible world, and to cater to the passions and fancies of the populace, that Plato made his famous criticism of them. Believing that the evanescent particulars of sense are shadowy and unreal, compared with the eternal verities that are apprehended by the mind, Plato could not consistently tolerate an art that remained wholly in the flux. Yet he realized that the poet could envisage the world of eternal verities and shadow it forth by means of concrete imagery; and so far as the poet did so, he won Plato's approval. Plato, of course, was not averse to concrete imagery as such, and had recourse to it when he tried to recount the mystical vision of the world of truth.[1] In his repulsion to the attitude that is content to scrutinize the immediate world of the senses, Plato was the foremost representative of many Greeks, philosophers and mystics. Because he saw the comic possibilities of an extreme antithesis between poetry as it was and philosophy as it would like to be, he did not choose to recognize the idealizing tendency of all the best Greek art, but only its directness.[2] But Aristotle was merely expressing the other side of the Platonic point of view when he observed that poetry is

[1] *Phædrus*, and *passim.* I have dealt with this matter more fully in "Plato's View of Poetry," in *Harvard Studies in Classical Philology*, XXIX, 1918.

[2] Cf. *op. cit.*, and my "The Spirit of Comedy in Plato," *ibid.*, XXXI, 1920.

more philosophical and more elevated than history because it deals with universal, not merely with particular, truth. So Wordsworth surmises that the Solitary Reaper may be singing of some

> *Familiar* matter of to-day . . .
> Some natural sorrow, loss, or pain,
> That has been, *and may be again.*

Plato's own influence on art and poetry was on the whole a good one, calling attention to the possibilities of idealism in treatment and to the value of the intangible verities realized only by thought. The course of Platonism in later literature is almost the course of thought itself. On the other hand there has been not a little formal rhetoric and sentimentality which derives from the same source. The greatest art keeps its hold on concrete reality, and deals with it directly; yet it contrives to see things as parts of a greater whole, and the temporal in its relation to the eternal. The best Greek art and poetry is at once direct and ideal.

In our observation of the directness of Greek art and literature, therefore, we must not miss, what some might consider even more characteristic of them, their idealism. Nothing could be more simple and direct than the way in which Homer tells of the expedition of the Princess Nausicaa with her companions to the river, of the washing and the game that followed it, and of the uncouth stranger who startled the gentle maidens. But if that simplicity and directness were all, Nausicaa and her companions would have been the only persons to whom the story would have been of interest. Homer has contrived, however, to invest the homely detail of the story with the charm not merely of the actual but of the permanently real and interesting. Every age is attracted by youth and beauty and adventure, every

age enjoys a picnic by the river. And what is true of this
episode is true of Greek art and literature generally; there
are stretches of human experience which are of permanent
interest to men, and the Greek instinctively treats of these
matters. So long as man feels rebellious against injustice,
Prometheus will appeal to him; so long as he feels that there
is a righteousness that is above human laws, or that the lot
of women is hard, or that war crushes the innocent, he will
find truth and enlightenment in Antigone and Medea and
Andromache. It is therefore in two different, though not
opposite, senses that we find pleasure in the literature of the
Greeks; its directness appeals to our love of the actual, yet
at the same time we find in it the tokens not merely of the
experiences of the Greeks, but of human experience. The
same words appeal to us, as it were, on different levels of ourselves. "Let us consider," writes Cardinal Newman, in a
famous passage, "how differently young and old are affected
by the words of some classic author, such as Homer or
Horace. Passages which to a boy are but rhetorical commonplaces, neither better nor worse than a hundred others
which any clever writer might supply, . . . at length come
home to him, when long years have passed, and he has had
experience of life, and pierce him, as if he had never before
known them, with their sad earnestness and vivid exactness.
Then he comes to understand how it is that lines, the birth of
some chance morning or evening at an Ionian festival, or
among the Sabine hills, have lasted generation after generation, for thousands of years, with a power over the mind, and
a charm, which the current literature of his own day, with all
its obvious advantages, is utterly unable to rival. Perhaps
this is the reason of the mediæval opinion about Virgil, as if a
prophet or magician; his single words and phrases, his
pathetic half lines, giving utterance, as the voice of Nature

herself, to that pain and weariness, yet hope of better things, which is the experience of her children in every time." [1]

Greek literature and art, then, keep their freshness partly because they deal with the experience that is of all people and of all times; *quod semper, quod ubique*. And how does this occur? Partly, as we have seen, because the Greeks themselves lived such a many-sided life that they absorbed much of human experience, and wrote and carved from the fullness of their experience; partly, too, because they deliberately chose to leave out of their work much that is accidental, and to express only the essential. Their artists tried to present, in the paradoxical words of Aristotle, "probable impossibilities rather than possible improbabilities." We need not, of course, take literally the word "impossibilities"; but the point is clear enough. Some creations of a poet — the character of Achilles, or the death of Antigone — strike us as in keeping with the nature of things, whether they ever found a place in the chronicles of history or not; they are more plausible than the best authenticated coincidence. This is the reason for the comparative repose of most Greek sculpture and its avoidance of the temporary attitude; the characteristic, rather than the possible phase that a camera might happen to catch, was sought. Even a *discobolos* in the act of hurling the discus was exceptional. Portrait sculpture came late; the head of Pericles by Cresilas [2] is evidently an idealization, rather than an attempt to render accurately his features. If we set such a statue, or the Hermes of Praxiteles, side by side with a modern realistic statue, we instinctively feel the difference; in the one case there is an attempt to express the appearance of man, in the other we have Tom, Dick, or Harry in some particular atti-

---

[1] *Grammar of Assent*, ed. 1901 (Longman's), p. 78.
[2] In the British Museum.

tude or occupation. Even the most highly idealized statue cannot help presenting its subject in some attitude or setting, even in a highly concrete setting. But idealism, as such, means the neglect of all that detracts from the concentration of interest on the permanent. The hero of tragedy, as Aristotle points out, is not merely the personality before us; it is man generalized. And the pupil of Aristotle, Theophrastus, wrote a series of sketches of typical characters,— all comic, because of some large defect,— which we can easily recognize as true to human nature to-day. The New Comedy, and its descendant the Roman Comedy, dealt largely in these comic types, — the miser, the surly father, the lover, the braggart soldier, the parasite; and dramatists of later periods, under their influence, tried, like Ben Jonson, to present "Every Man in His Humour" (i. e., in his character). Idealism, then, need not imply what we mean by idealization, as Plato would have preferred, but simply the presentation of what seems permanently significant in human nature.

Idealism has its dangers. If it means merely abstraction, the omission of detail and variety, it runs the risk of losing our interest. If the artist tries to leave out all the familiar traits of the everyday world, — the expression of countenance, the wrinkles, the characteristics which each personality has, — he may reduce his picture nearly to a blank, featureless and devoid of content. If the poet tries to lead us into the presence of eternal truth, he may lose his grip of the world about him, and give us only rhetorical commonplaces that fit all occasions but that have no especial fitness for the particular occasion. The Greeks and their imitators did not entirely escape these dangers. Some of the statues of the archaic period are mere types; some of the later sculpture is theatrical. The New Comedy repeated character, plot, and jest till they became merely so much stock-in-trade; and the Alexandrian poets and their Roman imitators had ready-made sentiments and phrases which could be introduced at any convenient moment.[1] But the best Greek artists and writers were saved from this danger by their directness. However much they lifted the actual into the light of the ideal, they did not cease to deal with it as they might with anything actual. They avoided shadowy abstractions; the universal was not something external, brought forcibly upon the stage, but the present seen as universal. War is terrible; but the Greek showed its terrors in the person of suffering Andromache. He tried to reduce the infinite and the vision-ary so far as he could to the finite and the visible. This world is neither perfect nor complete; but the Greek found that anything more perfect or complete could be best real-ized by being translated into terms of this world. Then the mind could pass from this world, as by an easy step, to a more perfect world; and the Greek could say, with Keats,

> Heard melodies are sweet, but those unheard
> Are sweeter; therefore, ye soft pipes, play on;
> Not to the sensual ear, but, more endear'd,
> Pipe to the spirit ditties of no tone.

3. CONVENTION AND ORIGINALITY

We are so much in the habit of thinking of the Greeks as pioneers looking at life with fresh eyes and expressing their experience without feeling the trammels of tradition, that it sometimes surprises us to find how much of their art and literature is in a sense conventional. In the subjects that they treated, as well as in their artistic forms, we are aware of a certain continuity, even of repetition. This need not imply a slavish attitude of mind. For any art is fundamen-

[1] Cf. p. 119.

tally a matter of conventions and accepted illusions. When we talk, we agree to attach certain meanings to certain sounds; and it is only by a similar acceptance that the painter's lines and colors represent objects of sense; they would seldom deceive us into thinking that we were looking at real mountains or people, and if they did so deceive us, we should not long find them interesting. Out of all the chaotic material before him, the artist selects certain elements, governed partly by involuntary racial or personal instincts, and partly by the particular purpose of the moment. The human mind, then, is the dictator that decides what things shall be used and how they shall be used.[1] More than this, it has been the experience of men everywhere that they enjoy formal relations of certain kinds, in space or in time; they instinctively find pleasure in symmetry of architecture, and balanced effects in sculpture, and measure or proportion in speech. Especially a recurrent theme gives pleasure, whether it be the regular succession of columns in a building, or of figures in wall-paper, or the refrains and the rhythms of poetry and music and the dance. It happens, too, that rhythmic language or action is the normal expression of great emotion; the regular beat of metre therefore gives to poetry the illusion of emotional excitement; but it is excitement confined by the will of the poet to a pattern; it is "emotion recollected in tranquillity." [2] This confinement is one of the economies of the artist; instead of allowing his material to

[1] It is a pure convention, if we choose so to consider it, that Homer's heroes pause in the midst of battle to make speeches that are too long to find a place in any real battle; their only justification is their appropriateness to the characters. We must know what is going on in their minds; this convention, in keeping with an inner, not with an outer propriety, gives the opportunity. Of such a nature are the visions and divine apparitions, the stock epithets, and the stock lines that are important in the epic machinery.

[2] Wordsworth, Preface to *Lyrical Ballads*, 1800.

sprawl at large, he gives it a vertebrate structure, subordinating details to the main purpose. Restriction does not necessarily mean loss of freedom; the explosion of gun-powder produces an effective shot only when it takes place in the confining barrel of a gun. Conventions in art may be not only natural and pleasing but the absolute condition of concentrated effectiveness.

Mere following of convention, on the other hand, and the endless repetition of forms, however interesting they once were, become monotonous and even meaningless. Order and unity must be brought out of chaos; but variety is a natural human craving. Much as we like to recognize the familiar and to welcome the recurrence of sounds or lines and colors, we are no less interested in the strange that offers a contrast with the familiar. Unrelieved rhythm becomes doggerel; constant repetition of the same design in architecture bores us. The task of the artist is to discover, without surrendering the advantages that his conventions have given him, how to give the pleasure of surprise. He may seek new subject-matter, new plots and strange people and settings and novel ideas, and original methods of presenting his materials; or he may even revolt against the conventions of his art. Probably it was Archilochus's originality in several of these fields that won for him his enormous reputation among the Greeks, — a reputation which his intrinsic merits hardly justify.[1] Usually mere originality, mere revolt, is wasteful; for conventions are ultimately based on experience and common sense; and originality simply satisfies our desire for a contrast with the known, keeping an undertone or ground-bass of the known. The subject-matter and the methods of the arts are always expanding, now gradually, now by leaps; but the process is more like the enlarging of a circle, whose

[1] Cf. J. A. Symonds, *Studies in the Greek Poets*, vol. i, pp. 276, 279.

centre is man, than like the progress of a man along a road. The discovery of the new does not always require the abandonment of the old. So originality often merely discovers something new in what seems familiar. The dactylic hexameter is made to reveal new rhythms; the drama, the sonnet, the symphony are proved to be no hindrance, but rather an asset to one who has ideas. The poet learns how to vary the regular beat of his metre by substitutions and inverted stresses and "run-on" lines, so that the more individual design of the sentence-rhythm shall be heard against the stiff pattern of the metre. A subject painted by many painters becomes, in a moment, when the master takes it up, absolutely new: we thought we had always known it, but it seems as if we were only now beginning really to become acquainted with it. An old story, told by countless poets, is retold in such a way as to seem fresh. The legend of Achilles was old before Homer touched it; Shakspere borrowed most of his plots, yet they are his own. Even a borrowed phrase may be used by a poet in such a way as to bring old associations into a new context. "Neither familiar things grown trite, nor things so new as still to be remote and alien, ever grip us as do those things which are at the same time old enough to touch the chords of memory, and yet fresh (if I may use a poet's phrase) with some unspent beauty of surprise. And the supreme test of originality is its power to give us the sense of a footing on trodden and familiar ground which all at once is recognized as unexplored." [1] In their essence, then, conventions consist of certain limitations, voluntarily accepted, because of a gain in pleasure and effectiveness; when these conventions are imitated as in themselves valuable, without regard for the occasion, we have conventionality. In the same way, a religious ritual which is at first

[1] J. L. Lowes, *Convention and Revolt in Poetry*, pp. 106 f.

spontaneous and expressive may by repetition become almost meaningless, unless its meaning is kept constantly in view. And in a somewhat similar way, the best works of the Greeks and the Romans, at a later time described as *classici*, or "first-class," because they were felt to be the most perfectly formed expressions of human experience,[1] became objects of admiration and study and imitation for many hundreds of years: yet "the classics," if merely imitated in their external features, will produce only conventionalities. Their true value appears only to one who realizes how they, and the conventions in which they abound, came to exist, and who can further distinguish in them the accidental and the permanent.

So much may be said in general of the relation between convention and originality; we must now examine a little more closely the experience of the Greeks in their finding of beauty, and see how it was that they were at once the most conservative and the most original of people. And first we must notice that much of Greek art, we might almost say most of all art, is in origin religious. The primitive man is anxious for success in the hunt or in battle; he instinctively goes through a dance that rehearses his actions in the hunt or in battle, or that recounts his past experiences. He draws or models forms that are prayers to dimly imagined gods. Now these are ritual acts, the repetition of which is held to be efficacious; but they are the beginnings of art. The often-repeated spring festival in honor of Dionysus, a ritual act, was the ancestor of the *drama*;[2] the votive image of the rain-god or of the sun-god, offered in the hope of getting rain or

[1] Cf. Sainte-Beuve, *Qu'est-ce qu'un Classique?* Causeries de Lundi, Oct. 21, 1850.

[2] It is even possible that the etymological connection between *dromenon*, as applied to a ritual act, and *drama*, a thing done, is an indication of an historical connection.

sunshine, was preserved in the typical gods of later days. Now few human activities are so conservative as religion; and ritual, which is constantly repeated, is the most conservative part of religion. It is not surprising, therefore, that drama and sculpture and the temples in which the images of the gods dwelt, should have perpetuated old types, even when their significance was almost forgotten. The chorus of the drama were nothing but the worshippers of Dionysus who in earlier times had danced about his altar; murder was not represented on the stage because the theatre was still sacred ground. The reliefs on Athenian gravestones tended to preserve an archaic technique, even when sculptors knew more developed forms. But the conservatism that is natural to religious rites was among the Greeks only one phase of an even more wide-spread conservatism. Not only religious activity but many other activities of the Greeks were social rather than individual. The artist was the spokesman for the collective ideas and emotions of many beside himself. Though he seldom, except during the fifth century at Athens, consciously worked as the spokesman of national ideals, he was always aware of old traditions,— myths, and customs, and sculptural forms,— which expressed to his fellow-men their common ideals; and many of these ideals had been expressed superlatively well by the poet who came first in time as well as in excellence. So it was no accident that Pheidias drew his conception of Zeus from Homer, and that Æschylus in his dramas pretended, as he said, only to serve up "fragments from the feast of Homer." [1] The later poets and artists therefore had to reckon with the fact that Greek life was institutional, and appealed, as it has been

---

[1] This is the usual interpretation of the phrase. But it is possible to hold that Æschylus meant that he used the large slices untouched by Homer; he did indeed draw much more from the Cyclic poets than from Homer.

said, to the "greatest common denominator" of their audience.[1] This is doubtless one of the reasons for Greek idealism, in that the universal and permanent was the constant in the tradition, and the accidental and the individual had less prominence. It also enabled the artist to take much for granted; an allusion in a play to something not fully stated was enough to awake old associations; a plot could be rapidly developed because the audience was familiar with all that went before. For this reason, too, the dramatist was able to introduce into his plot many a bit of "irony"; for the audience often knew what the characters on the stage were not supposed to know. The tendency to idealize was assisted by the usual avoidance on the part of poets and sculptors of contemporary subjects. The well-known story that tells of the condemnation and fining of Phrynichus, because he presumed in his play on the "Taking of Miletus" to deal with the recent sufferings of fellow-Greeks, shows that the Greeks resented too immediate an appeal to their sensibilities; the strain was too great for their endurance. But as bodies of old legends were treated again and again, the interest of the audience was held not by any notion that they were witnessing historical events, but rather by the lasting truthfulness of the ideas. If it is universal, not particular truth that we seek, what does it matter whether we have an ancient or a modern instance? The story of Agamemnon is as dramatic a case of fallen insolence as the most recent episode; and the struggles of the Lapiths and the Centaurs in the metopes of the Parthenon suggested, better than any realistic representation of Greek and Persian would have done, the old conflict between Greece and the Orient, between civilization and barbarism. Indeed the perpetuation of the old myths

[1] H. W. Smyth, "Aspects of Greek Conservatism," in *Harvard Studies in Classical Philology*, XVII, 1906.

and subjects served to take the preoccupations of the Greeks out of time and to lead them into that region where beauty and truth live in eternal youth.

Other conventions of the Greeks are more or less rationally explained. The circumstances of Greek life, which in classic times practically excluded romantic love and the marriage for love, excluded romantic love from classic poetry; only Euripides among the dramatists deliberately presented a woman in love. It may be mere habit that restricted the tragic poets to the writing of tragedy, and comic poets to comedy, and that in general limited rather severely the provinces of the several arts. Certainly from an early time there were distinctly defined literary forms, — epics and dirges and encomia and hymns and odes in honor of athletic victors, and the like, — and Plato went so far as to say that these divisions were inherent in the nature of things and should not be contaminated.[1] It may be partly accident that the forms which special conditions first called forth were so scrupulously kept distinct; but there was at least this advantage in the accident, that constant experiment within the several forms developed them intensively as far as art could go. In a later epoch, of course, it was easy for formalists without creative energy to go through the traditional motions of writing drama or epic, with all the proper conventions and sentiments; but the life was gone.[2] Except

[1] Yet the Socrates whom he professes to report in the *Symposium* holds that the genius of tragedy and of comedy is one in its insight into truth.

[2] The Greeks did not, however, go so far as did English poets of the eighteenth century in holding to a special "poetic diction," using some words as in themselves "poetic" and discarding others as "prosaic." Of course they realized that some human experiences and their associations touch the emotions more nearly than others, and they therefore had much to say, like modern poets, of home and fatherland, of death and things beautiful, of the sea and the stars; but there was no particular set of adjectives or phrases reserved, as in the age of Pope, to characterize them. Thus the Greeks were

for a few purple patches, not much of the literature of the Alexandrian Age greatly interests us. Its more characteristic excellences, the flavor of its personalities, rest on other foundations than imitation.

With all these forces making for convention, it may be hard to find a place in Greek art for originality. Yet the Greek was so closely in touch with the life that he expressed that traditions were for him only conveniences. "The same subjects are handed down through many generations of poets, but almost never are the newcomers enslaved by the authority of their predecessors. If they readily accept the given models, they also accept them in the right way; for example does not in any fashion cramp them. . . . The use of old subjects, and even of established forms, is for them like the use of language: every one avails himself of it without a thought that he is thereby imitating any one else."[1] "The Greek vase-painter in all periods works in schemes. He does not freely invent a new embodiment for a tale or a myth. He is dependent on the manner in which that tale had been represented in earlier art. He must satisfy the eye as well as the mind. But, on the other hand, though he accepts and repeats a scheme embodying artistic tradition, he does not, unless he be a mere workman and no artist, accept the scheme in a slavish way. He alters poses and details, omits figures, or introduces fresh ones; sometimes he merely

spared the long debate about the literary *cliché* versus the *mot juste* which has agitated French and English letters. (See passages from Wordsworth's Appendix of 1802 and from Coleridge's *Biographia Literaria* quoted in R. P. Cowl, *Theory of Poetry in England*, pp. 205–218.) But figurative language, the natural idiom of poetry, did become at times stereotyped; a given situation provoked a given simile. And tragedy did at times affect a certain pompousness of style.

[1] M. Croiset, "Histoire de la littérature Grecque" (by A. and M. Croiset), quoted by L. Cooper, *The Greek Genius and its Influence*, p. 95.

improves the lines of the composition. Here, as in every field of Greek activity, we find infinite variety of detail within limits cheerfully accepted by the poet or artist. An exceptional poet or artist pushes back the limits; a conventional spirit keeps far within the bounds." [1]

Let us, then, notice how the Greek tried in several of the arts to secure economy of effort by creating conventional types, and then to secure interest by variation from type. And first let us consider poetry. The materials of poetry are as wide-spread as life itself. It is hard to see what human experiences, what activities and emotions, what types of character, and what ranges of the fancy Homer could have known that he did not bring within the confines of his poems. But art imposes, or at least accepts, limitations. The emotions and the characters of the "Iliad" are subordinated to one episode and one man; order is thus brought out of chaos. In the briefer forms of poetry, naturally, only certain aspects of life were selected for song or satire or meditation. But it is in the drama that we find the most striking instance of life envisaged through a clearly defined window. Even in Homer we have seen the workings of the divine law by which sin and pride have their just reward. Paris brought suffering not only on himself but on countless others; the suitors of Penelope perished because of their own insolence. The note of *nemesis*, the sure retribution that follows guilt, is sounded constantly in most of the poets from Homer to the drama of the fifth century, as well as in Herodotus; and the theme of *nemesis* is the mould in which Attic tragedy is almost always cast. But the convention is differently treated by the successive dramatists. Æschylus shows us the progress of pride and insolence, leading to impiety or violence committed blindly, and ending in a retribution

[1] P. Gardner, *The Principles of Greek Art*, p. 239.

which involves, it may be, the third or fourth generation.[1] The majesty of fate, to which even the gods seem at times to be subject, and the merciless working of the family curse, almost overwhelm us. The generous act of Prometheus because it defies Zeus, condemns him to suffering; the sins of Tantalus and his son Pelops beget new sins, and the "House of Pelops," great but greatly guilty, passes from crime to crime till all is at last expiated by the blameless Orestes; the overweening might of the Persians meets its doom at Salamis. In the working of this *nemesis* there is something impersonal that affects us with a sense of helplessness. Sophocles accepts the convention; but he brings fate nearer to the tragic hero, making it in effect the unexpected result of his own character. Wilfulness brings its own reward. Œdipus is not a wicked man, he is merely headstrong; yet the outcome of his deeds is tragic for him and for others. And our interest is transferred from the impersonal fate to the workings of the will and of suffering in the soul. Antigone commands our admiration for her calm choice of duty, which brought her, as she knew, to her death. Philoctetes is a pathetic figure simply because of his undeserved suffering; and the interest of the play of which he is the hero is far less the working of fate than the working of different motives and emotions as they appear to the various characters. The wounded and deserted Philoctetes holds in his possession the only means of taking Troy; shall he be won back to his fellow-Greeks by force, by guile, or by persuasion, and how will he respond to each appeal? Intrigue and character are now part of the dramatist's capital. But the audience of Euripides, already accustomed to see again and again the same

---

[1] This is the burden of the old saying of the Jews, quoted by Ezekiel, XVIII, 2: "The fathers have eaten sour grapes; and the children's teeth are set on edge."

plots and the same problems, now expects to have its interest aroused by new devices; and Euripides does not disappoint his audience. Taking the same stories and the same dramatic conventions of chorus and dance and costume, he introduces into his plays the sophistic thought of his own day, with its scepticism about the gods and about austere morality, and its rhetoric and subtle logic. For an audience that is no longer so certain as before of the sure pursuit of crime by divine justice, a new tragic motive has to be found; and this Euripides finds in pathos. *Nemesis* is for him no more than an outworn convention; but he is deeply attracted by the human interest of the old stories, which reflect the mutability and the helplessness of life. It is no longer the pursuing Furies; it is just bad luck. So Euripides draws freely on the old legends, but makes the tragic heroes and even the gods more like ordinary men. They have lost much of their majesty; but they are often nearer to our life and our problems than are the austere figures of Æschylus. At the same time, they have externally the same pomp and splendor as before; and they stalk in statuesque poses on the same vast stage, and declaim to the same huge audience. Naturally the effect is somewhat "theatrical," as if children or marionettes were imitating a real drama; and we are often aware of melodrama and sentimentality and spectacular interventions of the gods. Sometimes the plot is so complicated that we really need the prologue that Euripides provides. At its best, however, the tragedy of Euripides by its transformation of the dramatic conventions has made itself the vehicle for new beauties such as his own day and every sophisticated age, like our own, can appreciate perhaps more easily than we can the severity of his predecessors; beauties of romance and sympathy and brilliant episode.[1]

[1] Cf. J. A. Symonds, *Studies in the Greek Poets*, vol. ii, pp. 15–33, 149–170.

The history of Greek comedy shows a similar development of convention and similar inroads of originality; but
our materials are so scanty that we cannot trace the development in detail. Like tragedy, it was originally associated
with the worship of Dionysus, and included the coarsest sort
of buffoonery. It was brought from the country to the city
festivals, and by degrees borrowed the stage machinery of
tragedy, substituting the grotesque comic mask for the
tragic mask, and the low slipper for the high-soled buskin.[1]
It always had, and generally exercised, the privilege of dealing with ordinary men or even with low life, rather than with
the exalted personages of tragedy; and even the gods were
liable to ridicule. Heracles never steps upon the comic stage
except as the good-natured buffoon. The comic chorus is apt
to consist of animals or of other strange creatures, and to go
through not only the usual evolutions of tragedy, with its
entering and retiring songs, but to take part in an *agon*, or
debate between two of the characters, in which a principle is
set forth or a quarrel is decided; and it even advances, in
the *parabasis*, to harangue the audience with the views of the
author. For in all the drollery of the old Comedy (which includes all the comedy before and contemporary with Aristophanes), there was a plentiful supply of ideas, particularly
of a satirical sort; any public character, any eccentric individual might expect to see himself pilloried on the stage;
and Aristophanes devoted plays to satirizing the absurdities
of the Athenian war policy and its democratic sponsors, the
new education and the sophists, the excessive love of litiga-
tion and of Utopian political ideals, the ethical and literary
creed of Euripides, the political claims of women, and, in a
word, all unsanctioned innovations. Sincere in his conserv-

---

[1] Cf. Milton, *L'Allegro:* "Jonson's learned Sock"; *Il Penseroso:* "Gor-
geous Tragedy . . . the Buskin'd Stage."

atism, and fearless in his criticism, Aristophanes by the
vigor of his exquisite but downright verse exposed to laughter every deviation from the sane tradition of Athenian life;
in technique we have nothing to-day that suggests him so
well as the operas of Gilbert and Sullivan, and there is something of his spirit in the ministrations of the London *Punch*.[1]

The Old Comedy was largely concerned with political subjects, and dealt much of the time with personalities; the
comic chorus was its life. But with the decline of political
life and the economies required at the close of the Peloponnesian War, the chorus was confiscated and the Old Comedy
died of starvation. The Middle and the New Comedy are
known to us chiefly from fragments and from Roman imitations, which were in turn imitated in later European literature. Travesties and burlesques on tragic themes were
common; romance and intrigue became increasingly prominent. Less vigorous and daring than the Old Comedy, the
New Comedy concerned itself more with average humanity
and above all with special types of character.[2] Though the
fragments of Menander usually disappoint us, he enjoyed an
extraordinary reputation in antiquity, largely for his insight
into human nature and his delicate art. Nor should we forget that comedy in the fourth century before our era supplied the place taken in modern times by both the drama
and the novel and in part also by the moving pictures; and
the combination of realism and romance and universality
achieved by Menander impressed the ancients as Shakspere
and Molière, Thackeray and George Meredith impress us.
The outward traits of the New Comedy, with their plots and

[1] Mr. Punch is the same stubborn, lovable, old-fashioned fellow, with his
heart always in the right place, as the old countryman Dicæopolis, the hero
of the "Acharnians."

[2] E. g., the soldier, the cook, the lover, or the slave. Cf. p. 125.

characters and pithy sayings, were singularly attractive to the imitator; and Roman comedy is little but a series of imitations or combinations of Greek plots, characters, and rhetorical commonplaces, within the narrow world of intrigue and self-seeking that the New Comedy had made its province. Greek comedy, like Greek tragedy, had found its natural limits, and ended in the perpetuation of conventions.

If we turn to the architecture of the Greeks,[1] we find again that certain purposes and certain material conditions determined the mould in which the architect was to work; these he accepted, and found the perfect form which the harmony of these requirements demanded; then, without discarding his conventions, he contrived by slight variations and adaptations to surprise the beholder with a sense of discovery. The temple was the abode of a god, the home of his image; as such, it was shaped not unlike the palace of an Ægean monarch, an inner chamber having an approach of pillars or being surrounded by them. The pillars at Cnossos, we remember, were of wood; and we have the testimony of Pausanias that wooden pillars persisted in Greek temples till a comparatively late time, being replaced by stone as they decayed; one wooden pillar remained when he saw the Temple of Hera at Olympia in the second century A.D. Indeed, the front elevation of a Greek temple is in its structure something like a wooden "frame" house, with uprights, transverse beams, and slanting gable-roof. This structure, later translated into stone, was the basis of some of the characteristics of the most noble Greek temples. For there was never any attempt to conceal the structural design; on the contrary, the skeleton always boldly met the eye, nor were its bones allowed to cross each other or to be lost in decora-

[1] The reader of the next few pages is advised to have before him some illustrations of Greek temples; the text will then be more easily understood.

tion. The upward thrust of the columns, and the solid mass
of the horizontal architrave that rested on them, and the incline of the roof, gave a sense of simplicity and power; it was
in the parts of the temple that had no strain that decoration
was allowed.[1] Much of its beauty, however, is quite apart
from its detail, and lies in the extraordinary care with which
the proportions of its structural members were planned.
Only the most accurate measurements have revealed with
what extreme subtlety the architect adapted the width and
the height of his temple to the diameter and the number of
the columns, and thus imparted a rhythm to the whole. In
the decoration, too, the functions of the members were considered; the grooved flutings of the pillars merely accentuate
their direction; the capitals effect a transition from the perpendicular to the horizontal. The triglyphs, which simulate
wooden beam-ends resting on the architrave, again have
perpendicular grooves, to suggest the direction of their
thrust. The wall of the temple inside the pillars "is primarily intended to divide or enclose; it is a curtain in stone,
and its decoration runs horizontally in narrow bands which
remind one of the hem or border of a curtain";[2] here we
have the frieze. The parts of the temple that have least
structural importance give the greatest scope for free decoration. The frieze, which is found on a flat wall, consists of
sculpture in low relief, and is apt to represent processions or
battles; the square spaces between the triglyphs, known as

[1] The secret of successful landscape gardening rests in a somewhat similar
preservation of a studied contrast between the formality of certain elements
— trim paths, lawns, and architectural members, and the less rigidly confined contribution of nature, in masses of foliage and flowers, with perhaps a
setting of untouched nature.

[2] P. Gardner, *A Grammar of Greek Art*, p. 34. I owe much to the sugges-
tions of this admirable book. The enlarged revision of it is entitled *The Principles of Greek Art*.

metopes, perhaps originally left open, and then filled in with
painted slabs, eventually received sculptures in high relief,
as befitted the depth of the cavity; and the two pediments,
the triangular gables at the ends of the temple, contain
groups of sculpture in very high relief or even in the round.
All these carvings are planned so as to fill their space. It
appears that the larger members of the temple, — the columns and walls and other unbroken surfaces,—were colored
only by the mellowing hue of the stone, which usually acquired a creamy or even a golden tint; the snow-white of
Parian marble was rarely used for temples. But certain
smaller parts, especially the sculpture and the borders and
cornices and other spaces and bands reserved for decoration
seem to have been painted with vivid touches of color, even
with tones that to modern eyes, accustomed to softer shades
and to the subdued light of more northern climates, might
seem almost garish. The effect under the bright sun of
Hellas may have been different to unsophisticated eyes; our
color-sense has been more educated than that of the Greeks,
though our sensitiveness to proportion is perhaps less acute.
At any rate, the brilliant contrasts of color that the Greeks
seem to have loved can hardly have surpassed those of nature in southern climates.

In these ways the Greek architect strove to discover the
natural and logical limit of his art. It might seem as if there
were slight opportunity here for originality, when once so
rigid a type had been developed. Yet a cursory glance at the
temples that remain will show how much variety was
achieved. Not only were the several orders, the Doric, the
Ionic, and the Corinthian, separately evolved, and endowed
with their peculiar characteristics of strength and grace and
ornate grandeur; but the architects learned how to plan their
proportions and their details according to the site that a

building was to occupy. Thus on the Acropolis of Athens alone we find the Parthenon, dominating the cliff and the whole landscape by its massive form; the Erechtheum, compelled by the site and its local cults to conform itself to an irregular plan, and throwing out its ever-charming Porch of the Maidens (Caryatides); the Propylæa, acting as the approach for the whole Acropolis, with columns wide enough apart to admit chariots; and the little Temple of Victory, perched on a lofty bastion of the rock, so perfect in its slender lines that it does not suffer from its proximity to more imposing structures. Nor is the Parthenon itself lacking in originality of design. Alone among Doric temples, it borrows from its Ionic sisters the frieze, and treats it with great informality; all its chief lines have a slight curve, and by this optical correction are prevented from appearing to sag; the columns are inclined a little toward the centre, and are nearer together toward the corners than elsewhere, so that the impression of strength is enhanced;[1] and the columns themselves, though tapering as they rise, swell a little at about one-third their height, in order to avoid the appearance of concavity. Thus there is no mechanical or rectangular regularity; subtle curves and varying distances abound, and the shadows caught by the many-shaped recesses, as the sun moves across the sky, give an ever-changing relief from the monotony of straight lines and conventional details.

Architecture, it may be said, is by its very nature bound to find what originality it can within narrow limits; for it is almost always used in order to answer unchanging needs for

[1] A similar device is noticeable in the Maidens' Porch, in which the inner knees of the maidens at the outer corners are bent, so that the weight of the roof appears to be the more firmly sustained. Many of the variations and the curvatures (known as *entasis*) in Greek temples were in modern times first noticed by H. Labrouste and by F. C. Penrose as recently as the first half of the nineteenth century.

shelter, and can merely vary the details of wall, support, and roof. Sculpture may seem to have a greater freedom. But apart from the obvious limitations of the material, wood or stone or bronze, the sculptor has always worked within no wide circle of conventions. He has chosen subjects usually from the world of nature, plants and animals and human beings, treating them frankly according to accepted conventions, or at least from definite points of view. The Greek sculptor was influenced in almost every period by religious considerations; his subject was often a god or a votive-offering to a god, and he was frequently occupied with figures designed as adornments of a temple. The conservatism that religion usually inspires had its full effect. Even in the figures of athletes, which were often carved to commemorate athletic victories, the attempt was less to strike some new effect than to render again the typical or characteristic beauty of the runner or the wrestler. In this striving for the ideal, rather than the accidental, we can undoubtedly see the results of a long tradition that perfected single types instead of chronicling novelties; the god or the athlete was in a sense a composite of many beautiful models, not the record of a single one.[1]

It was only after centuries of development, of course, that these types were perfected. The earliest figures, of wood or terra cotta, were little but crude pillars or doll-like images;

[1] We know that some, at least, of the Greek artists worked in this way, unlike Rubens, and Charles Dana Gibson, and other modern painters, who constantly painted their wives. An interesting ideal portrait of the Red Cross nurse was painted in 1920 by F. Luis Mora, who used as his model the photographs of many nurses, endeavoring in this way to represent the composite nature of American womanhood. Dr. Tait Mackenzie has made fine composite statues of young athletes, using the measurements and photographs of large numbers of young men. Probably every artist unconsciously makes his work partly thus "representative," even if he dispenses with these mechanical aids.

and many of the early stone statues preserve the almost cylindrical form of a tree-trunk. By degrees certain types were evolved; a standing or a seated, draped, female type, and a standing, nude, male type were among the most common. From the latter in the course of time developed the various gods and the forms of athletes. At first the gods were very near to their functions as nature-divinities: Apollo's flowing locks symbolized the rays of the sun, and Hermes bore the wings of the messenger. More and more, however, the symbolic attributes were discarded, as the sculptor learned to represent their natures in more human ways. The "maidens," too, were differentiated into the various goddesses. In looking at statues of the archaic period, we soon become accustomed to many conventions that are due simply to the sculptor's lack of technical skill. In accordance with what has been called the "law of frontality," the standing figures are posed so that a plane might pass through the head, the nose, the back, and the navel; and the position of the arms and legs is usually symmetrical. A similar convention is often observed in Egyptian and Assyrian art, with which archaic Greek art has much in common. Later, where there is an attempt to render figures with a twist in their pose, a part being in profile, there is no transition from the front to the side view. Even at a fairly late period the sculptors in relief and the painters found it hard to represent the eye in profile; they were so much accustomed to think of it as looking toward them that they introduced the frontal eye into faces seen in profile. Another difficulty in anatomy that occurred when motion was attempted consisted in the proper proportions of a kneeling or a running figure; it was solved, arbitrarily enough, by allowing the legs to be of different lengths! In the attempt to give expression to the face, the early sculptor resorted to a grimace, the "archaic smile" that is found even on the faces of the wounded warriors of the Ægina pediment. The hair was treated with conventional lines and spirals.

By slow degrees these technical difficulties were surmounted. The sculptor learned to vary the frontal pose by resting the weight of the figure chiefly on one foot, and so to discover at last the graceful curves of the body that win our admiration in the "Marble Faun" and the "Aphrodite" of Melos. Different schools perfected different types of athlete; the Dorians developed the massively built figure, with heavy shoulders and jaw; the Attic school brought forward a more refined type, with a larger brow and more slender frame. The "canon" of Polycleitus was supposed to embody the most perfect proportions of the human figure. It was not till the time of Praxiteles that sculptors learned how to leave the hair in masses, treating only parts of it in detail, and of Scopas that they learned how much could be gained in expressiveness by sinking the eyes deeply beneath the brows. Drapery, at first rendered stiffly by conventional folds, now hung or fluttered at the sculptor's will, and was even introduced for the sheer beauty of its varied forms. By the Hellenistic Age, sculpture had reached the stage of virtuosity, and the great virtues of the sculptors were a playful grace and a fidelity to human nature; gods and men were hardly different in beauty and majesty. The funeral monument, with its conservative technique and its restrained but tender pictures of everyday life, is full of quiet charm.

When the sculptor's task was to provide the decorations for a temple, he found still other problems in choosing subjects and arranging figures in such a way as to fit into the space at his disposal. Especially the triangular shape of the pediment was hard to fill. Naturally the centre was usually occupied by a standing figure of some god; but as the sculptor proceeded toward the outer corners, all his resources were called into play to arrange seated or crouching or reclining figures, so as to leave no awkward gaps, and yet so as to let every part contribute to a harmonious whole. A convention which assisted in this task was the assignment of greater moral dignity to the important personages by giving them larger stature. The device to us seems quaint, though not offensive, like some early Italian paintings that show a similar convention, or like those Italian paintings in which the hero appears several times in the same picture in successive adventures; the naturalness is the gift of the mind, not of outward fact. We may compare with it, too, the convention by which the heads of the figures in a frieze were apt to be at the same level. But the whole management of the pediment sculptures is astonishing. The outer corners are filled by reclining figures of nymphs or river-gods, that suggest the scene of the action, or by the rising or the descending heads of the horses of Apollo or of Selene, marking dawn or sunset. From the corners toward the centre the action rises in intensity and the figures increase in importance till we reach the commanding figure of Apollo or Athene or Zeus, who directs the combatants or presides over the assembly. In the pediments of the Temple of Zeus at Olympia there is an absolute symmetry of the groups of figures on each side of the centre, each single figure or pair or group of three figures having its counterpart on the other side, and the figures balancing each other in their poses: at Ægina a similar grouping is found. In the pediments of the Parthenon, Pheidias achieves a more subtle effect; group does indeed balance group, but it is two seated and one reclining figure that balances one seated and two reclining figures, a man that balances a woman, or a bearded man that balances a stripling. It is this carefully wrought variety of detail within the confines of a tradition that constantly occupied the attention of the Greek artist.

Another test of the sculptor's skill was provided in the metope; but the rules of the game were somewhat different. Instead of a wide space to be filled with figures to be brought into relation with each other, there was a series of unconnected squares, in which two or three figures sufficed to fill the space; the metopes were therefore particularly adapted to be used for a series of single combats or for the several labors of Heracles. In the frieze, on the other hand, there was no attempt to give such a harmony of effect as could be taken in by the eye at one glance: the figures were merely to be related so harmoniously that the eye should be drawn from one part to another, perhaps with a rising interest toward one end. And this is the effect which Pheidias gains in the frieze of the Parthenon; the Panathenaic procession is seen as it forms at the western end, and moves, now gravely, now rapidly, till it comes into the presence of the gods, the northern and the southern sides of the frieze keeping pace with each other.

We must not forget that the decorative sculpture of temples, and for that matter probably most of the marble statues of the Greeks, were painted, whether in delicate tints or in such strong tones as would harmonize with their painted settings; and some accessories, such as weapons, were often added in bronze. The total effect of a temple like the Parthenon must have been both of austere grandeur, as we can see from its ruins, and at the same time of elaborate detail; each member, however perfect in itself, was only a part of the whole.

In the paintings of the Greeks, of which we have few fragments, in their countless painted vases, and in their coins alike, we can see again the conquest of one technical difficulty after another. Color was never so important or so pleasing an element in their art as the definite delineation and the modelling of human forms. Their drawing was concerned chiefly with the simplification of the figures to be drawn, and with the placing of them in the spaces, often of irregular shapes, at their command. Perspective and setting were of an awkward and undeveloped nature; shading but slightly indicated. As in the temple, so in the vase; the parts that had most strain, such as the handle, were least decorated. Certain bands and borders were covered with formal designs, whether of geometrical figures and "mæander" patterns, or of lotus and palmette and animals; but the larger spaces were "reserved" for pictures, usually of human beings. And here the following of certain conventions tended to produce a formalism not unpleasing in decorative art, that enabled the artist to direct all his attention to the careful drawing of forms. The figures were drawn in comparatively few attitudes, generally in frontal or in profile view, and were placed, as it were, at an equal distance from the spectator, hardly ever overlapping each other. Their shapes and the axis of their main lines tend to conform not only with the "reserved" space that they fill, but with the lines of the whole vase, whether rounded or elongated. The vase-painters of Attica learned how to draw their figures in black against the orange-red clay of the background, and later to fill in the background with black so as to enhance the statuesque silhouette of the reddish figures, whose draperies were delicately drawn in black; other colors were less often used.

In this discussion it may seem that a good deal has been said about matters of form and technique and convention, and that we are almost in danger of losing sight of the sources of inspiration of the poet and the artist, of their in-

dividual experiences and their genius. But there is a reason
for this emphasis. The Greeks realized, none better than
Plato, that a half of art and the creation of beauty lies in
that uncharted region that we variously call inspiration or
intuition or creative energy, that is as irresponsible as the
wind and as precious as the sunlight. It flames up in some
men and in some races and ages, in others it smoulders or
dies. Clearly to give any account of it here would mean
nothing less than to rehearse the history of Greek literature
and art, dwelling on the several names of the great figures
and their special experiences. But that is not the purpose of
this discussion. What we have done is to consider some of
the channels, natural or artificial, into which the Greeks
directed their creative energy, and by which they saved it
from being dissipated. The substance of Greek literature
and art,— the legends and myths, the heroic characters and
the stirring events,— must be sought elsewhere. But we
have seen that the limitations and conventions of Greek art,
accepted or even self-imposed, were in reality no repressive
bonds; like the scheme of the sonnet or the rules of football,
their limitations were the very making of their art. Even
the outward conditions of the theatre, which made quick
motion and facial expressiveness impossible, were utilized to
form the drama on the grand scale; the rigid requirements of
the temple taught the architect the power of large masses
relieved by elaborate but restricted detail. We used to wonder at the marvelous skill with which the bees build their
hexagonal cells, until it was pointed out that the shape of
their heads makes it impossible for them to build any other
form of cell. The fact is no less wonderful for being explained
and pushed further back; and the cell is now understood as
the natural development of the bee's energy. So we are inclined to see in much of Greek art the more or less conscious

development and perfection of their repeated attempts to find beauty. The crude seated figures found at Branchidæ, figures that seem almost to be part of their seats, and that "have sat down so hard that they cannot get up," as it has been said, represent a type that was repeated many times; and the perfect development of the type confronts us in the Demeter of Cnidos, one of the great statues of the world, whose attitude of resignation does not suffer by comparison with the Madonnas of the Christian era. So in the pedimental sculptures it was by repeated experiment within a convention that the sculptors acquired the technical skill that enabled them, when the moment came, to express in the Parthenon the glory of Athenian history: the mould was now ready, they had only to pour into it the newly fused substance. Form and technique are only the half of art; but they are a necessary half, without which the substance is often lost. Each of the masterpieces of Greek literature and art that have survived presupposes the work of countless pioneers and experimenters, whose blunders and whose uninspired imitations the world has let die.

There are moments when the Greeks do not wholly satisfy us; we remember Lowell's complaint, "The Grecian gluts me with its perfectness." The very fact that the Greeks limited their art to the things that they could perfectly express may seem actually a sort of imperfection, if we crave expression of the vague and the unknown. This is in part a matter of taste; there will always be some to prefer Rodin to Praxiteles, the spirituality of Giotto's ascetic saints to the healthy paganism of the Theseus of the Parthenon pediment, the mysticism of Wordsworth to the realism of Sophocles. With them we shall not quarrel. The Greeks will have sufficient glory if we recognize how their exquisite tact and their balance of thought and instinct per-

meated every kind of art,— making, for example, the secondary characters of the "Iliad" unforgettable, yet secondary,
causing the emotional strain of a play to be relaxed before
the close and the violence of opposed characters to be
softened, as it were, by the interpositions of the chorus.
Here the touch of the Greek is sure, and each part of the
poem and each part of the statue wins us because it is in perfect harmony with its neighbors. And this touch lasted
through the natural sequence of austerity, mature perfection, and graceful decline that marked the development of
the arts in Greece, as it has marked those of other countries.[1]

For Greek art suffered decline and temporary eclipse, nor
will any servile imitation of its conventions or even of its
masterpieces avail us now; true art must rise from real experience. Yet art that rose from experience so large and so
nearly universal as that of the Greeks can never lose its
appeal. The Greeks still have much to teach us; and if we
have the power to distinguish in their work the vital from
the accidental, they may be our best masters in all that
comes from example.[2] One thing remains; originality there
must be, and originality must come of itself or it will not
come at all. "It must be quite a poor intellect that cannot
dare to find out something further for itself, but stays always on an old path, only follows others, and cannot understand how to think on for itself. It becomes, therefore,
every understanding man to follow another thus far, that he
need not doubt that he will be able to find out also, in time,
something better for himself. Then it will happen, there can
be no doubt, that art will again achieve perfection, as it did
in ancient days." [3]

[1] Cf. J. A. Symonds, *Studies in the Greek Poets*, vol. ii, pp. 33–36.
[2] Cf. G. Murray, "What English Poetry may still learn from Greek,"
in *Essays and Studies by Members of the English Association*, vol. iii, col-
lected by W. P. Ker, 1912.   [3] A. Dürer, *Proportionslehre*.

CHAPTER VI

INDIVIDUAL AND SOCIETY

1. From Custom to Reason

GREEK life tended to find expression in human terms. The Greeks themselves were aware of this, and soon lost interest in anything in which man and his welfare did not somehow hold the centre of the stage. We are therefore at the very heart of Greek life and thought when we ask how the Greeks contrived to live together and what they thought of man as a member of society.

We remember in the first place that the Greeks were, and are, an intensely sociable people, who can hardly conceive of life except in communities, even the farmers gathering in villages, sometimes at a distance from their farms, rather than in solitary homesteads. They have always loved the pleasures of conversation, of story-telling and personal banter. On the other hand they were from the beginning stout defenders of liberty and the rights of the individual. Again, like any early people and like most modern people, they were much concerned with the winning of their daily bread; and their economic position as masters or slaves, as land-owners or artisans, colored much of their thought. Yet, as we have seen, the Greeks at their best were far from being the pawns of economic circumstances. How, then, did they reconcile the rival claims of individual and society, of property and personality? In the present age these opposing interests are in such violent conflict that any reconciliation, however partial, must be of value to us.

The Greeks, though attached to many smaller groups, — family, clan, religious brotherhood, and trade-guild, — hardly thought of society as existing in any other sense than as the state. Any smaller body derived its right to exist from the all-inclusive body, the state, which was the sovereign of all within its borders, not merely the arbiter between groups. And since society was nothing but the state, economics was subject to politics.

Now we realize that a state may derive its unity from more than one element: a common territory, or race, or religion, or language gives a natural unity to a people, which may be further bound together by community of laws and government. Above all, a common sentiment may make a nation of people otherwise very diverse. Few nations have every other kind of unity; but without unity of sentiment, no nation can remain one. Nature did much to bind together the ancient Greeks in land, race, religion, and language; but community or equality of government and law had to be won by centuries of effort; and community of sentiment between the separate states, though fostered by the Homeric poems and by the oracles, by athletic festivals and by the Persian Wars, was always precarious. But however rare was Panhellenic unity, the unity of the city-state was for a time almost perfect.

Since we have already traced the stages by which the Greeks passed from monarchy to democracy,[1] we need only remind ourselves of the course of their political progress. In Homer we found the raw materials of the state: a king, whose prestige was largely personal, though he claimed divine descent, and a populace, consulted only formally, so that it had, as we might say, the referendum but not the initiative. The individual Greek counted for almost noth-

[1] P. 36.

ing, unless he was one of the privileged few. Yet the kings were responsible for gathering together in a single state, for mutual protection and help, the clans of those who claimed common blood and common worship; so that it was really true of the Greek states that they were consciously founded for the attainment of an end. And what began merely for the preservation of life was continued for the furtherance of a good life, as Aristotle later realized. When through some weakness or some overweening act on the part of a king he was shorn of his functions, they were taken over by the other nobles, though the king or his successor might hold a nominal position. The political changes that followed were in effect the result of a series of challenges against the pretensions of the aristocracy to a monopoly of ability and virtue and patriotism. Largely against lack of economic rights, but partly against their lack of political privilege, the common people revolted. Sometimes the laws were codified and published; sometimes economic inequalities were removed at the same time that political privileges were extended, so that there should not be voters without settled interests at stake.[1] New classes of citizens received recognition. Often it was through the good offices of a "tyrant" that these rights were won; but the democracy survived the tyrant. The quality of democracy became most clearly apparent, superficially, at least, in the opportunities that every citizen had to take part directly in some of the manifold duties of state,[2] and in the enhanced sense of personal dignity thus achieved. Though the idea of developing expert or professional politicians only gradually gained ground, the more

[1] Cf. W. Fowler, *City State of the Greeks and Romans*, p. 133.

[2] It has been calculated that there were in the Athens of Pericles some 1900 offices, so that by the use of the lot in awarding offices the places "would circulate among the whole body of citizens about once in sixteen years." Cf. Fowler, p. 168.

gross forms of inefficiency and corruption were avoided not
only by requirements of examinations and reports before
and after the term of office but also by publicity and opportunities for the impeachment of illegal proposals; above all,
the people became conservative because they felt that they
had won "equality of law" by their own effort, and therefore felt a genuine respect for the law because it truly represented them. Strangely enough, they did not go farther and
extend the same privileges to foreigners and to subject populations. At home, however, the democrat was no longer
hostile to the state, but felt that in it he was reaching his full
development as an individual. The wealth of the state, and
much of the private wealth of rich citizens, tended to be
used for the public welfare; indeed, before the end of the
fifth century, Athens was largely committed to state-social-
ism. Yet the Greek states fell at last, partly because of their
proneness to civil discord among themselves, and partly because of their inability to outgrow the type of state that was
confined to a single town and the surrounding country; so
they fell a prey to the monarchy of Macedon and to the
military strategy of Rome. Under foreign rule the political
freedom of the Greeks was, save in petty details, practically
dead.

Each period of Greek history thus had a character of its
own, both with regard to the actual position of the ordinary
citizen in society and with regard to the prevailing theory of
human nature. Progress, to be sure, is a comparatively modern notion, and, it may be remarked in passing, a dangerous
notion unless very carefully defined. The Greeks were little
concerned with it, though they were much concerned with
personal and national endeavors for certain definite ends.
Yet the Greeks did conceive of a golden age in the past, an
age better than their own, and it was not till they had suf-

fered much and had built a better world that they thought of the possibility of a golden age in the future.[1]

The Homeric poems already presuppose a more barbarous age in the past; some have thought that they show traces of attempts to expurgate or explain away traditions of cruelty and immorality. But if we ask what it was that guided the Greeks of Homer's own age in their belief that some things were base and beneath the dignity of their manhood, the answer must be that even more than any direct relation to the gods it was a pair of emotions or direct intuitions.[2] A man felt a sense of *aidos*, or shame, at the thought of committing unnecessary cruelty, for example; it acted like a personal conscience. And if he saw others committing such acts, he felt *nemesis*, a righteous indignation. These sentiments acted as a code of social responsibility, even if wholly in a negative direction, and contributed to the dignity of the individual man. Of course they could hardly suggest very definite or far-reaching programmes of social reform; but, like habit and tradition, they were the safeguard of whatever advance was made. Again, they were emotional, rather than rational. But the greater part of our lives still consists of instinctive acts of habit, which we seldom stop to rationalize. And among ordinary Greeks, even in the age of philosophy, *aidos* and *nemesis* were potent influences.

Something of this instinctive, or if we prefer, this inspired morality was to be found, too, in the utterances of the wise men of the succeeding centuries; the seven sages, the lawgivers, the oracles of Apollo, with their insistence on temperance and limits, on law and the mean that lies between two excesses, were more the product of the Greek racial

[1] See also pp. 303 ff.
[2] Cf. G. Murray, *Rise of the Greek Epic*, pp. 101–114.

genius than the work of conscious reason. For the average Greek of the sixth and even of the fifth century, wisdom was sought chiefly in the poets who preserved the traditions of the race; and law was regarded as the codifying of ancient practice, which rested formerly on the will of the gods (*themis*) interpreted by the priests and kings, and later on the common usage of the people (*nomos*). In the latter sense law amounts almost to convention, not that it is artificial, but because it states what is always done, without any inquiry into the reason why it is done.[1] Even after law and political ideas were being subjected to the criticism of reason, there were stanch conservatives like Aristophanes who defended the good old traditions against innovations; the country squires and the elderly men of affairs were constitutionally opposed to change, and much of the radicalism of the hour seemed dangerous.[2] So they depended on sound tradition and honesty and conventional religion, and were more interested in bodily activities than in the education of the mind. For a beautiful and sympathetic interpretation of such a man one need only turn to Plato's picture of the serene old age of Cephalus, in the opening pages of the "Republic." Cephalus is tranquil in the consciousness of a life well lived according to the standards of his age; he is not much troubled when it appears that he cannot give a rational account of its basis.

But the Greeks of the old school could hardly shut their eyes to the fact that conditions were rapidly changing in the fifth century. They had done great deeds; but the Greek character demanded a balance between energy and thought.

[1] It reminds one of the tribal spirit of the Dodson family in George Eliot's *Mill on the Floss;* see Book I, chap. 6; Book III, chap. 3.

[2] Cf. M. Croiset, *Aristophanes and the Political Parties at Athens*, Eng. translation, Introduction, pp. 1-7; C. D. Burns, *Greek Ideals*, chapter on "The Old School."

And for several reasons the Greeks were now thinking much of political and social questions. For one thing, most states had done away with kings; the divine right of kings followed suit. The change gave cause for reflection. But some states now had democracies and others had aristocracies or oligarchies, and each was not too large to have a distinct character capable of close scrutiny. The very differences tempted men to compare their qualities and to discuss the merits of government by the many and government by the few. Political power in the hands of the citizens of a democracy was in itself a political education. Above all, the thinkers of Greece were turning their attention from physical problems to human problems; the Sophists professed to train young men for public life. Sometimes they merely retailed the prevailing notions; oftener they tended to criticize the very foundations of the popular conventions; at any rate they showed that there were two sides to a question, and so provoked thought. In particular, they attacked the conventional morality and politics for its very conventionality; their appeal was sometimes to the example of the natural world and sometimes to reason. The appeal to Nature is always ambiguous; for Nature at times appears to be a blind and cruel force, and so to justify the right of the stronger; at other times she is the bountiful mother that counsels her children to live in the harmony of kinsmen. "Break away from the artificialities that you have imposed on yourselves, and live as Nature would have you," is the burden of Hippias. "But that means only life after the manner of the beasts," replies Protagoras, and so becomes the champion of a life that is distinctively human, conventional in that it recognizes restrictions, but always capable of development.

The influence of the Sophists was electric; not only the philosophers, the historians, and the dramatists, but through them the general public were induced to find a new interest in morality and in political philosophy. In the plays of the three great tragic poets moral problems had become ever more prominent; some of the dramas of Euripides might well be described as "problem plays," and the conservatives were shocked by his scepticism and iconoclasm. Even Herodotus goes out of his way to put in the mouths of Persian nobles living two generations before his time an up-to-date argument with regard to the respective merits of democracy, oligarchy, and monarchy; both the efficiency and the irresponsibility of monarchy are set forth; the enlightenment of oligarchy, it is explained, is balanced by its proneness to dissension; and to democracy is ascribed fairness and responsibility, secured by equality of opportunity and the use of the lot, but offset by ignorance. So far as the argument goes, it is admirable and not without value to-day.[1] But it is in Thucydides among the historians that we feel the full power of the sophistic criticism of politics. Speaking sometimes in his own person, sometimes through the mouth of one of the actors in his drama, he lays bare the theory of empire, its rise, its means of preservation, and its justification; he shows why it involves expansion, and what dangers expansion brings; he discusses the place of clemency and generosity in an empire, and the reason why it is safer to leave subjects free. He asks what causes lead to rebellion, and when rebellion is justified. He considers the question of the rights of the individual against the state, and shows why it is better to belong to a state than to remain isolated. He exposes the effect of war on a people's temperament, and the danger that it brings to political stability; he asks pertinent questions about the value of eloquence, of education, and of a critical spirit in politics. He even poses the query whether clever

[1] Herodotus, III, 80–82.

men or stupid men make the better citizens, and upholds expediency over justice as a motive in statecraft. He estimates the limits of effective punishment, weighing the influence on character of revenge and of hope; and notes the effect on human nature of sudden disaster and of sudden success. In all this he reveals a keen insight into psychology, and occasionally deals with the abstractions of political philosophy. He realizes that the national spirit is even more important than the form of government.[1] Yet brilliant as his genius is, his attitude is always that of the student confronted with the task of accounting for a certain definite phenomenon, or of the advocate entering his plea for a particular institution or person. We need not regret, perhaps, his lack of a detached point of view; for he deals with situations so various that from them one can construct a fairly comprehensive philosophy. But Thucydides is more the political adviser of statesmen than the disinterested seeker after truth and righteousness in social relations that we find in Socrates and Plato. And so, even though it is perhaps Thucydides more than any other writer who sees the inner character of the age in which he lived, and who preserved his vision of its temper and its possibilities (in the immortal words of the Funeral Oration of Pericles), it is not to Thucydides but to the poets and to Plato that we turn when we wish light on the ultimate values and the permanent character of human life. If we wish to know whether a certain thing can be done, and what will be the result, Thucydides has much to tell us; but if we wish to know whether it is worth doing, Plato is a better guide. Fortunately we have both; and Aristotle has some of the qualities of them both.

---

[1] Thucydides, III, 37 ff., 82 ff. Parts of the paragraph above borrow points from R. W. Livingstone, *The Greek Genius and its Meaning to Us*, pp. 215 f.

So far as it was possible to give any reason for the extraordinary achievements of the Great Age of Greece, we found it[1] in the happy union at the right moment of a multitude of influences; not least of these is the fortunate balance between energy and thought. And for some years it actually seemed possible for the world to see government carried on by men whose minds and muscles were equally developed. Then, through the inner weakness of the city-state, came the disillusioning lesson of the Peloponnesian War. Political life was not yet dead; but the best in political thought was now to come to fruit no longer in the busy assembly and the market-place, where Pericles had thundered and Socrates had questioned, but in the quiet walks of Plato's Academy and the Lyceum of the scholarly Aristotle. Even so, there was some interplay between energy and thought; Plato himself and some of his pupils tried, with varying success, to apply philosophy to statecraft; Demetrius of Phalerum, a statesman of the fourth century, studied the Aristotelian tradition to advantage. Yet the vigor of political thought waned, and only among the learned did it have great influence.

2. THE RULE OF REASON

The Greeks were both sociable and politically minded. Though Xenophanes and Isocrates, each in his day, complained that the athlete received more honor than the statesman but was less valuable to the state, it can hardly be doubted that the average Greek fully recognized the importance of sound statesmanship and gave honor to the successful statesman. But the statesman, of course, was not necessarily a theorist in politics; nor was the political philosopher necessarily a practical politician. It would be interesting to know how far Themistocles or Pericles could

[1] P. 46.

have explained by abstract principles the foundations of their power and their policies; we can only conjecture what they would have said. For there are in politics two different and often opposing elements. There are on the one hand the material conditions of geography and economic resources and the existing habits and institutions; all these we conveniently refer to as "the facts." On the other hand there are the less obvious but no less real motives of human beings who think about "the facts" and set before themselves goals for action; these may be described as "ideals," — "mere ideals," we sometimes call them, if we are inclined to look down on all that is not tangible. Mere ideals they often are, and even undesirable ideals; nevertheless they do often become so much a part of the life of men that they become facts and even determine the course of history. It is possible to consider democracy, for example, as a fact, and to notice where it is an existing form of government, and what are its present merits and defects; or we may consider it as an ideal of the imagination, only partially realized, and inquire what its full possibilities are. Much of our difficulty in understanding Greek political theory comes from our failure to distinguish when the Greeks supposed themselves to be describing "facts" and when they were frankly dealing with ideals. Often they give no indication of the transition, nor is there any reason why they should have done so; for facts should lead to ideals, and ideals should be based on facts. In particular, we shall see that the Greeks passed, perhaps unconsciously, from the description of laws and existing states to the inner nature of law and of political obligation. It is sometimes hard to say whether Plato or Aristotle is giving the result of observation of "the facts" in the city-state or whether he is reasoning about the nature of government.

In early times law (*themis*) was a simple fact, and rested either on the supposed will of the gods, interpreted by priests or kings, or in custom and tradition; it was not rationalized. It did not present a harmonious system, but consisted of a number of independent judgments. Long-continued acceptance of such law, however, gave it the majesty and the force of eternal principles of right and wrong. So for the work of legislators like Lycurgus and Minos, given the authority to set forth constitutions for states, was claimed a divine guidance, very different from the special acts and decrees passed by states for ordinary matters. By the fifth century, therefore, two kinds of law existed; there were divine laws, permanent and fundamental, rarely if ever to be amended; and there were the human statutes of ordinary legislation, declaring the will of the democracy, and deciding cases on their merits. Rapidly the human statutes assumed a larger part of the province of law, so that it might be argued plausibly enough by some of the Sophists that right and wrong was wholly a matter of human judgment, or, in a democracy, of the popular will, and that might made right. And in these times of rapid change, man seemed an unstable thing; it was easy to argue that man-made law was only artificial, compared with the uniformity of Nature, and that the state was only the tool of the strong for the guarding of their strength. Such arguments seemed to derive considerable support from appeals to "the facts" of contemporary history, — the power of the Athenian democracy to make and unmake law, and the ruthlessness of the Athenian Empire in dealing with lukewarm or revolting allies.[1] The appeal had been made from divine sanctions and from tradition to human reason, from convention to Nature. The force of the appeal was not to be denied, nor did Socrates deny it; he rather asked per-

[1] Cf. pp. 44 ff., 51 f.

tinent questions with regard to the nature of the man whose reason was to be the arbiter of political right and wrong. True knowledge, he agreed, is to be the standard; but it must be the knowledge of the expert, and the expert in political affairs is hard to find, for he must have an understanding of the true welfare of the citizens which the citizens as individuals do not possess. And though Nature is superior to convention, Socrates maintained that man's nature is social and can realize its proper end only by the rule of the common reason in an organized society. Nominally a sceptic in attitude, Socrates was so positive a believer in the duty of man to obey law, even the imperfect law of his own time that had not yet been brought into accord with ideal law, that he despised the opportunity to escape from prison, and died a martyr's death. His work was that of a pioneer; without leaving any writings, he succeeded by his stubborn questionings in causing the whole tendency of Greek political thought to concern itself with the potentialities of man's social nature, — with ideals rather than with "mere facts." This is indeed in the normal current of Greek thought, for the state had always been assumed as natural; but it was for Socrates and his followers to show in what sense the state was not merely natural but rational.

The position of Socrates was extremely simple, — so simple that the most diverse people could claim some point in common with him. The soldierly, practical Xenophon learned from him chiefly sincerity of mind and the importance of education, as well as of innate ability in the making of a good monarch.[1] The pamphleteer Isocrates, not strictly a Socratic follower, was content with a less abstract political philosophy than Plato demanded, and hoped only to ap-

[1] These points are illustrated in Xenophon's *Cyropædia*, an historical romance dealing with the life of Cyrus the Great.

proximate the truth by the free play of intelligence; a conservative in domestic politics, he turned his aspiration toward a Panhellenic union. The Cynic philosophers went still further in their cosmopolitanism; not merely all Greeks, but all men are by nature equal, they believed, and wise men need no state to control them. The Cyrenaic philosophers agreed with them in dispensing with the state, but merely because pleasure seemed attainable by the effort of the individual. All these thinkers represented imperfectly and inconsistently the Socratic emphasis on the intelligence of man; only Plato reckoned with all the previous currents of Greek thought, and pressed them with Socratic courage to their ultimate conclusions. His earnest eloquence, his poetic imagination, and his gift of comedy captivate our minds, so that even when his thought requires critical revision it is still usually the most rewarding approach to any of the multitude of subjects that he discussed. By birth an aristocrat, Plato by no means inherited from his ancestors any prejudice against democracy; indeed he felt respect for his ancestor Solon, who was in a sense the founder of Athenian democracy. But from his master Socrates he learned to distrust inefficiency and ignorance in any form; and nothing seemed so hopelessly ignorant as the people that could persecute Socrates. Plato's interest in politics from the first was ethical; he was the reformer, to whom the bare facts of Greek politics in his day appeared ugly; and his aim was beyond doubt a practical one. Several of his pupils were more or less successful legislators, and he was himself persuaded, though reluctantly, to undertake to put into force at Syracuse his political tenets; his failure proves not the utter falseness of his principles but rather that, as he well knew, any true reform takes measures more thorough than average human nature will readily tolerate. Dionysius, the young tyrant of Syracuse, became impatient when he found that sound statecraft was supposed by Plato to depend on a sound knowledge of mathematics. Some have thought that it was because of his failure in Syracuse that Plato's later writings show a willingness to make a compromise between the ideals of the reformer and the facts of everyday existence.

Though most of Plato's dialogues, and practically all of the earlier dialogues, present Socrates as the chief speaker, it is clear that Plato's own thought tends more and more to take the place of a chronicle of others' views. In the early dialogues we can see Plato's repudiation of the claims of this unregenerate world and his approach to Utopianism. In the "Apology," which professes, perhaps with some degree of truth, to give us the defense of Socrates against those who accused him of impiety and the corruption of the young, Socrates appeals to reason as something higher even than existing law; yet in the "Crito" Socrates accepts the claims of the state that has brought him forth to take away his life, though not to silence him.[1] In the succeeding dialogues [2] the existing state is accepted only under the strongest protest; statesmen act, it is argued, merely by virtue of instinct or opinion, right or wrong, without any coherent plan or any complete understanding of their objects that can be reduced to a clear statement of principles. They flatter the people, who are only less ignorant than themselves; they are amateurish, and aim at power and external success, rather than at truth; they use rhetoric rather than reason. True statecraft is a subject not for amateurs but for scientific experts

[1] Plato (Socrates) would have us defy the law only if some spiritual issue is at stake, not, as Hobbes holds, only if our life is at stake. Cf. E. Barker, *Plato and his Predecessors*, p. 123.

[2] Especially in the "Euthydemus," "Meno," "Protagoras," and "Gorgias."

who have an understanding not only of fragments of life but
of all reality, and who therefore can see parts in their relation to the whole. But states as they are will not tolerate the
rule of reason and the expert; they must be reformed. Meanwhile, reason can rule only in a Utopia, an ideal of the
imagination.

Plato's "Republic" is much more than a treatise on
politics, though it professes to be an account of a discussion
between Socrates and half-a-dozen of his friends about the
nature of justice. The question as to justice in the individual leads to a question as to the sort of state in which just
men are trained; and this leads to the further quest for an
understanding of the meaning of true knowledge and of the
effect of its application in society. During the night of talk
we are led from what at first seems to be only a small point
of definition to the most fundamental questions of human
life; and we are lifted out of the world of time and change till
in the end we become the spectators of pure existence.

The discussion arises from a question about the reason for
the happy old age enjoyed by the host, the pious Cephalus.
He soon shows that though he is good by force of habit he
has never really thought about these matters; yet his son,
Polemarchus, for all his confidence, is shown by Socrates to
have only a few second-hand maxims that enjoin particular
acts but that give no all-embracing and consistent definition
of justice, the quality that all attribute to the father. Thrasymachus, the Sophist, flings into the discussion the familiar
argument that justice is merely what the strong command:
but this leads to the admission that there is such a thing as
an art of government, not necessarily in the interest of the
ruler. Thrasymachus therefore shifts his ground and appeals
to "the facts"; the real interest of rulers is not justice but
injustice. But Socrates points out that there must be an

honor even among thieves, and that internal harmony or
moderation of some sort is the condition of any principle
that is to succeed; injustice pure and simple does not pay.
Socrates has answered Thrasymachus, so far as verbal argument goes; but young Glaucon and Adeimantus, the brothers of Plato, are not satisfied that Socrates has quite proved
that, as they believe, justice is good on its own account, not
merely for its consequences. Some would consider justice
not really good yet nevertheless better than being exposed to
injustice, and would therefore be willing to bind themselves
not to injure others; [1] others would say that justice is to be
pursued not for itself but for the respectability or the material prosperity that the appearance of justice brings. The
rest of the dialogue is Plato's attempt to show that justice is
worth attaining for its influence within the soul.

In order to exhibit the true nature of justice in man, Socrates investigates its place in the state, which is "man writ
large"; this he can do because man's social needs and instincts require him to live with his fellow-men and to express
the various elements of his nature in social institutions.
Accordingly, Socrates traces the steps by which, logically
rather than historically, human fellowship passes from the
satisfaction of the most elementary physical needs, in what
strikes Glaucon as a "city of pigs," to the elaborate state in
which provision is made for all the cravings of luxury and of
intellectual refinement. At every stage it is found profitable
to take advantage of the natural differences of capacity in
the citizens; this means the division of labor by which separate classes of farmers and artisans and tradesmen, of
soldiers, and of rulers, each with its own virtues and its own
peculiar technical ability, are to carry on their specialized
functions. The soldierly guardians and the rulers will need a

[1] This is the earliest statement of the theory of the "social contract."

thorough training both of the body ("gymnastic") and of the mind ("music," which includes literature and all the arts over which the Muses preside), to give them good habits and good standards of conduct. Almost imperceptibly Plato has been drawing our attention from the average state to the ideal state; and his Socrates now discusses the principles of government in the ideal state. More depends on the strength of character and the disinterestedness of the rulers and on the spirit of the citizens than on the form of government; accordingly much is said of the choosing and testing of the rulers, and of expedients for removing temptations from them even at the expense of leaving them few ordinary pleasures; corruption of manners must be prevented by laws guarding against innovations in music and dances. Compared with fundamental matters like these, ordinary details are unimportant and may safely be left to the good sense of the rulers.

Now that the state has been established, Socrates reverts to the original question, about the nature of justice. Obviously the difference in capacity of the various classes in the state leads us to find in each a characteristic virtue; the rulers have wisdom, the soldierly guardians have courage, and the workers have a self-control that causes them to concern themselves only with their own business. If all the classes in the state exhibit their proper virtues, the state is just. And as the state shows on the larger scale the work of human nature, the individual is just if the several parts of his personality exist in a harmonious relation to each other: the reason should rule, aided by the higher emotions, and holding in check the lower, bodily passions.

In a sense the quest of the "Republic" is now over; yet the outlines of the argument need to be filled in with greater detail. Socrates has made the stability of the ideal state depend on the devotion to duty of the rulers; he now suggests ways and means of securing this devotion. He argues that their life can best be merged in the life of the state if they have as little private life and private property as possible. He finds no essential difference of kind in political capacity between men and women; he therefore holds that women should have the same education and occupations as men, for their own good and for the good of the state. And now Socrates is confronted by the urgent question whether his ideal state, however desirable, is practicable. Of course it is the very nature of ideals that they can be only approximated; yet Socrates thinks that his ideal state can be approximated if in the same person can be united the power of the statesman and the insight of the philosopher; a king must become a philosopher or a philosopher must become a king. Not, to be sure, the ordinary sort of philosopher, who is, as a matter of fact, an unpractical and rather ridiculous sort of dreamer, unappreciated if not actually dangerous; he must be the complete man, who though not lacking in practical experience, understands the abstruse theory of existence; who has clambered out of our cave of ignorance and superstition and beheld the sun of truth, and yet is willing to return to the cave in order to help his fellow-men. And Socrates sketches the sort of education that it is necessary to add to the training already described in order to produce the philosophic ruler, — an education beginning with mathematics and ending with pure logic, drawing the mind away from the observation of visible things to the contemplation of the unchangeable principle of goodness and existence.

As Socrates traced the logical growth of the state from primitive society to the ideal state, he now traces the steps by which it must decay if inferior elements gain control of the state. The disorganization of the state arises from the debasing of the human nature on which it rests; the rulers begin to care not for reason and the welfare of the state but for property; other desires surge up and vie one with another, so that the undiscriminating mob-rule of a democracy follows; finally the worst passions are enthroned, and the government has become a tyranny. All harmony and unity of purpose are lost; and the tyrant, who has set the lower over the higher instinct, cannot possibly feel the happiness of the philosopher who alone has had a complete experience of life. Justice, then, and real happiness are internal, and are valued because they are signs of a healthy condition of the individual or of the state, not because of outward consequences. Indeed, if, as a matter of fact, the just man is debarred from political activity in the city of his birth, he can still feel that he is a citizen of a heavenly city in which he can live even a higher life.

Now that Socrates has vindicated the claims of justice and the philosophic life to exist in their own right, he proceeds to satirize the claims of contemporary poetry to impart truth. And he ends by suggesting in a myth the blessedness that the just may hope for in a future life.

The "Republic" is an amazingly daring work; yet its courage is the courage of despair at the shortcomings of an imperfect world. It may well be asked whether it takes greater courage to have faith in a Utopia or to have faith in the world as it is. But to suppose that Plato regarded the two as absolutely distinct is to miss his chief point. What always interests Plato most in man is not what he is at a certain moment but what his latent personality is capable of becoming; and these potentialities to him are more real than the merely temporary phases that are visible at a given moment. Human nature, he believes, is not what it seems to be just now, but what it is trying to become, what it would be if it were awake to its destiny. That is Plato's criticism of those who argue that the state is merely a contract between hostile persons to abstain from hostility; he replies that man is not by nature permanently selfish, but that his true nature is social and unfolds all its powers most fully in the midst of organized society. The state, therefore, far from being an alien and repressive agency, is the expression of the more highly developed, that is, of the real nature of man. Its characteristic is not merely that of a geographical unit, or of an agency for economic production, or of a military establishment, though it may include all these; it is the embodiment of the spirit and the moral aims of a people, and rests not on force, though it may use force as a means, but on the will of the people rightly understood.

But how is the will to be made known? Surely not by a count of hands, Plato believes; for there is nothing of which he is so thoroughly persuaded as the ignorance and inefficiency and lack of disinterested motives natural to a democracy, since it is guided by whims or conventions or passions, not by the light of reason. Men are fundamentally unequal in physique and still more unequal in mental ability; and it is the height of absurdity to rely on the beliefs of all men alike. Just as in economic production a division of labor is to the advantage of all, so in the management of the state Plato thinks that different men should have different functions, according to their capacities. Since a man cannot be regarded as a self-contained unit but only as a member of society, justice is wholly a social matter; in fact, there are for Plato no strictly self-regarding virtues and no absolute rights of the individual. Accordingly no man has a right to feel aggrieved if the task to which his ability assigns him is that of an artisan or of a soldier, rather than that of a political leader. As the reason rules the body of the individual for its good, those members of the state whose reason is preëminent should rule those whose reason is less developed than their physical and emotional powers. Plato is not thinking of the expert rulers as subduing the wills of a subject population, any more than he conceives of the reason of a man as tyrannically oppressing the emotions; just as in the individual it is not a single emotion that should prompt action, but the whole personality, so the state should be mastered not by the desires of a single class but by the whole mind of the community. And Plato assumes that only a few experts can be fully aware of this mind, because only they can think not as individuals but as members of the state; and the state can express itself only through human minds.[1] At the same time, Plato's eagerness to carry out to its logical conclusion the principle of the division of labor leads him into the fault of forgetting that though a man's personality acts as a unit it expresses various motives; reason does not, as a matter of fact, wholly exclude desire. It must be admitted that Plato's psychological basis in this discussion is an argument in a circle: he "begins with an implied psychology of the individual, constructs a state accordingly, and argues from the state to an explicit psychology of the individual."[2] The reason is that Plato has not sufficiently determined in his own mind how far the rulers should take into account the wills of the lower classes in the state. Although some individuals are more rational than others, there are none who are wholly rational and none who are wholly irrational; and it is an arbitrary and too precisely mathematical solution of the difficulty to divide people into separate, water-tight compartments.[3]

---

[1] "States do not come out of an oak or a rock, but from the characters of the men that dwell therein." *Rep.* 544d; cf. 435e.

[2] E. Barker, *Plato and His Predecessors*, p. 178, n. 1.

[3] It has been well said that Plato "trichotomizes with a hatchet"; he

At the heart of Plato's plan for the unfolding of man's powers is naturally the educational system, which extends from the cradle to old age; his state is largely a public school system crowned by a state university. The earlier training, with its attempt to inculcate habits of action and emotion in keeping with the national character, strikes one as Spartan, rather than Athenian; but the emphasis on literature and music as more productive of the desired character than laws, and the superiority of the spirit over the letter are Athenian. Each citizen will proceed in the curriculum only as far as his abilities warrant; those who pass through the advanced and abstract studies reserved for the training of the ruling class will have passed in review all the phases of human experience from the most concrete and emotional to the most rigorously intellectual.[1] At the end, after an ecstatic vision of the intellectual and moral principle that governs the universe, the philosopher is ready to rule. In theory, at least, he has a perfect understanding of all things and their relations, and Plato is careful to prescribe that for fifteen years after attaining the age of thirty-five the future ruler shall take part in practical affairs, and that his life shall have included numerous tests of strength of character; even when he is allowed to rule he is to spend his time alternately in practical affairs and in study. Plato intends that he shall be no mere theorist; yet it strikes us as curious that the subjects of the statesman's study are not such matters as history, or taxation, or the principles of the suffrage, but mathematics and metaphysics. Probably Plato believed in the disciplinary value of these studies for the inculcating of good reasoning

lacks the patience to recognize different degrees of intelligence and different kinds of claim to political value.

[1] This is essentially the application of what biologists mean by saying that each individual's experience "recapitulates," of course to a variable extent, all the experience of the race.

and a disinterested attitude of mind; even more, he believed that these studies give insight into the real nature of things, and that good government is largely a matter of insight, since virtue, as Socrates had held, is knowledge. In the ordinary sense, however, Plato's rulers are experts not by reason of their philosophic pursuits but because of their large measure of practical experience. They have not ceased to be ordinary men of affairs because they have added to this experience a reasoned understanding of all experience. And the actual functions of government that are contemplated in the scheme of Plato seem to involve only such supervision of the routine as is necessary to prevent any violation of the constitution, together with minor details that call only for honesty and common sense. But even if Plato had been acquainted with the vast machinery of modern government, made necessary by complicated economic conditions, it is doubtful whether he would have revised his educational system; he would hold that the spirit is more important than legislation, and that technical matters can be best managed by subordinating the technical specialists (experts in our sense of the word) to the control of those who are experts (in the Platonic sense) in all the objects and principles of life.[1]

In order to be sure that the rulers will devote themselves whole-heartedly to the service of the state, without thought of private aggrandizement, Plato provides that they shall use in common a small amount of property and that their life shall be a sort of military monasticism, somewhat like that of the Spartans. In this way the temptation of worldly gain is to be removed; at the same time their modest stipend is to free them from anxiety about material things,

[1] This is the ground, *mutatis mutandis*, for the control, in the British and usually in the American government, of departments by well-educated laymen, all-round men, rather than by technical specialists in the narrow sense.

so that all their attention may be liberated for the public welfare. They are not even to have families of their own; for them marriage and the care of children is to be socialized. Under this supervision Plato hopes not only that a better race of children may be bred, but that the rulers, women as well as men, may be set free from the excessive preoccupations of domestic life. For the communism of property Plato had precedent in several early peoples, both Greek and barbarian; and in Plato's day the notion of the equality of the sexes was not unknown. The striking point in Plato's use of them is that his whole aim is moral, not economic. Industry and trade in the Platonic state are still left to private initiative; it is only the governing class that is subject to communism. Plato's communism, then, differs from that of modern socialism because it is ascetic and does not aim at greater production or at a more equitable distribution of wealth; it is strictly a means toward the attainment of the great political end, the unification of the state. It is surprising that Plato's usual confidence in the spirit of his citizens did not lead him to suppose that the minds of his philosophic rulers would be above material temptations without socialistic regulation. Yet it is perhaps an open question whether those who have done most for human welfare during past centuries have achieved because of, or in spite of, their material surroundings; or, again, whether they have more often been helped or hampered in creative work by having a family. Whatever the testimony of history, we must not forget that everything in the Platonic philosophy tended to magnify the importance of the unseen world and to look down on the solicitations of the material world. The rulers, if true to their mission, would hardly feel the absence of wealth or of family life; if they were in danger of defaulting, the precaution was not wholly absurd. The real flaw in

Plato's reasoning is his assumption that as the individual finds happiness in the harmonious condition of his whole personality, so the rulers will find their happiness in the harmony of the whole state; he forgets that the rulers are not only the rational part of the state but are also themselves individuals with complete personalities of various elements, as he forgets, too, that even the less intelligent citizens are not wholly devoid of intelligence and of desires that deserve recognition.

The "Republic" represents Plato in his most idealistic or Utopian mood; in this dialogue Socrates craves permission "like an idle wayfarer to indulge his imagination without inquiring too closely whether his dreams can come true." [1] When Plato said that his state could be realized *if* the philosopher were to become a king, he had no illusions about the "if." So it is hardly fair to say that he shows disillusionment in the later dialogues in which he sketches a state that reckons more with the "facts." In the "Statesman," Plato still defends the absolute rule of a monarch and ignores the will of the citizens; but he is less hostile to democracy. His ideal statesman is not so much an actual ruler as a trainer of rulers; his is the art of weaving together in a harmonious whole the varied materials of human nature. Because of his living intelligence he is more flexible than rigid laws; and he is capable of reconciling the conflicting interests of different classes and groups of society. And yet, artist though he is, there is grave danger that he may be tempted to be arbitrary or even selfish; and Plato recognizes that law, though less flexible than a living personality, represents the experience of many men, and is perhaps safer in the end. If the ideal monarch cannot be found, the rule of law must prevail, either constitutional monarchy, or aristocracy, or a moderate democracy: such is the order of Plato's preference.

[1] Cf. *Rep.* 458a.

In his old age, Plato considers anew the whole problem of
the rule of law. He still believes that the philosophic legislator is best and that the spirit of the citizens is more important than legislation; but he is willing to outline a "second-
best" state, taking more account of human nature as it is.
Accordingly the "Laws" deals more fully than the "Republic" with constitutional and legislative details. Law is
not opposed to reason; it is rather the expression of reason,
and personality finds its scope in the details of administration. So Plato returns to the earlier Greek conception of law
as something fixed and fundamental, even though he provides that the several laws shall be accompanied by preambles justifying them on rational grounds, and so appealing
to the intelligence of the public. The state is to include all
the social life of its members, and is to be the sponsor of education and of morality. With less emphasis on specialization
of function among the citizens than in the "Republic,"
Plato is equally insistent on the need of discipline and self-
control to curb too great aggressiveness within the state and
in foreign relations; for it was the growth of lawlessness that
caused the decay of those Dorian states whose prime Plato
so obviously admires and regards as in many things his
model. Yet all forms of government have their defects as
well as their merits; the best practicable form is a "mixed"
constitution, combining some of the elements of each form.
Even democracy is recognized in the preambles, which imply the consent of the governed. The officials are to be
elected by the assembly of all the citizens, but in such a
way as to give the wealthy classes the greater opportunity,
because of the greater merit which they are likely to have;
yet all the citizens have equal votes, and the lot is to be used
in choosing among nominees, for there is no infallible
method of measuring merit. As in the "Republic," educa-

tion is the heart of the state; and the official in charge of education is the most important official in the state. Thus Plato hopes to combine Spartan training with some of the constitutional forms of Athens, the prevailing influence being nominally democratic but really aristocratic. Representative democracy is not even considered. The economic system of the "Laws" is nearer to that of the ordinary Greek state; but Plato is anxious to make politics the chief concern of the citizens, and therefore, though he does not deny them private property, he reduces business and economic production to a minimum, intrusting it so far as possible to slaves or aliens; for he holds that money is the root of evil. Marriage is still to be regulated by the state, but is now to be wholly monogamous; and women are still to engage in the same occupations as men, extending their skill in housekeeping to the larger household of the state. The whole picture of life under the rule of the "Laws" is one of quiet regularity and orderly habit, with due provision for amusement and worship, but always according to accepted ordinances. As we might have expected, religion is strictly controlled, and Plato is willing even to hold inquisitions against heresy. So far is Plato carried by his zeal for order, and so far is he willing even in his last years to sacrifice the liberty of the individual to the supposed safety of society; even in political and moral matters he reverts to a system of censors and examiners and espionage, with a "nocturnal council" to act as a court of last resort. In spite of much practical wisdom,[1] Plato points in the "Laws" to an ideal almost as static as that of the Egyptians. But before we attempt to decide wherein the value of Plato's thought consists, we must review the contributions of later thinkers.

[1] For example, the discussion of the reformatory motive in punishment, and of the value of imitation in producing habits.

When we turn from the writings of Plato to those of his. pupil Aristotle, we are conscious of a complete change of atmosphere; we have turned from the pulpit to the laboratory. It is not only that Plato's dialogues hold the breath of the Muses and that the treatises of Aristotle seem to be bare lecture-notes; it is even more a difference of temperament. Whereas Plato's bent is Utopian, Aristotle is the practical man of the world, interested in the systematic investigation of facts. He is therefore conservative[1] and inclined to limit his political vision to typically Greek institutions, and is sceptical of much in Plato's idealism; he considers Plato's proposals for communism and for the segregation of classes not practicable. But Aristotle has an idealism of a different kind; he is more patient than Plato in his observation of average human nature, and more sanguine in his hopes of what can be done with ordinary men. His ideal for a state is a constitution that permits not merely a few enlightened men but all the citizens to lead as complete a life as possible; and for the realization of this ideal he cannot say in advance just what form of government is best. Theory must wait on facts.

Like Plato, Aristotle finds in the state no artificial or arbitrary union, such as some of the Sophists had supposed it to be, but a rational scheme for the realization of man's nature. "Man is by nature a political animal," he says; it is the community of man's interests and needs that produces not only every partial association, such as the family, the trade-guild, or the village, but the all-embracing association, the state. The developed state is therefore no less natural than a primitive society; in fact it is even more natural, for it carries out more perfectly the imperfect beginnings and in-

---

[1] Indeed he devotes considerable attention to methods of avoiding political revolution.

tentions of nature.[1] Politics is always concerned, then, with the question, "What does nature intend?" Since society begins for the sake of mere existence, but is continued for the sake of a better life, the individual finds his true nature in organized society.

Aristotle believes that the state is the highest institution in society; but he does not believe that it excludes other institutions. There is room for lesser allegiances, such as the family, or the village; and the state acts as the directing influence when lesser institutions conflict. Here Aristotle recognizes more fully than Plato the diversity in human nature; and though he sees that the state must have unity if it is to be efficient, he does not try to reduce men to moulds, as if they could ever be identical. The state, then, is a unity, like a living organism, so far as its members have a common end and a fellow-feeling one for another; so far as they differ in motives and character, it acts as a mechanical agency for the minimizing of friction. On the whole, Aristotle is inclined to emphasize the organic nature of the state, which implies that as the several members of the human body can fulfill their functions only as parts of the body, and vary in importance, so the members of society are not self-sufficient, but derive their powers and their importance from the body politic. Obviously this view supports a conservative attitude, for it implies that the state has naturally, almost by divine intention, grown to its present condition, and it thus resists any pretensions of individuals that cannot clearly be shown to issue from the whole organism. On the other hand, the opposing view, by which the state is merely a mechanical

[1] To put the matter differently, Aristotle regards the state as logically prior to the individual, as the whole logically comes before the part. This is Aristotle's answer to the Cynics, who began with the assumption that man is naturally solitary; only a beast or a god, he holds, can exist without society.

compact between individuals or groups, encourages the idea that change or revolution is natural.

Not only does Aristotle consider the individual and therefore the state wholly from the point of view of their end, but, like Plato, he regards this end not as something materially determined but as moral; for man's nature differs from that of the lower animals in his rational and moral powers, and the state's aim must then be to secure for its members the most complete and the most intelligent use of their powers. Mere life in a common territory, or association in economic production is not enough to constitute a state; the state is needed to secure order and peace and the enjoyment of man's manifold capacities; above all it is needed to control by education the moral ideas of the citizens so as to train their natural aptitudes by instilling good habits. Though material conditions are necessary to produce a healthy man or a healthy state, they are not all that is needed; they must be guided by the whole moral purpose of society. In other words, wealth and the rights of property and the conditions of industry must prove their claims at the bar of social justice. Wealth is not good in itself, and poverty is not good in itself; all depends on the use that is made of what resources exist. In this matter, Aristotle agrees with Plato that there is no limit to the power that the state may legitimately use; but he finds, unlike Plato, that practical experience shows that it may be wise for the state not to exercise all the rights it has over the activities or the property of individuals, not because the individual has superior rights, but because the good of the state exists only in the good of its members. How far the state should go in suppressing or controlling the private activities of its members is a question, Aristotle believes, to be decided not by abstract reason but by observation of facts. And he thinks that experience shows that such

communism of property and of the family as Plato desired
for his rulers would not increase the unity of the state enough
to compensate for the loss in personality of these rulers;
their affections, instead of being strengthened, would be
diluted and become "watery." [1] Even more would Aristotle
criticize the proposals of modern socialism, not merely because he fears that common ownership means loss of initiative and efficiency, but because his faith is less in change of
ownership than in such a changed spirit as would mean the
use of private property for the common good. Probably the
answer of common sense as well as of experience is that
Aristotle is right in seeing the ultimate possibilities of private ownership but perhaps over-sanguine in hoping that
any but a radical change of heart will cause most men to use
private property for the common good; and that Plato,
though aiming in his communism not at material production
but only at the liberation of a few rare souls for the employ-
ment of their minds, probably exaggerates the gain that
would come from his plan. Aristotle in this instance, at
least, sees more clearly than Plato the moral possibilities of
property and of the family as aids to social welfare; and he is
right in holding that true unity is a thing of the spirit, to be
won by the education of all the citizens.

Since the end of education is political, in that it aims at the
development of the will and the character in accordance
with the national temper, it should be controlled by the
state and should be uniform; so far Aristotle agrees with the
practice of Sparta (not of Athens) and with Plato's conception of elementary education. But it should train the reason
as well as the will, and should be effective for peace as well as
for war; here Aristotle surpasses the Spartan ideal. He bases

[1] Aristotle has in mind what we mean by saying that "everybody's business is nobody's business."

his education on a sound psychological foundation, in that he makes its stages correspond with the gradual unfolding of man's various faculties. Some supervision of marriage is advisable for the safeguarding of healthy children. The early training of the body, not to be carried so far as to produce professional athletes, is to be followed by training in literature and the arts; these should be studied less for any utilitarian ends than for their power to produce good habits and emotions, sound standards of action, and pleasant means of recreation. Last of all, as in Plato's plan, the reason is to be fed by mathematical and philosophical studies. At every point the emphasis is on the type of character that is to be produced.

As the state tries by education to stamp its character on the citizens, so conversely the character of the citizens determines the form of the state. All the free citizens constitute the state,[1] and, as in the average Greek democracy, Aristotle considers citizenship to imply direct participation in government, with as little delegation of duties as possible; this brings about, as we have seen, a further education of the citizens in practical politics. But he believes in the separation of legislative, executive, and judicial functions.

Since those who hold political power may govern either for the good of the whole state or for their own ends, and may be either a single person or a small group or a large number, Aristotle finds that there are six possible forms of government. Those that aim at the good of the whole are monarchy, aristocracy, and polity (or constitutional republic); in theory, monarchy would be the best, but perfect rulers are

[1] Slaves, manual workers, and aliens are denied political rights, on the ground of fitness and specialization of function; some men engage in productive labor, others in government. So far as the citizens govern for the good of all, this amounts practically, though not in form, to representative government.

seldom if ever found; and even a smaller number of men with the right qualifications is not often available; in practice, therefore, the best form of government is usually the constitutional republic, which gives the control to the whole electorate and relies on their patriotism. Each of these forms may be perverted, if the class in power considers only its own interests; and the corresponding forms, in the order of their badness, are democracy, the counterpart of the constitutional republic, oligarchy, corresponding to aristocracy, and tyranny, the corrupted form of monarchy. In this classification of states it is important to notice that Aristotle's criterion is not primarily numerical but moral; it is the spirit in which the ruling element regards its opportunity. The case for a constitutional republic or for democracy, Aristotle thinks, is the superior wisdom that is likely to be found in numbers of citizens; individually they may be in error, collectively their judgment will probably be right, if they are disinterested.[1] Of course Aristotle's attention is turned chiefly to the city-states that he knew, and does not reckon with nations on the modern scale, or with representative government, or with complex systems of government. Yet the bare principles of his classification are not without value when we compare Czarist Russia with England, or Soviet Russia with France, or analyze the seat of political power and its nature in the United States.

Aristotle's conception of an ideal state is colored by his shrewd observation of Greek states as they existed. He judged democracy, for example, not, as Plato did, by its ignorance and the evil human nature on which it seemed to rest, nor, as we do, from experience of representative democracy and in the light of a theory as to the rights of the in-

[1] Aristotle points to the fact that popular judgments were actually of value in literary and artistic matters.

dividual; he looked at democracy as it was actually working, and found that it was affected by special circumstances. Granted that the farmer had the suffrage, had he the time to vote, or would he not incline to let government become the concern of those who lived in the city? Did the democracy respect the fundamental laws, or were they inclined to tinker with legislation? Did they govern for the good of the state, or did they expect the government to despoil the rich for the benefit of the poor by padding the payrolls and making paupers of the citizens? Did oligarchies, by restricting the numbers of those eligible to office by standards of wealth, or heredity, or force, secure real merit, or did they encourage party strife?

With these observations and questions in mind, and remembering that an ideal state can exist only under ideal conditions both external and internal,[1] Aristotle comes to the conclusion that the form of government that is to be sought in any given circumstances is the one that gives most power to the middle class in the state and that causes it to increase; for the middle class is the centre of stability and the chief seat of virtue and intelligence and wealth. Since it has most at stake, it is least likely to favor any kind of revolution; Aristotle therefore commends its supremacy as the best remedy against sedition. For political stability is certain only when those who have an interest in maintaining the *status quo* are either more numerous or more powerful than those who would be likely to gain by a change; it hinges on giving to as many as possible a "stake in the country." From this point of view, rather than from any notion of the fundamental equality of man or of the dependence of the

---

[1] Aristotle further believes that it is only in the ideal state that the good man and the good citizen are identical; in imperfect states there must be compromise.

state on the consent of the governed, Aristotle is inclined to favor as a practical expedient the "mixed" type of state, in which political powers are to be distributed among all parts, taking advantage of the collective average wisdom of the many voters, the expert knowledge of the magistrates, and the conservatism of the laws. By this blending of extremes, with the fostering of a *bourgeoisie*, Aristotle thinks that the greatest practicable unity of the state is to be found.[1] And by suggesting that the same individuals might be soldiers in their youth, statesmen in middle life, and priests in old age, he guards against setting classes against each other. He nevertheless excludes laborers and slaves from political life, as we have seen, on the ground of a division of labor; nor does Aristotle discuss economic measures for the prevention of revolution. He merely argues that men will not wish to revolt if their consent is asked in the government, so far as their ability and worth warrant, if public office is not made very profitable, and if the citizens are educated in the spirit of the constitution.[2]

Particular forms of government, then, are in Aristotle's opinion always a compromise between an ideal and the facts in the case. Law in the abstract is the embodiment or crystallization of men's moral ideals removed from any selfish considerations; it is reason without passion, and as such is not arbitrary or conventional but the expression of man's best nature. Yet it is only the legislator who can see

[1] The "mixed constitution," with various expedients of "checks and balances," may be traced in Stoic doctrine, in the observations of Polybius and of Cicero on the Roman constitution, in Montesquieu's account of the British government, and in the elaborate provision in the Constitution of the United States for preventing excessive authority in any part of the government.

[2] Aristotle's arguments for the encouragement of the middle class, with a broad basis of citizenship, sustain the policy of the statesman Demetrius of Phalerum, who was trained by Aristotle's pupil Theophrastus. Cf. W. S. Ferguson, *Hellenistic Athens*, p. 39.

law in this light; he has to adapt law to particular conditions; the judge occasionally must in appearance correct it, in order that essential justice may be done. This is the argument for the government of men, rather than of impersonal law; men are more flexible than laws. But they are also less disinterested, and it is dangerous to leave justice to them, unchecked by a fundamental law; it may even be wise to ostracize men of great ability. On the whole it is safer to hold to the government of law, remembering that law is ultimately the lasting expression of society's whole nature, and that only to its recalcitrant members can law seem arbitrary. There is wisdom in numbers; and the character and habits of a people is the court of final appeal which slowly creates and modifies law, and without which law is powerless.

The habit of obedience to law is therefore justice in the largest sense; in particular, justice means the distribution of political rights and privileges to men according to their deserts and the correction of any encroachments on such a distribution. Men's merits are not equal, and their political rights are therefore not equal, Aristotle argues; true justice aims not at absolute equality but at a proportional balance. When we ask on what grounds Aristotle would assign rights to some individuals and deny them to others, it appears that his answer depends on their moral worth as measured by their past services to the state or by their use of wealth. In theory little can be said against a moral standard for the distribution of political rights; in practice it is very hard to determine who are morally worthy; and our tendency in electing officials is to emphasize the qualifications of mental ability and practical experience, but to extend the franchise as widely as possible, on the assumption that only the exercise of the vote can develop the capacity to vote, just as the only way to learn to swim is to swim. No man has "rights" except by anticipation of the use that he will make of opportunities; and the only way to learn what a man's capacity is, is to give him a chance to show it. We are more willing to take a risk than Aristotle was, for all his faith in average human nature. But the difference is not so great as it seems; Aristotle does extend the franchise to all free citizens, and we try not to elect to office clever rascals.

Later schools of philosophy, interested primarily in the life and character of the individual man and the basis of his happiness, were forced to consider his relation to society. The Stoics, who thought of the universe as a divine order governed by reason, found in the laws of nature the model for human life; the wise man is the man who lives in harmony with nature, and to him no evil can happen. Men can live together because they have the common gift of reason, and have therefore common rights. At present, because of the accidental differences between states, we are imperfect citizens of the world; but we may find what good we can in these states, remembering our spiritual citizenship in the divine order. What the Stoic means by the "law of nature" is really the physical laws disclosed by the reason, which seem uniform and absolute, and to which human law can be only an approximation; but the relation is confused. None the less the growing uniformity of law in the various parts of the Roman Empire was supposed, in accordance with Stoic doctrine, to be an evidence of the fact that the law of Rome, interpreted by the reason of her prætors, was in accordance with nature.

The Epicureans, striving to attain happiness by the temperate use of all man's faculties, taught that man's social nature and the state were to be utilized so far as served convenience, but discouraged active participation in political life. Stoics and Epicureans thus agreed in treating the state as a mere stepping-stone, not as the highest embodiment of human nature; but the Epicureans were much more inclined to be indifferent to the state.

Despite the views of the Stoics and the Epicureans, the normal Greek view in every age, making much of the social nature of man, thought of the state as logically prior to the individual; ethics therefore, which considers the moral ideals of the individual, was for the Greeks only a special aspect of politics. Moreover, since the Greeks relied for their standards of conduct less on the supernatural revelations of religion [1] than on instinct and habit and on the sovereign reason, we shall do well to consider at this point some of the qualities that the Greeks desired in their lives.

In the world depicted by Homer we find, as we should expect, that the more rugged virtues predominate; the strength of Ajax, the fierce and brilliant heroism of Achilles are pre-eminent; then come the wiliness of Odysseus and the mellow wisdom of Nestor. Achilles shows in his fervent friendship for Patroclus and his pity for stricken Priam that he has a gentler side; and in Penelope and Andromache we find beautiful examples of loyal feminine character. But the whole basis for such moral qualities as we find is not rational but instinctive and emotional; [2] when Homeric personages debate, how often they appeal to pride, or anger, or pity, how seldom to the reason! The Homeric heroes were for centuries the pattern of manly virtue among the Greeks. In the sixth and the fifth centuries the typical gentleman, the καλὸς κἀγαθός, regarded health and personal beauty as possibly the highest goods; he wished for sufficient wealth to set him free from the need of working at a trade, but thought it

---

[1] The gods of the Greeks, not unlike the deities of many other nations, were only gradually moralized as the national ideals became higher.

[2] Cf. p. 157, on *aidos* and *nemesis*.

no disgrace to be compelled to do so; he was fond of country life and simple living; though fond of athletics, he kept the standing of an amateur; he set a high value on friendship and social intercourse; without being especially intellectual in his tastes, he took a lively interest in the arts and could meet the demands even of Attic tragedy; he worshipped without question the gods of his fatherland, as he served without question his term in the army; he was kind to his slaves, but never thought of slavery as wrong,[1] and fond of his wife, though not sentimental and not regarding her as in any sense his equal; temperate in his use of wine as of all things, he acted consciously or unconsciously in accordance with the precept of the Delphic oracle and sought excess in nothing.[2] It might seem as if he were treading a calculated path between opposing vices (as in fact Aristotle later explained his conduct); but his prudence was largely a practical sense of the utility of certain things, with a rooted dislike of those excesses that seemed to him ugly. He had no fixed standards of conduct except for such matters as were laid down by custom and by the state; in all others his desires and his own experience determined his course.

It was only when the validity of any sort of fixed moral standard had been challenged by some of the Sophists[3] that it occurred to the Greeks to establish it. To Plato it seemed that the challenge came from the lower instincts and passions in man, which claimed equal rights with man's higher nature; the obvious remedy seemed to be to enthrone the reason, and to subject the emotions as far as possible. Even courage, for example, does not deserve the name of courage

[1] Cf. C. B. Gulick, "Greek Notions of Humanity," in *Harvard Essays on Classical Subjects*.

[2] Cf. R. W. Livingstone, *The Greek Genius and its Meaning to Us*, pp. 114 ff.

[3] Cf. p. 159.

if it is the blind indifference to danger of the beast or the fool, but only if it means the determination of the rational man who has counted the cost.[1] Plato thus tended to make all virtue synonymous with asceticism; he who deserves praise and envy is not so much the man who can combine in a harmonious life all the good things of body and of spirit as the man who, like the athlete in rigid training, can subject all else to a single end; and that end, for Plato, is the rule and the pursuit of reason. He was not alone in feeling that the body and its passions are an impediment to the soul's progress toward truth, and that the philosopher is he who *par excellence* succeeds in rising above the claims of the body; asceticism was an important movement in Greek life and thought, and was destined to exert a strong influence on Christianity.[2] But Plato was ready to go further than his contemporaries in starving the flesh and committing his saints to celibacy and monastic communism and military discipline. Moreover, he intends to enthrone no mere practical sense, — the cunning of an Odysseus, the instinctive balance of the καλὸς κἀγαθός, qualities never lacking among the Greeks. His supreme ruler is nothing less than the austere reason that is forever seeking the ultimate abstract principle of existence and goodness. And Plato never doubts that to know goodness is to love it and to practise it. The ideal is a stimulating one not unlike that held out to us by the Hebrew prophets in the "love of God"; for average mortals, however, it often seems a little remote and forbidding. Instead of commanding certain definite acts, which is what childish natures demand, it enjoins an inward harmony; and

[1] Cf. S. H. Butcher, *Some Aspects of the Greek Genius*, chap. 1.

[2] Cf. C. H. Moore, "Greek and Roman Ascetic Tendencies," in *Harvard Essays on Classical Subjects*. Livingstone does not seem to me sufficiently to recognize this movement in his otherwise excellent book, *The Greek Genius and its Meaning to Us*.

when it is asked of what elements the harmony is to be composed, the explanation seems at first sight to strip away a good deal of the content of ordinary life; it seems to be a compromise in which the reason gives up nothing and the desires give up everything. Such a criticism is superficial. Plato does recognize the claims of the natural man; but he shows that his personality is a contradiction and that it dooms him to unhappiness unless some sort of balance is struck, and, finally, that the greater the rule of reason, the greater the harmony and the happiness.[1] Now for man in general, though not for all men in the same degree, this is undoubtedly true. Self-control, which is another name for the rule of reason, is the price of even the least noble sort of success; and self-control contains at least an element of negation.

As one might have expected, Aristotle is critical of the rigid and absolute goal that Plato would like to set up.[2] He holds that the end of human life is not Plato's transcendental good (he assumes, perhaps too hastily, that it must be transcendental), but the happiness which comes from the complete activity of the powers of a personality both emotional and rational, during a lifetime. The emotional nature with which man is born is converted, by rational training, into good habits, or character; the intellect requires similar training. Emotions are in themselves not bad, but become bad when allowed to go to extremes; the path of virtue is therefore a middle course between two extremes. So courage stands between cowardice and foolhardiness; nobility of soul is the mean between humility (by Greeks generally con-

---

[1] It is worthy of note that not before Plato do we find old age regarded as not wholly gloomy, clearly because its bodily disabilities are of slight consequence compared with its intellectual resources.

[2] For the intellectual basis of Aristotle's criticisms, cf. pp. 256 f.

sidered a fault) and arrogance.[1] If we ask how we are to know at what point between the extremes to seek the mean, Aristotle refers us to no absolute standard, but to the discretion of the man of sense who has made some moral progress and who therefore might be said to have moral insight. We are all pacifists when we are at peace, Christian Scientists when we are well, and Socialists till we have tax-bills to pay. It takes experience and common sense, in addition to abstract reason, to tell us how to apply our principles to a given case, or, indeed, to be sure just which principles to apply.[2] And moral insight is not wholly a matter of emotion or instinct, though it grows out of emotions and instincts that have become habitual; nor is it, as Socrates had held, the same thing as knowledge. It is emotion directed by reason, or reason made effective by emotion, and becomes at last not momentary impulse and not intellectual cunning but moral purpose, the will that is determined by its perception of a moral end and that carries out its end in the details of conduct.[3] So morality neither begins from absolute nothingness nor is derived from a perfect principle of goodness, but, like any biological fact, is a growth from something to something more. The higher the stage in this moral growth, the greater the exercise of man's highest faculty, the

[1] We have already referred (p. 125) to the "Characters" of Aristotle's pupil Theophrastus, which depict with comic exaggeration various types of men who err through excess of one quality.

[2] Viscount Bryce speaks of the "fond illusion that to confer a right is to confer therewith the capacity to exercise it. In politics it is not false principles that have done most harm. It is the misconception of principles in themselves sound, prompting their hasty application without regard to the facts of each particular case." *Modern Democracies*, vol. ii, p. 173.

[3] This is what Aristotle means by προαίρεσις, the term in his vocabulary that comes nearest to what modern psychologists mean by the "will." It is an attitude of the whole personality, not, like Plato's "reason," a mere part of the personality.

reason; and the life of reason or contemplation, which differentiates man from the animals and brings him nearest to God, is more pleasant and lasting than the life of action, which is always a means to an end. In this conclusion, Aristotle seems not far from the philosophic life praised by Plato; but the moral and intellectual life that Aristotle holds up for emulation is at best rather self-centred, not to say selfish. Even if we acquit his "magnanimous man" from the charge of being a prig, still the coolly calculated balance of his life strikes one as little more than a glorified sort of worldly wisdom or prudence. We miss the ardor of Plato's perfervid adoration of a better world, and the reckless self-sacrifice of the Christian saint. Prudence is much; harmonious self-development is much; we need a better appreciation of them to-day. But they are not enough.

In principle, the utilitarianism of Aristotle's ethical system is not very different from the utilitarianism of the Epicureans, whose aim was to gain happiness by realizing as fully as possible their various powers; in effect, however, because the emphasis of the Epicureans was on the individual's gratification of his personal desires as far as is possible, with only incidental recognition of social relations and ends other than convivial, Epicureanism was apt to find its consummation in immediate pleasure, whether coarse or refined, and seldom attained sufficient forgetfulness of self to end in the contemplative life. It was the Stoics, men immersed in the universal reign of law that men's common gift of reason could investigate, who were able to sink their individual wills in the common task. The Epicureans were individualists by choice, and members of society by convenience; the Stoics were soldiers in a common cause, and in their devotion to the highest good they were inclined to ignore any imperfect or merely personal good.

The average Greek hardly had what we call a moral sense to any uncomfortable degree; though not without con- science,[1] he was not haunted by the Puritan's sense of sin. The Cretans were notorious liars; the Spartans applauded theft, provided that it was undetected. The Athenians un- der the stress of war were capable of brutal treatment of the Melians. Compared with the moral earnestness of the Jew, the self-satisfied attitude of the Greek seems almost child- ish. But that does not mean that the Greeks were immoral or even unmoral. The ordinary Greek of the Homeric world compares favorably in character with the ordinary Jew of the Old Testament, though he lacks the leadership of a su- perior moral nature. But the Greek towers above the Jew of the Old Testament in his intellectual command of the prob- lems of conduct. It is the Greek who shows the logical basis of conduct in human nature, and who clearly formulates a notion of an end to be realized and of the best means for realizing it. The whole structure of Greek tragedy and the moral problems which it presents are permeated by intellect- ual conceptions; the hero falls through excess of a quality. There is something almost quantitative about Aristotle's theory of virtue as a mean, or of distributive justice, that reminds one of the striving for mathematical proportion in Greek architecture and sculpture. And if Plato and Aris- totle, following Socrates, seem at times almost to over- emphasize the intellectual element in ethics, and to have less to say about the will, we must remember that the will was already fully recognized in current opinion, and was the foundation of the theory of Athenian democracy.[2] It was

[1] Cf. p. 157 f., 191.

[2] Also, we may add, of the tragedy of Sophocles. Fate was a part, but only a part, of Greek drama. See Miss Leach, "Fatalism of the Greeks," *American Journal of Philology*, XXXVI; also reprinted in L. Cooper, *The Greek Genius and its Influence*.

rational criticism, the rule of reason, that Greek practice most needed and that we greatly need to-day. And as Greek art by its innate tact keeps a clear line between sentiment and sentimentality, Greek thought about the problems of individual and society keeps a golden vein of common sense mediating between fact and ideal. If Greek political and ethical theory does over-emphasize the intellectual element, our tendency to-day is in need of this corrective. It is therefore worth while to notice several of the larger aspects of Greek thought with our own problems in view.

3. Freedom and Control

In all periods of history there have been two opposing tendencies in human nature: one, arising from the love of liberty and of personal opportunity, we may call individualism; the other, recognizing the mutual dependence of men, may be called social cohesiveness, or political control. The general prepossession of the Greeks was in favor of liberty: "Hellenes do not like to be called slaves," says Aristotle, "but confine the name to barbarians." [1] It was the boast of the Athens of Pericles that there was no interference with the daily life of any man.[2] The very word "obey" in Greek is $\pi\epsilon i\theta\epsilon\sigma\theta\alpha\iota$, which means literally "to be persuaded." [3] Nothing was more valued at Athens than the freedom of speech which subjected even the most distinguished personages to the pitiless criticism of the comic poets.[4] Even Sparta, the home of military discipline,

---

[1] *Pol.* 1255a.

[2] Thuc. II, 37; cf. VII, 69.

[3] But we must not press words too far; the word for a deserter is $a\dot{v}\tau\acute{o}\mu o\lambda os$, which means simply one who moves of his own accord.

[4] Until this criticism went so far that it had to be curbed, during the Peloponnesian War; even then the comic poets found ways of evading the law.

boasted of freedom of speech.[1] Unlike the early Republic of Rome, which was too much occupied by wars waged to defend its very existence to value highly the toleration of eccentricities, the Greek states, infinitely varied in form and spirit, felt that they existed primarily for the good of their several members. It was this love of freedom that not only made away with the tyrants but kept alive in a patriotic song the memory of the tyrannicides Harmodius and Aristogeiton; for as Americans are suspicious of political bosses, and yet tolerate them, the Greeks were opposed to the principle of tyranny, and put their trust in institutions rather than in powerful rulers, and tolerated the tyrants only during their good behavior.[2] Under Roman rule, Greek love of liberty was at times troublesome to the governors; and the Stoic philosophy gave support to any revolt against tyranny.[3]

One result of the extreme individualism of the Greeks was the fact that not merely did they live in isolated communities, coöperating imperfectly in national causes, but even within their narrow boundaries they were particularly liable to those violent civil riots and wars that Thucydides has so eloquently described. Aristotle has preserved for us the oath of the oligarchic party: "I will hate the Demos (the popular party) and do it all the harm in my power." [4] Individualism in the selfish person of the brilliant Alcibiades is hard to distinguish from tyranny. Such manifestations as these persuaded Plato that unity must be won at any cost; he was willing to rid the hive of its "drones," and even

---

[1] Herodotus, VII, 135.

[2] Cf. B. L. Gildersleeve, "Americanism and Hellenism," reprinted in L. Cooper, *The Greek Genius and its Influence*, esp. p. 249.

[3] Brutus, one of the murderers of Cæsar, was a Stoic. Cf. J. P. Mahaffy, *Problems of Greek History*, p. 172.

[4] *Pol.* 1310a.

to let invalids die, since they could contribute nothing, he thought, to the social good. Yet unity is not wholly an end in itself, and may be purchased too dearly if it loses all the richness and variety of individual life. Plato hardly realized that "liberty need not be sacrificed to gain fraternity"; [1] and it was Aristotle who saw more clearly that the safest cure for dissension is not repression but the recognition of whatever is sound and capable of useful development. Few things in Greek history are more instructive than the way in which the Greek army of Cyrus the Younger, a hopelessly undisciplined body of troops, by modern standards, resolved itself from time to time into a parliamentary body, debated the issues of its march, and voted sanely what course to take. And we must never lose sight of the tremendous debt that the world owes to the richness of experience that the Greeks won through their lack of conformity to a mechanical type. In our world of huge states, quantitative production, organized activities, narrowing personal liberty, and converging customs, we feel the loss of something vital and spontaneous that was possible in the earlier world of little states and unhampered individualism.[2]

We feel a loss, but we are conscious also of a gain; for Greek individualism could be very wasteful in its tolerance of friction. Solidarity and organization were needed to curb the power of supermen and to direct to useful ends the aimless or conflicting energies of lesser men; and coöperation culminated in the state. It was good economy; and ordinary men found that their personal opportunities were enhanced, or, as Aristotle expressed it, that they realized their full natures. But in their attempts to combine and form larger

[1] E. Barker, *Plato and His Predecessors*, p. 231.
[2] Cf. the very stimulating discussion in "The Value of Small States," by H. A. L. Fisher, *Oxford Pamphlets*, 1914; see especially pp. 9–12; 15–18.

units than the city-state the Greeks failed. Unity of spirit was at times achieved; but a permanent union of states was feasible only if one state formed an empire or a hegemony.[1] Alliances and federations fell apart because without a system of representation there was no method for recognizing the will of a dissenting minority. Empires and hegemonies lasted only as long as the leading state could hold its military preëminence.[2] It is interesting to read the Athenian claim to leadership in a speech of Isocrates.[3] Athens has won her position by virtue of having been the leader in every good work of war and of peace; her supremacy has lasted long, and has brought prosperity and the establishment of democracies; only those who resisted her have been punished. And in the second century B.C. other Greeks were ready to declare, in an Amphictyonic decree, that Athens was the "inaugurator of all human blessings."[4] The several states, and especially the leading states, therefore, were the political units that held the imaginations of Greeks; even Aristotle could conceive of no larger unit. And cosmopolitanism became an important fact only when the city-state, which long supplied all social needs, had been superseded by the empire of Alexander and later by the empire of Rome. Greek thought was therefore dominated for the most part by the conception of an extremely tangible state; citizenship was emphasized, and the only rights that were thought of were

---

[1] A hegemony is a loosely organized group of states under the leadership of one state.

[2] A. Holm (*Hist. of Greece*, Eng. tr., vol. iii, pp. 447 ff.) believes that the reason why there is no abstract noun corresponding to the word προστάτης, which was used of a state that acted as the champion or leader of other states in time of peace, is that such a relation existed only temporarily for an emergency.

[3] *Panegyricus*, esp. pp. 100–109.

[4] Quoted more fully by W. S. Ferguson, *Hellenistic Athens*, pp. 308 f.

not those of the human being as such or even those of the citizen of the world, but those of the citizen of the Greek city-state. Even Plato rarely stepped outside of the Greek world, and spoke, for example, of the wrongness of harming one's enemies.

The Greek theorists, finding the city-state already organized and of use in safeguarding the interests of the individual, were concerned above all to preserve its unity and to protect the national character against the revolt of individualists who might endanger it. As we have seen, Plato's distrust of inferior or merely average elements inclined him to favor a benevolent despotism without the consent of the governed; a revolutionary at heart, he used the weapons of the reactionary to achieve his ends. Aristotle's end is not different, but is achieved by more moderate means, since it hopes to substitute for the absolute rule of the best the co-operation of all, on the assumption that at least a majority will be sound at heart.[1] But both Plato and Aristotle find a problem in the minority. They do not hope to make them good or to make them agree by act of Parliament. In a word, their supreme hope is that by education and by environment all citizens may be sufficiently imbued with the spirit of the national character to offer no serious impediment to harmony. Supposing such measures to fail, the disaffected must be treated with greater severity. But here it is hard to draw the line. When Athenians felt that a political leader was too much at variance with the spirit of the government, they were apt to ostracize him, — that is, to debar him from further political activity by temporarily exiling him; when it became evident that one statesman might thus

---

[1] The same assumption lies behind the law of Solon against neutrality in time of dissension; he expects the majority to support the established order. But this expedient does not meet a danger till the crisis is passed.

become the victim of a coalition of two rivals, a form of impeachment for unconstitutional policy was substituted. If the views of a public man seemed too outrageous, he might be fined, or exiled, or even put to death; Pheidias, Anaxagoras, Pericles, and Socrates are only a few of the distinguished men who suffered from this practice. In modern times the censorship of the press and of speech, the restriction of immigration, the expulsion of dissenting members from a legislative body,[1] and the various acts of control assumed by many countries under stress of war are in varying degrees comparable; for they are the attempt of the body that claims to be sovereign to deal summarily with any attempt of a minority to influence the national course or the national character. The extreme case is a civil war, either to prevent secession,[2] or to decide whether the constituted government or a revolutionary party is to control the state.[3] The appeal to arms does not mean, for Plato or Aristotle, that the state is merely the embodiment of force, but that the state may in self-defense have to use force if its character is not to be altered. But here comes the all-important question; have the minority no right to criticize, or even to claim that their understanding of the nature or end of the state is better than that of the majority? Granted that there can be no satisfactory common life without some organization and controlling policy, why should the present organization and policy be assumed to be final, and the minority, reactionary or revolutionary, be treated like naughty children? The modern answer is somewhat different from that of the Greek thinkers. We act on the assump-

[1] E. g., the dissolution of the Parliament by Charles I and of the Duma by Nicholas II, and the expulsion of the Socialist members of the New York Assembly in January, 1920.

[2] E. g., revolts from the Athenian Empire, or the American Civil War.

[3] As in the French and the Russian Revolutions.

tion that, except in times of grave national danger, there should be little restriction of free discussion; and sometimes by proportional representation we give a voice to a minority. We hold that in the end the wisest view will prevail; men are after all a good deal alike. The Greek view is more objective and ethical; it fixes our attention on the end, the welfare of the state and its citizens, and tries to find those men, the experts, who can best advance it; men are after all rather different, and cannot be equally treated. The problem is one of selection and education; selection of men by their fitness for certain tasks, and education for these tasks.

The search for the expert in politics is the natural reaction from the faith of Greek democracies in an aggregate of impulses. So far had this gone that for many offices at Athens men were chosen by lot; originally this was probably supposed to leave the choice to the gods; later it was a method of ensuring widespread training and practice of politics and of avoiding unscrupulous rivalry among candidates who might be regarded as equally fit for election. The officials were simply a cross-section of the electorate. But were all candidates equally fit? Indeed, are all men equally fit to vote? And could a democracy based on the absence of discriminations rule an empire or wage a war? It seems to be the experience of modern as well as of ancient times that in the face of subject populations and in time of war democracies become less democratic. Mobs are unwieldy; even under the most favorable conditions of peace, it is hard to know what a people really desires till issues have been sifted and formulated. It is a choice, then, between demagogues or bosses, who profess to give the people what they want, and expert statesmen who interpret what they really want, or what they would want if they knew better. For there is a difference between the collective wishes of all the citizens, a mathematical aggregate, and the considered purpose of them all, which may be a compromise and may not be exactly what any individual desires. No man, alone, wishes to pay taxes; but just taxes are the expression of what Rousseau calls a "general will." It requires an expert to perceive in all the confusion of different preferences a possible ground of agreement. Yet that is not Plato's conception of an expert. His expert is the man who knows what a people ought to wish, not merely what it actually does wish. We have seen reason to believe that Plato does not do complete justice to average human nature, even if he does not quite postulate, as Mill said, "either infallibility in his rulers or comparative imbecility in the rest of mankind." The Platonic expert is not concerned with the interpretation of mass movements or with the focussing and expression of a general will; he descends from the heights to deliver the law to those in the valley. It is easy to object that if the welfare of the people is the goal of the legislator, the people know better than he where the shoe pinches, so that the initiative must frequently, at least, come from them. Plato would answer that his expert is not a mere expert but also a man like other men, only with heightened experience; if their shoes pinch, so must his, and he is better equipped than they to discover means of relief. But does his shoe really pinch in equal measure? May not his whole training have deadened his sensibility to some of the experience of ordinary men? [1] Aristotle would think so, and would try to arrange a partnership of the expert and the average man. Intellect is not the sole criterion for leadership, nor is practical experience, nor even moral character, but a happy combination of all. There may

[1] The chief source of power of our "bosses" is their understanding of the motives of ordinary men, — the "facts" of modern politics.

be a presumption in favor of certain types of men when political careers are at stake; it may be the men of wealth, or the college graduates, or the lawyers, or those who know intimately a particular community. But the predominating element is apt to be one that is little recognized in political theory,—the element of personality. And there we confront again the danger of unfettered individualism. Our present tendency in representative democracy is to trust mainly to the inertia of a constitution, altered only when public opinion has decidedly changed, and to treat our representatives as hirelings engaged to get what we want for us, and to relieve us from the need of giving personal attention to the innumerable details of modern government; this is especially the case since modern states are on such a large scale, and other interests occupy most of our time.[1] This division of labor is a thoroughly Platonic one, except in the attitude of the politician, who, if he is in any sense an expert, is now usually a technical expert, rather than an expert in the Platonic sense. The division is safe only if some of the functions of the Platonic expert are taken over by a public that is educated in some conception of its best course.[2]

Modern society is centrifugal; the state means less to us than it did to the Greeks. The various interests which in our day compete successfully with politics are mainly expressions of the acquisitive instinct, concerned with the production and the use of property. Acquisitiveness is only a phase of self-preservation; but it is also liable to become selfishness. The mind cannot live without the belly, but the

[1] "To judge well of men is, in a democracy, more essential than to judge well of measures, for the latter requires more knowledge than can be expected from the average man who must be mainly guided by his leaders." Viscount Bryce, *Modern Democracies*, vol. ii, p. 175; cf. pp. 594–604.

[2] Cf. *ibid.*, p. 536.

belly would like to rule the whole man; society depends in part on the increase of material things, but the greed for increase may defeat its aim, if it is not subjected to the will. The desire of the capitalist to get as much as he can in return for the use of the money that represents past production, and the desire of the laborer to get as much as he can in return for the labor that he is doing, are equally selfish. Especially under modern industrialism is it hard for the average man to think of himself first as a citizen and only secondly as a member of an economic group. Thus economics is apt to encroach on politics, and the result is lobbying and bribery and various forms of special privilege. Property is dangerously apt to become the master instead of the servant of humanity. The Greeks knew this, and tried resolutely to subordinate economics to politics, recognizing first of all the man as man and secondarily the man as producer. So at Athens political power gradually ceased to be the monopoly of those of superior economic position; yet the Greek saw the danger of giving votes without giving at the same time some measure of economic opportunity. A man with a vote and without property or a fair chance of winning property is inflammable material for demagogues.[1] The Greeks, believing that the state existed for a moral end, held that economic matters, too, were subject to regulation in the interest of this end. Whether this was to mean a socialistic system of production or only the supervision of private industry seemed wholly an incidental problem, to be decided on the basis of the practical results in production and in the effect on human nature. State socialism was very nearly a fact in fifth century Athens; but it was seriously modified by the fact that it drew from a subject empire and from newly discovered mines, and that slavery took the place of modern

[1] Cf. W. W. Fowler, *City State of the Greeks and Romans*, p. 133.

machinery. Yet if any kind of socialism was to be approved, the Greeks would have assumed that it must be state socialism, with the direction of men's productive energies toward a common end. In modern times there have been attempts to begin with separate groups of producers, — guilds, or soviets, men interested in particular conditions or prices for a certain product or amount of labor,—and to regard the state as merely a council representing these groups and reconciling conflicting interests.[1] The Greeks would have feared that some group or combination of groups might tyrannize over the rest, — that one selfish instinct might organize and strike against the whole, and that there would be no effective "representative of the public"; and they would have held that only the political state, expressing the whole nature of all its citizens, can be sovereign. If the state does not truly recognize the whole of society, with all its economic interests, it must be made to do so, by departments or commissions that are responsive to conditions. We might add that economic and social interests to-day are so intricate that they are no longer confined to single states, but cut across national barriers; difficulties can now be settled no longer by single states or even by diplomatic bargains between states. There is good reason for international conferences and associations of those interested. Nations can be as selfish as individuals or as economic groups; but economic groups and individuals can be as selfish as nations. If international economic groups are not to tyrannize over mankind, they must be subject to somebody that can truly express not merely an aggregate of selfish interests but the

[1] It is sometimes argued that laws giving special privileges to certain groups may be necessary to correct the inequalities inherent in the modern system of industry. Cf. G. Clark, " A New Road to Equality," *Atlantic Monthly*, July, 1921.

general will of all men. Whether this will be a League or Association of Nations or in the course of time a world-state, it is too early to prophesy.[1]

As the selfish acquisitiveness of men, uncontrolled, brings class warfare, the greed of nations brings international war. And war, the Greeks thought, is inevitable exactly to the extent to which greed is inevitable. If the "economic man," who is presumed to be perfectly selfish and to act only from motives of acquisitiveness, is a mere bogy of the imagination, because men really do act from a variety of motives, the aggressive state is equally capable of subjecting its expansive instincts to rational ends. The only method of preventing war is not ultimately material, but is the use of the will to prevent undue aggressiveness on the part of nations; it is the attitude of the Quaker applied to national issues. But it takes two parties to keep the peace, and only one to open hostilities; unless the attitude of the Quaker proves contagious,— and this often has been the case,[2]—a certain preparation for defensive warfare will be necessary. Yet nations are notoriously prone to carry chips on their shoulders; and a great insurance against war is the submission of differences to any international body that can act as the acknowledged representative of mankind. This submission can come about only by an act of self-control, an absence of selfishness, a morality or rationality more common among individuals than among nations; for we are still at the tribal stage of development that lets one regard the land of one's birth as better than other lands no less confidently than Hellenes claimed to be above barbarians. Only the rarest spirits, among Greeks or among modern men, have risen above the myth of national infallibility; and nothing but

[1] Cf. R. C. Jebb, "Attic Orators," on Isocrates, II, pp. 13 ff.
[2] E. g., W. Penn and the Indians.

education of peoples and free intercourse of peoples will ever show the folly of the myth.

One form of selfishness with regard to which the consciences of the Greeks were tough was slavery. The average Greek never questioned the institution, and accepted it as legal because it was rooted in custom. Euripides, to be sure, protested against slavery;[1] but Plato took slavery for granted, merely holding that it should apply only to barbarians, who in fact greatly outnumbered native Greek slaves. Aristotle justified slavery not because it was legal, but because it was founded on the natural inequalities of men's abilities. Some men are by nature fit for nothing else than the work of slaves, and are actually better off as slaves; and it is only a useful division of labor for them to perform it. It is easy to accuse Aristotle of neglecting every element in the humanity of the slave except his capacity as a worker, and of forgetting for once that a man's potentiality for development is an essential part of his nature;[2] nor is it here to the point that, as we have seen,[3] the Greek slave was generally well treated. But the important point is that Aristotle has based his view of slavery not on the legalizing of an accidental fact but on an ethical conception of natural fitness for an end; and that is a step in advance. The next step is to show the impossibility of determining even on Aristotle's ground who are fit only to be slaves; and, further, to deny that any men are mere bodies without spiritual or political possibilities, and that they may therefore be denied political status, any more than any men are mere intellects devoid of bodies. The current conception of a "living wage"

[1] Cf. P. Decharme, *Euripides and the Spirit of His Dramas*, Eng. tr., pp. 116 f.

[2] This is the conception of the position of women that Plato and Aristotle generally take.

[3] P. 81, and A. E. Zimmern, *Greek Commonwealth*, pp. 377–397.

(i. e., bare subsistence) as an adequate return for labor is not very different from the notion of the dole of the slave; but it is mitigated by the fact that the laborer may have a vote, and by the extent to which he has a chance to rise to any kind of work of which he is capable.[1]

Any principle must be judged not more for its inherent reasonableness than for its capacity to reckon with new conditions. Judged by this standard, the political thought of the Greeks deserves only a qualified approval. As a matter of fact the Greek state, though self-contained, was incapable of growth and adaptation except by the sacrifice of its very nature; its formula was "unicellular."[2] The ideal state of Plato is mathematically perfect, like an Egyptian pyramid; but it is no more capable of suffering change or development than was the "wonderful one-hoss shay." Only Aristotle recognized sufficiently the need of adapting methods to the case in hand. Yet it is easy to go to the other extreme and to suppose that judgments can be made entirely on the basis of "the facts." But this is palpably false; the same facts in Greek history seemed to give support to Mitford in his Tory principles and to confirm the democratic views of Grote. All facts require interpretation by the application of the principles that have been derived from the consideration of similar facts. Some of these principles, first reached by the Greeks, are now commonplace. And among these principles it is dangerous to lose sight of the ideals of Plato; in themselves too static, by their effect on us who are immersed in the world of facts they may become dynamic.

[1] At another point, too, Aristotle's ethical interest leads to a disappointing conclusion; his attention to the evils of usury and of middlemen's profits blinds him to the possibilities of a developed system of exchange and finance. Cf. E. Barker, *Greek Political Theory*, pp. 373 ff.

[2] W. S. Ferguson, *Greek Imperialism*, p. viii.

We cannot apply directly to our own problems any of the formulæ of Greek thinkers, any more than we can treat any kind of principle as a panacea to be taken in large doses. But many contemporary problems can be classified by being considered in the light of Greek thought. We may apply to the ugly fact of lynching the probability that justice can be done only by the law of the state, which is reason without passion. The spoils system of appointing officials is directly opposed to the efficiency of the expert that is sought by a classified civil service. Only by a budget system can the aggregate of selfish interests be subjected to the will of the whole body of citizens. In discussions of a protective tariff, the point to be discussed is whether a tariff is going to mean special privileges for favored economic groups or is capable of bringing advantage to the whole population. The rights of small or backward nations in an empire can be appraised only by losing sight neither of their backwardness nor of their racial and sentimental desires and their capacity for development. In considering the desirability of merging national states in a larger federation, we should weigh the possible loss of individuality,—even of racial integrity, as races multiply at different rates,— against the possible gain in security from waste and friction. Granted the right of a state to appropriate its resources and to develop them for the common good, the question whether this right should be exercised is wholly one of expediency, to be decided by observing how far private initiative is serving the common good, how far resources are still open to new initiative, and how efficient the government is in its present functions. The form of government that should be preferred cannot be decided wholly on abstract grounds, but will depend in part on the stage of development of the citizens and their capacity for self-government.[1] Democracy is the expression of our faith that all men become not very different in capacity and character, and must rest on a wide foundation of education that trains not merely men's bread-and-butter faculties but their characters and their imaginations. Nevertheless we know that men do differ greatly, and we do well to intrust much of the detail of government to experts who act as our agents. And though democracy rests on education, it is not the sole end of education; rather than try to make all men conform to a single type, we hope, to be sure, to emphasize their common humanity, but also to develop their various powers in different ways and in different types of institution. However much the wise man subjects his life to the control of a single aim, he tries to include in it rich and even apparently irrelevant experience; so, too, the ideal society will rest on a common substratum of humanity, but will leave as much room as possible for the play of individuality. If human nature is all that we need reckon with, the hope of achieving a good society is measured precisely by the extent to which our faith in human nature is justified.

The hope of the Greeks, at least, was usually concentrated for better and for worse, in human nature. It was not the worship of brute force, or even a mythical noble savage, that was the standard; nor on the other hand was it such a

[1] After democracy at Athens had failed in crucial tests, and while Aristotle was praising the middle class, monarchy almost of the Homeric type survived in Macedonia; at Rome the rule of the Republic ended with the rule of Cæsar. Political development proceeded faster than the education of the people that should have accompanied it. Perhaps it is not after all too much to say that the national character and the spirit of those most closely concerned with government are more important than the precise forms and institutions of government. "If we ask under what kinds of government letters and arts and science have flourished, history answers, under all kinds." Viscount Bryce, *Modern Democracies*, vol. ii, p. 572. Cf. also p. 568.

conception of a deity as could lead to theocracy and the control of a priestly caste. So far as practical conduct was concerned, ordinary Greeks were hardly influenced by faith in the gods and a spiritual world and the hope of a future life; even the Orphic religion was largely a matter of ceremonial. What could be done, they thought, could be done by rational human nature in this world; and by a happy combination of circumstances some of the Greeks often succeeded in realizing their ideal in this life. This ideal could not include all men, and meant the realization of one's own personality to the fullest possible extent by the control of things and by the exercise of rational self-control; it was an exalted sort of selfishness. It was really against this code that Plato, in his most visionary mood, revolted, and tried to substitute for a compromise between relative goods the rule of an absolute good. But even Plato's approach was fundamentally rational, and only subsequently an act of intuition; man remained the worker of his destiny. And few men could fully enjoy the blessedness of the kingdom within the philosopher's breast. Average Greeks found the demand of an absolute too exacting.[1] It might, and did, serve as an ideal of the imagination, a counsel of perfection, — no visionary, even in defeat, is entirely defeated, — but after all the typical Greek found his ideal firmly rooted in reality.

The typical Greek therefore could not think of men as equal in any spiritual sense. The Orphic mysteries gave them a common experience and a common hope, and the Stoics taught them that they were partakers in a common reason; but the conception of the intrinsic and infinite value

[1] They would have agreed with Portalis, one of the chief authors of the Code Napoleon: "It is absurd to abandon oneself to absolute ideas of perfection in matters which are susceptible of only a relative degree of good." We may recall also the remark of Cicero about the impracticability of Cato: "He talks as if he were in Plato's Republic, instead of in the dregs of Rome."

of each human soul was alien to the Greek, because it is reached not by the reason but by a different kind of perception, the conviction of the existence of an infinitely loving God. That is the reason why the Greek pauses at the limit of humanism, and does not step across the boundary into humanitarianism; he loves his fellow-men to a measured extent because his personal life is incomplete without them, not because they have an absolute claim on him regardless of their characters and their personal merits. So far as material conditions and human nature carry him, the Greek is safe; where they fail him, there remains only pessimism or Stoical endurance.[1] Though Plato's philosopher agrees with the Christian in believing in a kingdom not of this world which may yet be present in his own soul, it is for the philosopher only in his breast that it may become incarnate, because only he has toiled to the heights of vision; whereas the Christian believes that the beatific vision is for the humble as well as for the wise. The danger of the Greek lies in too great exclusiveness and in pride of intellect; the danger of the Christian comes from indifference to personal effort and to all distinctions. The reconciliation between the ideal of humanism and the ideal of Christianity is most apparent not in theory but in the concrete form of personality; the self-control of a Socrates and the self-sacrifice of a Christian saint are but different aspects of a single paradox, the losing of one's life in order to save it. But these are matters not so much of politics as of religion; to them we must return when we have considered the Greeks' experience of religion.

[1] Cf. p. 280.

CHAPTER VII

MAN AND THE UNIVERSE

1. MAN AND GOD

LIKE other peoples, the Greeks were busy much of the time in winning their bread, and in social undertakings and pleasures. It seems at times as if their life was so far self-contained that they had little or no need of going outside of human activity for the satisfaction of all their needs. But if there is truth in such a supposition, it is not equally true of all periods of Greek experience, nor is it wholly true of any period. Such independence as the Greeks achieved was slowly achieved; and even in the end it was only a qualified independence.

All primitive peoples, living in a state of insecurity, liable to lose suddenly their sources of food in drought or flood or pestilence, are awed by the presence of powers greater than themselves; powers which befriend them, but which may become unfriendly. Fear begets the craving for a closer and more friendly relationship with these unknown powers. If it is impossible to understand them, the primitive man wishes at least to do such deeds as may propitiate these powers and win their aid. So worship and ritual acts precede understanding; they may even precede the conception of distinct deities with personalities. Most early peoples, however, tend to think of the powers that surround them as in some way like themselves; thus the world becomes a more companionable place. Like the child who sees the work of Jack Frost on the window-pane, and who feels more confidence in the dark if he takes a toy to bed with him, like the man who prefers to take his dog when he goes for a walk rather than go alone, man naturally tries to people the universe with personalities. "All men have need of gods," says Homer.[1] "If there were no God," remarks Voltaire, "we should have to invent one." Further, if fear begets gods, wonder creates stories about the gods, to explain the strange doings of the universe, and to delight men's minds. But the conceptions of the gods and the stories about them necessarily bear the marks of the imperfect human beings who create them. "In the beginning," a cynic has said, "God created man in his own image; and man has been returning the compliment ever since." That is the difficulty that confronts even those who are far from cynical. All men hold some sort of belief in a power greater than themselves, generally in a personal God; but this God is apt to be only a shadowy outline, a form, whose content is exceedingly difficult to fill in. "Fear God. Love God." Yes, but what sort of God? The answers to this question have been striking indications of the qualities most approved or most desired by the answers. It could not be otherwise without the assumption of an inscrutable God whose qualities bear no relation to the faculties of the worshippers that seek him. A time comes when men awake to a realization that their gods are much like erring men, and that the traditional stories do not account for the facts. When such an enlightened people as the Greeks awake to this realization, the result is a critical attitude that gives rise to science, to philosophy, and, it may be, to a nobler and a truer religion. It is this growth that we are now to observe; a growth that may be observed partially in many peoples, but that can in no people be observed with a greater measure of completeness than in the case of the Greeks. And if we find that we must begin by borrowing

[1] *Od.* III, 48.

from the lore of the anthropologists, who are interested in primitive man with all his crude acts and imaginings, we shall find ourselves at last on the familiar ground of Christianity. So true is it that religion and science and philosophy, like all other phases of human experience, are nothing fixed or inherently good or bad, but grow and decay and put forth new life, always with the power of becoming more vital and more true.

The earliest phase of Greek religion belongs perhaps in a sense to the pre-Hellenic period; but it concerns us because of its survival and its influence in later times. It is clouded with obscurity; and scholars disagree in their interpretation of it. Yet by noticing the instincts of children and by learning what anthropologists have to tell us about other primitive races, we can with due caution surmise something of its nature; for children and backward races represent simply an early stage of man's development which the Greeks rapidly outgrew.[1] Further, we find among the Greeks of historic times many survivals of earlier rites and cults, often fused with later institutions; and many articles have been discovered by the archæologists. From all these scattered bits of evidence it appears that the earliest religion of the Ægean world was, like other early religions, a form of animism. All sorts of objects were supposed to be alive, to be the abode of spirits good and evil; unwrought stones ("fetishes"), or stones carved into pillars,[2] trees, and caves; the powers of nature, sky and earth; and many kinds of animals. Why some of these objects should have been chosen it is hard to say; the choice was often apparently arbitrary. It would not

[1] From children and from backward races, too, we learn not to be surprised at beliefs that seem incredible or even self-contradictory; we must therefore not hope for a wholly coherent idea of the religion of early Greece.

[2] So the lions on the gate at Mycenæ guard a pillar; and the statues of Hermes were once mere pillars.

be right to say that the early inhabitants of Greece thought
of these spirits as distinct personalities; such a notion was a
later development. Nevertheless they felt that these spirits
were powers to be reckoned with, and they sought by various dances and offerings and ritual acts to secure their good
will; this projection of a people's desires is, in a word, what is
meant by "sympathetic magic." If some animal was associated with the fortunes of a particular group of people, and
was thus regarded as sacred, he was carefully protected; [1]
yet men might at times try to assimilate his strength by
eating him.[2] Especially the bull was supposed to be the
abode of mysterious powers; when men turned from grazing
to agricultural life, not only animals, such as the pig, but
plants were used as emblems of the death and the resurrection of the crops. Rites of initiation and of pretended marriage between a human being and a god were supposed to
secure the fertility of the tribe and of its fields.

Since spirits might be either good or bad, offerings were
made either to avert the influence of bad spirits or to gain
the friendship of good spirits. Particularly the offerings to
the dead are characteristic of this stage of religion. As the
old men of the tribe were wiser than the rest, the spirits of
the departed might be supposed to keep the gathered power
and wisdom of the tribe; it was therefore natural to call up
the dead in times of distress,[3] or at least to pay them the
debt of respect in the form of libations that would trickle
down to their abode beneath the ground. And some animals
would be associated with the cult of the dead; such is the

[1] I. e., he became in some respects like what anthropologists call a *totem*
animal, protected by a *taboo*, or arbitrary avoidance. But *totemism* in the
narrow sense of the word can hardly be said to have existed in Greece.

[2] They would thus acquire what is called by the inhabitants of Polynesia
the *mana* of the animal.

[3] As Atossa calls up the spirit of Darius in the "Persians" of Æschylus.

serpent, who lives underground, and who by sloughing his skin gives an indication of his rebirth.

Though we have said that the spirits worshipped in this ancient religion were at first hardly conceived as personal, they must have tended constantly to become more personal. The powers of nature seem to be doing such things as we do; winds blow, and the thunder shouts,— why not think of them as like ourselves? Only, what we think of as figurative language is for children and for early peoples a statement of fact.[1] If the ritual act or the man dressed in the skin of a beast failed to produce the desired result, one conclusion might be that the dance and the man were not in themselves powerful, but that behind them stood the god himself. Gradually the gods took on more and more personality, and were distinguished: there were maiden goddesses, mother goddesses, gods in the form of men, young or old. Each region would have its divinity; and it would be only after some time that settled communities would tend to compare their several gods with each other and to distinguish them. Probably this tendency showed itself long before the various foreign influences and the Greeks came into Greece; but it was so slow, and the Greeks themselves brought so fluid a form of religion, that Herodotus could say with a considerable measure of truth: "But as to the origin of each particular god, whether they all existed from the beginning, what were their individual forms, the knowledge of these things is, so to speak, but of to-day and yesterday. For Hesiod and Homer are my seniors, I think, by some four hundred years and not more. And it is they who have composed for the Greeks the generations of the gods, and have given to the gods their titles and distinguished their several provinces

---

[1] For a beautiful suggestion of the way in which myths arose, see Wordsworth's *Excursion*, Book IV, the lines beginning, "In that fair clime."

and special powers and marked their forms." [1] From this account we learn that the raw materials of Greek religion are older than the coming of the Greeks, but that the details of belief and especially the individuality of the gods is the work of the epic poets. We can indeed trace the growth of the god Hermes stage by stage from the rude, square Herm, a mere pillar, to the graceful god whom Praxiteles carved. Or we can find in the cult of Zeus Meilichios, who is now god, now serpent, or in the festival of the Thesmophoria, not only the worship of a highly developed god but the survival of an earlier chthonian cult,[2] a parasite on the new religion. The new god took over the old sacred places; but with them he took over also something of the old rites, perhaps with a sacred beast. So the old religion did not altogether perish; though driven underground and forced into a humbler position, it still persisted and through hidden channels it fed the needs of men; it was even able in the seventh and the sixth centuries to emerge again in a striking manner in the religion of the mysteries. Crude and childish though it may seem, it was nevertheless the expression of men's social instincts; it gave them the conception of powers greater than themselves, and of life enduring beyond their own lives; it taught them to seek communion with these mysterious powers and to feel a personal relationship with them; it caused them to refrain from much, no doubt, that was harmless, but also from much that was evil. Through channels not very different from these an experience far deeper was at a later time to reach the Greeks.

Although the strata of Greek religion are never wholly distinct, the gods of the Homeric poems are very different from

---

[1] Herodotus, II, 53.

[2] A chthonian cult is one that deals with the gods or spirits of the underworld.

their shadowy predecessors. Heroic, boisterous, even cruel at times, they are the gods of conquerors whose pride is in deeds of arms, rather than in the peaceful occupations of grazing or agriculture or city life. At first Zeus was merely the Achæan sky-god,[1] worshipped as enthroned on the Thessalian Mount Olympus that seemed to pierce the clouds and touch the sky, and on many other mountains in other parts of Greece that bore the same or similar names; gradually he assumed many other characters and attributes, as his worship supplanted other cults; so that at different shrines different rites and epithets predominated. So Apollo, the Hyperborean god, was worshipped under different aspects at Delphi and at Delos.

If it is hard for us to think of gods in merely human form as anything but degrading to their worshippers, let us not forget that such gods mark a great advance over the animistic religion that they supplanted. The Olympian gods were members of the same society with the Greeks; if they were not merely the social equals of men, they were at least not so far removed from men that they could not enter into their lives and their ideals of human conduct. They shared the common meal of their burnt offerings, as the savor of the sacrifice was wafted up to Olympus; they moved in common processions with men at their festivals; they could be bargained with, and could show their approval or disapproval for deeds done well or ill. Though only glorified human beings with human feelings, they were at any rate glorified; if they were only superior members of a club, they were superior, and served the purpose of a permanent aristocracy that might help and warn lesser men. They reminded men that there is something beyond the furthest horizon. There was no need

[1] See A. B. Cook, *Zeus*, vol. i; convenient summary of conclusions, pp. 776 ff.

of driving them away like evil spirits or monsters, nor of magic rites of purification to rid men of the taint of bloodshed, as in older days.[1] The Olympians upheld the ideal of monogamy and the patriarchal society against the ideal of the older society, with its glorification of fertility and procreation. The gods of Olympus, in a word, are the representatives of men who are attaching a greater importance to human excellence in its conflict with merely animal forces and instincts; the myths of the battles of the gods and the giants, of men and centaurs, reflect this conflict. As men grew more civilized, their gods became more civilized and idealized; doubtless the influence was reciprocal. Traces of an attempt to expurgate the grosser deeds of gods and men from the Homeric poems are still to be found, as some scholars believe. So at a later time Isocrates wrote: "Those of the gods who are the source to us of good things have the title of Olympians; those whose department is that of calamities and punishments have harsher titles. To the first class both private persons and states erect altars and temples; the second is not worshipped either with prayers or with burnt sacrifices, but in their case we perform ceremonies of riddance."[2] It was the Olympian gods, then, that were tamed and rendered fit to become the patrons of a society that now lived in city-states and was engaged in politics and in the arts of peace. And since they were worshipped in many parts of Greece, and had shrines, as at Delphi and Olympia and Delos, to which all Greeks resorted, they became, in a way in which merely local or tribal gods could never have become, the champions of the Hellenes against the barbarians.

[1] The solution of the moral problem of the Orestes trilogy of Æschylus shows very well the triumph of the new standard; blood no longer cries eternally for blood, but may in the end find atonement.

[2] Isocrates, Orat. V, 117.

As soon as the Greeks thought of their gods as persons, they began to tell stories about them, whether for the explanation of all that was strange in the world or for sheer enjoyment. Lacking even a notion of scientific investigation, they resorted to myth to account for the origin of the world, for the heavenly bodies and the phenomena of nature, for their own forgotten past and the origin of the rites and the images that they venerated. The gods, too, needed to have their descent and their relationship explained. Myth, like poetry, is spontaneous; like poetry, it is seldom a consistent whole. It rises wherever men are curious and have the gift of childlike imagination. No one can be compelled to believe in any particular myth; for it is not the pronouncement of an official institution. Myths need not even be consistent with the religious practices of a people, or with the prevailing standard of morality. Many causes account for this discrepancy among the Greeks. Some myths arose at an early date, and survived after the moral standard of the Greeks was raised. Sometimes an apparently immoral story represents nothing more than the attempt to reconcile conflicting legends. Zeus was not essentially a wanton polygamist; but in the attempt to reconcile a single conquering sky-father with the earth-mother worshipped at many scattered shrines it was natural to make him in each region the consort of the earlier goddess. In this attempt, too, may be found the explanation of the unedifying quarrels between Zeus and his jealous spouse Hera; their lack of harmony perpetuates the feud of the conquering northerners and the older people who had worshipped Hera. Many stories of the metamorphosis of a god into the form of a beast seem to be inverted accounts of the supplanting of a sacred animal by a god. Other myths rest on misguided attempts to explain the meaning of primitive works of art; so a statue of Sisyphus engaged in the beneficent task of building might be misinterpreted as Sisyphus performing an act of penance.[1] The very freedom with which myths could be invented or changed for the gratification of curious listeners, and the ease with which they were spread, kept them from remaining in accord with the conceptions of the gods that were instilled by the cults at the various shrines. Amusing, even scandalous stories about the gods would shock their pious worshippers no more than the legend about Washington and the cherry-tree affects our opinion of his statesmanship. But if myths did become fixed, as certain myths told more for entertainment than for edification were fixed by the Homeric poems, a later age would find much in them to blame; and the Homeric gods are actually less moral than the best human beings either in the Homeric poems or in Greece of the historical period. And when a higher standard of morality and wisdom had grown by the interplay of human minds, the Greeks tended either to bring the charitable offices of allegory to the interpretation of their myths, or to reject them, or perhaps to think of them frankly as inventions useful for the purposes of the arts, but as nothing that they need hold sacred like a creed. They could be the more easily sceptical about their myths because their priests were concerned solely with the conduct of ritual, and had little to do with dogma; persecution for agnosticism was almost unheard of.[2]

For many centuries the Olympian religion was mainly and at least superficially the dominant force in Greek life. It provided the sanctions of a somewhat improved morality, it lent itself to the highest developments of sculpture and architecture and poetry; infused with new vigor by the re-

[1] S. Reinach, *Orpheus*, Eng. tr., p. 88.

[2] Most of the persecutions of which we know appear to be complicated by personal or by political issues.

vival of mystical experience in the sixth century, it provided many of the legends for drama. Because it was tolerant of change, the dramatists could use the myths to convey new meanings and aspirations; and much could be read into the personalities of Zeus and Athena and Apollo. The gods thus became the symbols of something nobler in human nature; the outlines received a finer content. If we wish to gain an idea of what the Olympic religion meant to Greeks of the Great Age, we must think of the odes of Pindar, with their glittering imagery and pomp, of the Attic stage, on which human destiny and character stand in the shadow of the gods; of the Pan-Athenaic procession moving with music to the Parthenon. It was a religion that in itself gave scope for all the joyousness of a sunny race, all its gift of humanity and beauty and sociability. It provided gods and rites for almost every occasion. Yet doubtless it had its shortcomings. Not merely were there immoral elements, — some of which, as we have seen, are due simply to the attempt of the myth-makers to reconcile different elements, or to give free rein to their imaginations, — but the very anthropomorphism which at one period marked an advance became in time a hindrance. The gods might be in some respects better than men; but they could not be far better than men. Sometimes the explanation of nature in terms of man gave rise to positively bad myths; Zeus, the lightning god, appears capricious; the humanizing of the productiveness of nature, as well as the reconciliation of myths, leads to polygamous gods. Outside of the more progressive states the Olympian religion had little effect on morality, and only in the highest ranges of Greek thought was anything like monotheism to be found. Above all, the Olympian religion was a religion for the noble, the wealthy, and the strong; it was the defender of a stable society and the *status quo;* it had little to offer the

humble and the sick; it was not a religion for the poor in
spirit, nor for any who might feel themselves to be sinful. It
gave hardly any hope of a better world hereafter. Any cravings for satisfaction of such a sort were to be fed by new
kinds of experience.

Nevertheless, though the Olympian religion in itself was
only a framework, it served as the framework for the
thought of poets who succeeded in expressing through it the
most profound experience of life and death, of good and evil,
of fate and the human will. Through the lack of moral grandeur of Homer's gods, his men are the more imposing. In
Hesiod we find the gropings of a mind perplexed by the evil
of the world, and inclined to believe that it has degenerated
from a previous Golden Age; yet he feels that good and
evil are in conflict, and there is some hope of a fair outcome.
The lyric and elegiac poets, still more the tragic poets in
their several ways, emphasize the sovereignty of Zeus and
the necessary consequences of sin. The Zeus of Pindar is a
righteous god, who rewards justice and punishes transgres-
sion, especially the wanton insolence (*hybris*) of which men
in prosperity are often guilty. Pindar has even learned
from the Orphics (whom we shall presently discuss) to hope
that the righteous may enjoy hereafter the "Blessed Isles." [1]

The Zeus of Æschylus, so far lifted above the other gods
as to be almost the sole god, is the upholder of the moral order of the universe. If at times his authority appears to rest
only on his superior might, as in the "Prometheus Bound,"
he tends to become the embodiment of justice; it is even possible that the sequel of the "Prometheus," of which we have
only fragments, showed that the justice of Zeus is in the end
tempered by mercy. But even Zeus cannot act contrary to
Fate (*Moira*),[2] the innate structure of the universe, which is

[1] Pindar, Ol. II, esp. 63 ff.   [2] *Prometheus*, ll. 515 ff.

hardly to be distinguished from his own conscience; he can only ensure the workings of justice. We have already followed [1] the treatment of sin and its inevitable consequences in the three great tragic poets. It is important to observe that Æschylus believes that men suffer not simply because it is fated that they shall suffer, but because some act of folly that they presumptuously commit draws in its train far-reaching and unavoidable retribution. Yet even so the tragic hero may be taught and ennobled by his experience; "Learning comes by suffering." [2] Our interest is not therefore so much in the power of the moral order as in the struggle of the hero. Especially is this the case when, as with Orestes, the conflict is not between evil and good but between two moral duties. Orestes must avenge the murder of his father, but he can do this only by killing his mother. The final solution of this problem rests not so much on justice as on a myth that reconciles the Olympian gods with the Eumenides (Furies), those representatives of the older dynasty of gods that have persecuted Orestes.[3] But even this lame conclusion does not requite the blameless Orestes for all that he has suffered. Probably Æschylus never really faced the problem, which is the outcome of the growth of myths apart from morality and religion.

Sophocles does attempt to deal with the problem; and his solution is that of a conservative. Himself fortunate in all things, pious, and a defender of all that was sanctioned by custom, he accepts substantially the old myths. Finding that in this world those who are innocent or who sin unintentionally often suffer far beyond their deserts, he resorts to

[1] Pp. 135 ff.

[2] *Agamemnon*, 177.

[3] J. Adam, *Religious Teachers of Greece*, p. 152; and B. A. G. Fuller, "The Conflict of Moral Obligation in the Trilogy of Æschylus," in *Harvard Theological Review*, October, 1915.

two conclusions. He draws attention from the outward act
to the inner character of his hero in its struggle against adversity; there is something noble, as well as something
pathetic, in the soul that resists temptation courageously.
Like Æschylus he believes in the moral value of suffering:
"much is revealed to the soul that is cradled in calamity." [1]
So Sophocles goes further than Æschylus in asserting that
the will of Zeus is ultimately good, and that the sufferings of
the individual must be considered as only parts of the whole
moral order. So even Antigone, who has appealed against
the man-made law of Creon that forbade her to bury her
brother, to the eternal unwritten law of Heaven, suffers
death, that the will of Zeus may prevail in the burial of her
brother.

Euripides, whose restless mind has absorbed the sceptical
and rationalizing thought of his day, is at once thoroughly
iconoclastic and profoundly religious in his treatment of the
gods. In play after play he brings forward the old myths,
displaying the cruelty and immorality of the gods; hardly
one of them is as admirable as are many of his human characters. Some of the same myths have been treated by
Sophocles, but in a far different spirit. Sophocles has tried
to "justify the ways of God to man" by finding in them a
beneficent purpose; he says, "Nothing to which the gods
lead men is base." [2] Euripides declares, "If the gods do evil,
they are not gods," and thus suggests that the immoral gods
of the old mythology must be mere fiction. This is the revolt
of a new stage of human reason and morality against the
crystallized conceptions of an older world. So far is Euripides an iconoclast. But he does not dispense altogether
with the gods; for dramatic ends, if for no other purpose, he

[1] Frag. 600.
[2] Frag. 226.

must have gods worthy of the new moral dignity of man, and they must be spiritual gods.

> O Earth's Upbearer, thou whose throne is Earth,
> Where'er thou be, O past our finding out,
> Zeus, be thou Nature's Law, or mind of man,
> To thee I pray; for treading soundless paths,
> In justice dost thou guide all mortal things! [1]

Euripides is not quite sure, then, whether to dispense with all but human explanations. He even recurs, in his last splendid play, the "Bacchæ," to a glorification of the life of inspiration and enthusiasm, of mystical experience without the slow processes of reason; for such appears to be the meaning of the death of Pentheus at the hands of the women who are inspired by Dionysus. Not being certain as to the principles of the moral order, and yet seeing that men do suffer even though they are apparently innocent, Euripides falls back on the sheer pathos of suffering; and he is indeed, as Aristotle called him, "the most tragic of poets." When men suffer unjustly and are not even sure that they are assisting, however blindly, in the purposes of Providence, all that they can claim is a larger measure of sympathy for heroism.

Much of the iconoclasm of Euripides may be traced to the rationalistic spirit of his age, of which we have already [2] taken some notice; his idealization of enthusiasm in the "Bacchæ" goes back to the religious revival of a century or more before his day. That the Olympian religion had little hope to offer the humble and the unhappy is one of the causes for this revival. The seventh and the sixth centuries witnessed the emergence of rites of expiation and purification, of a new devotion, aroused by danger and fear, to the

[1] *Troiades*, ll. 884 ff., tr. A. S. Way.
[2] Pp. 158 ff.

worship of dead heroes who might be supposed to act as mediators for unhappy mankind. At this time, too, the worship of a new god spread from the East, through Thrace, and entered Greece, where under different epithets, — Dionysus, Zagreus, Sabazios, Bromios, Bacchos, names originally of distinct divinities, — he was the head of a triumphant cult. Bringer of the vine, and protector of all living things, he was the god of a blessed release, through intoxication, from the troubles of life; he stood for the call of the wild, the return to nature, the death and the rebirth of vegetation. He was even supposed himself to have suffered death and resurrection; and his worshippers hoped that by union with the god they might themselves become "Bacchoi," and so win a release from mortality and the trammels of the flesh. So, too, in the worship at Eleusis of Demeter and her daughter Persephone, who died and rose every year, the death and the revival both of the grain and of mankind were symbolized; and the brotherhoods who claimed Orpheus as their founder, and the communities that were supposed to have been founded by Pythagoras, hoped through purifications and an ascetic life to set the soul free from the body. The cult at Eleusis and the cults of the Orphics were commonly known as "mysteries," and tried by rites of preliminary initiation, — baths in the sea, and sacrifices, and participation in ceremonies, — to bring their adherents into a state of mind in which they could come into direct communion with the god. There was at first no elaborate theology, but merely a number of ritual acts to be done and a secret drama to be beheld. If we find the acts rather crude or even ludicrous, — the use of a pig, of a dish of "first-fruits," and of various taboos, — we must remember that very ordinary objects and deeds may become sacraments of the greatest sanctity, and that poetry is forever appropriating the raw materials of life for unexpected purposes. The tendency, among at least the better adherents of the mysteries, was to forget the physical origins of their cult,—the intoxication, the rending of wild beasts and the devouring of their raw flesh, the trivial objects and taboos and purifications,—and to recount highly imaginative myths that pointed toward a purification not physical but moral, and of a release from the body that was but the sepulchre of the spirit. The subjugation of the body thus became the condition of a better life, even of a future life such as the Olympian religion had never offered.

The mysteries at first seem far enough from the sober enquiries of such men as Socrates; their appeal is not to the sure-footed processes of the intellect but to emotion and to immediate intuition. "The initiated," said Aristotle, "do not learn anything so much as feel certain emotions and are put into a certain frame of mind." [1] There is no little value in this potentiality, which is not to be slighted because it is not identical with reason. "Mystical experience," a modern witness tells us, "does not supply concrete information. . . . It is the awareness of a Presence, the consciousness of a Beyond." [2] Without such an awareness, of what value are reasoned conclusions? On the other hand, of what value is an awareness without the ability to make clear, at least to one's self, of what one is aware? Again the difficulty is of finding a content for the conception of God. The reason cannot be thrown away; yet one of the hardest things in the world is to realize when reason has done its utmost and we must depend on something else, be it poetry, or faith in another person, or blind

[1] Quoted by Synesius, *Dion*, p. 47d.
[2] R. M. Jones, "The Mystic's Experience of God," *Atlantic Monthly*, November, 1921.

chance. If we trust only to intuition, to be sure, we run the risk of becoming irrational; but if we trust only to reason, the universe shrinks to the size of our own brains, which at times seem pitifully small. What we need is not to forego the use of the mind, but to realize that few people act solely by reason; it is even doubtful whether a logical process alone was ever sufficient to set in motion a single act of a single individual. If men act because of anything more than habit and emotion, it is the force of definite images, persons or vividly conceived ideals, that turns logical assent into action. That is the value of poetic imagery, of personality in religion, of the Greek mysteries. It is beside the point to object to the crudities of the worship, to the foreign origin and alien character of much of it, to the unsatisfactory content of the conception of Dionysus. The significant fact is that, parallel with the scientific and philosophic thought which we are about to observe, the religion of the mysteries persisted, with its emphasis on immediate intuition. We must not forget, for one thing, that it was the worship of Dionysus that gave rise to Greek drama. It is something, moreover, that the mysteries taught that there is a hope of salvation open to ordinary men, to be won by a life well lived; it is much that the conception of a god, suffering and reborn (even if he was not incarnate solely for the good of man), was kept alive in mysteries that exercised on the imagination possibly something of the effect of a "Passion Play" or of a religious procession in modern Italy. And it is highly important that this form of religion, with its mythology and its conception of soul and body, stood ready for the use of the philosophers; for we shall see that Plato recognizes its importance hardly less fully than the value of logical discussion. And through Plato this attitude passes into Christian thought.

In the fifth century the traditional forms of religion less and less affected the lives of the Greeks as other influences replaced them. Though the gods of Olympus still kept their outward ascendancy, the mysteries rapidly gained new adherents; they existed like dissenting chapels beside an established church. Foreign cults multiplied. Religion was not organized or codified so severely that differences of belief were taken seriously; there was no thought of exacting belief in a creed or a myth. Only the formal worship of the gods went on; and this survived long after the invasion of other religions. Indeed, when Christianity finally triumphed, the old shrines were not destroyed but were adapted to the new religion. The Parthenon was still the abode of wisdom, but under the protection of St. Sophia, and later of the Virgin Mary; a shrine of Apollo was often given to St. George; Dionysus became St. Dionysius. The Easter celebration of the modern Greek Church preserves much of the atmosphere of the old mysteries. All this and much more was handed on to later ages. But for Athenians of the fifth century, two new circumstances caused the old religion to suffer eclipse. At all times religion had been not a separate phase of existence tolerated or recognized by the state, but had meant simply the social group, small or large, including its patron god. So the state religion meant simply the body of citizens united under the worship of Athene, whose image appeared on its coins and other symbols. When the might of human hands had built the greatness of the Athenian Empire, and humanism was in full flower, the men of Athens almost forgot their dependence on the goddess who bore the name of their city; patriotism took the place of the national religion, Athens of Athene. Many readers of Thucydides have been struck by the fact that the noble "Funeral Oration" of Pericles, which epitomizes the greatness of Athens, says much of the character of its citizens and not a word about the gods.

The decline of religious faith was hastened also by another circumstance; this is the growth of rationalism which we have already [1] had occasion to notice. It is only another aspect of humanism, for it is the recognition of the world disclosed by the inquiring mind and the attempt to dispense with the supernatural. Naturally the average man was for a long time but little affected by the scientific and philosophical inquiries of the day, except as they reached him through the increasing subtlety of the orators and the dramatists. It is with the exceptional men that we must now deal.

2. THE LAW OF THINGS

The courageous criticism of the old religion showed the stirrings of a new spirit. Xenophanes, the first rebel against anthropomorphism, who objected that gods in human form were hardly more plausible than the gods that oxen would conceive in their own likeness, and Heracleitus and the poets with their ethical criticism, did much to undermine the primitive notion of the gods, and to introduce the idea of a single, beneficent power controlling the universe. But this criticism did not yet reach the bottom of things. The Greeks needed the positive contribution of a genuinely scientific attitude. They needed an accumulation of observed and demonstrable facts; they needed some sort of theory to reconcile the conflicting evidence of the senses and to reduce to unity the multiplicity of phenomena; and especially they needed to realize that no account of nature, the world of things, is complete that does not explain how man

[1] Pp. 158 ff., 230.

can know it and to what extent his knowledge of it is affected by his own nature. They must create science and philosophy.

The Egyptians and the peoples of the Near East had made a beginning in science, especially in an astronomy cultivated wholly for practical purposes. The Greeks carried these branches much further, and really created science in the modern sense of the word. Partly by observation, partly by reasoning, and partly by fortunate guesses, they arrived at many conclusions that are still valid. Thales foretold an eclipse; other Greeks learned that the earth is a sphere; the Pythagoreans guessed at its motion; Anaxagoras held that the sun is a mass of molten iron larger than the Peloponnese, — perhaps not so bad an account, compared with the prevailing mythological explanations of the sun, — that the heavenly bodies are centrifugal, and that the moon shines by reflected light. In the Alexandrian Age, Aristarchus anticipated Copernicus in the heliocentric doctrine of the solar system, and made a shrewd calculation of the relative size of the earth and the moon. Unfortunately the heliocentric doctrine was rejected by his successors. Yet remarkably exact measurements and calculations of the size of the earth and of the angle of its axis were made by Eratosthenes, and of the length of the year by Hipparchus, who also discovered the precession of the equinoxes. The astronomy of Hipparchus, developed by Ptolemy, was accepted universally till the sixteenth century. Meanwhile geometry and mechanics were being developed by Euclid and Archimedes and their followers up to trigonometry and integral calculus; biology, based on the most careful observation of animal and plant forms, was carried further by Aristotle and Theophrastus and their successors than by any scientists till within very recent times; and the practical phases of chem-

istry and medicine were carried on subtly and nobly. The
work of the fifth-century physician Hippocrates in diagnosis
and in prognosis was masterly. The "Hippocratic Oath"
that medical students took was used till modern times.[1] The
temples of the god of healing, Asclepius, were comparable to
a modern sanatorium; nor were the priests ignorant of methods resembling modern psychoanalysis and suggestion.

These notable results, achieved only in the course of centuries, rested partly, to be sure, on guesswork, but more on
observation and mathematical calculation. No true science
can exist without observation; only the descriptive sciences
can dispense with mathematics. But if we turn back and
trace the speculations of the Greeks in other fields, we are
struck by their dependence on pure theory and on conjecture. We find them still speaking the language of myth and
poetry; indeed, many of the early philosophers wrote in
verse, for prose was still considered unworthy of any important message.

The problem of the early thinkers of Greece, who were impressed by the manifoldness of natural phenomena, was to
find a single essence which should explain the physical universe. Water, the boundless, air, — such solutions were
successively proposed by the speculators of Miletus. The
Pythagoreans fixed upon number as the counterpart of
reality, and therefore as their chief study. Heracleitus,
speaking the language of the inspired poet, proclaimed,
"Wisdom is one thing. It is to know the thought by which
all things are steered through all things." This "thought"
or law (*nomos*), he held, is the unity of the many conflicting
things that we perceive, and the plurality of the one. At
times he called it Logos, — a term that we shall meet again,
— the divine word or reason, immanent in Nature and in

[1] It is quoted in R. W. Livingstone, *The Legacy of Greece*, p. 213.

man; but this he sometimes identified with fire, the ever-changing reality of things. So Heracleitus is after all at least half a materialist. Again, he personified under the names of Hate and Love the repulsion and attraction that he saw in this mutable universe. Yet much as the strife and flux of things impressed him, — and his most commonly quoted saying is, "All things flow," — his most characteristic belief is in the underlying unity, a harmony symbolized by the stress and repose of the bow and the lyre. Speculations so highly poetic and so hard to reduce to a consistent system were naturally interpreted differently: some found in the notion of the flux the warrant for holding that knowledge is only relative; others saw that the necessity of obedience to law, to the guiding Logos, is quite as characteristic.[1]

Against the notion of change, Parmenides and his followers revolted, bluntly protesting that what we see about us must be one and must be changeless; for if it changed it would become what it is not,—which is absurd. So far as that argument goes, it is sound; and in order to account for change it is necessary either to deny that reality is one or to deny that it is merely sensible (as Parmenides apparently believed it to be, despite the fact that it can be apprehended only by thought). Accordingly, later thinkers attempted a reconciliation between the extreme monism of Parmenides and the pluralistic tendency of Heracleitus.

[1] With this conception of law may be compared the saying of the physician Hippocrates, in answer to those who supposed a certain disease to be supernatural: "As for me, I think that these maladies are divine like all others, but that none is more divine or more human than another. Each has its natural principle, and none exists without its natural cause." It was a great step forward in the history of the world when men could avoid appealing to supernatural explanations whenever their understandings were baffled, and could conceive of everything as governed by natural principles, and as being on that account, not less, but more wonderful. Not that we can expect to understand or explain everything!

Empedocles supposed there were a number of physical elements, two of which, Love and Strife, caused change, through cycles of union and dissolution. Here we have at last an attempt to distinguish between matter and its organization; and the conception of deity that meets us in Empedocles is far from anthropomorphic; "he is only a sacred and unutterable mind shooting with swift thoughts through all the world."[1] Yet Strife, the efficient cause of physical change, is not different from matter; Empedocles "makes it part of the mixture," as Aristotle observes. Aristotle's criticism is doubtless based on the fact that Empedocles inclined toward a view of causation and necessary development that anticipates modern evolutionary theories; whereas Aristotle himself, being more interested in certain phases of biology than in physics, was apt to find a teleological reason for events; and in this preference he was followed, with momentous consequences, by most thinkers till recent times. The solution of Anaxagoras turns out to be less different from that of Empedocles than it at first appears to be. Anaxagoras conceived of an infinite number of "seeds" or elements, different in kind, corresponding to the various substances, as wood, flesh, and the like. Their motion and arrangement he accounted for by Mind (*nous*). Perhaps he thought that he was thus attributing the government of things to a non-material, spiritual agency; yet such were the limitations of necessarily figurative language that he could not describe its operation in terms other than material. Moreover, when Anaxagoras undertook to account in detail for physical change, he apparently made no use of Mind. Mind thus turns out to be for all practical purposes either only another and more subtle material ele-

[1] Frag. 180 (Ritter and Preller); J. Burnet, *Early Greek Philosophy*, p. 259.

ment or an omnipotent yet perfectly useless spiritual agency, like a God who does nothing. So much we may say without in any sense minimizing the great achievement of Anaxagoras in conceiving of a distinction between matter and mind; the interrelation of the two has baffled all later thinkers who have begun with the assumption that mind and matter are wholly distinct. He was no more inconsistent than many men of to-day who keep their theology and their scientific pursuits in water-tight compartments. Yet if we wish to see the results of thorough-going materialism, we need only turn to Leucippus, the real founder of the atomic theory, who took pains to deny the existence of any non-material principles. Although his brilliant conjecture had far-reaching results in later thought, and within its proper limits has been in a large measure confirmed by modern science, neither he nor Democritus had any way of accounting for the grouping of atoms save the assumption that motion is their innate property. Nor does modern science as such, with its theories of ions and electrons, accomplish much more. But scientific hypothesis could not arise till logic arose. So on every side, however unsatisfactory the immobile unity upheld by Parmenides had been, the unaccountable multiplicity set forth by his opponents led to results no less absurd.

The preoccupation of these thinkers had been mainly with the physical universe; and they had failed to attain exact results, because of their lack of scientific methods, or to account for what they saw, because they could not explain the relation of mind and matter. Science was for a time discredited. It happens that this disillusionment fell in with the sophistic movement, with its emphasis on human interests; inquiry into the unity of the world of sense was abandoned for an inquiry into the principles of human conduct. Yet here, too, there was confusion and disagreement; opinions and customs vary. When settled traditions and standards have once been questioned and rejected, it is not easy to replace them at once with anything so stable. Many Greeks of the fifth century were ready to agree with the Sophist Protagoras that what appears to each man to be true is for him true; there are no absolutely true statements which are true for all persons, and judgments about particular objects are all that we can make. Not only is the particular man the measure of all his experience but he cannot go beyond the experience of the moment. So irresponsible ethical and logical judgments became the counterpart of the irresponsible elements of the physicists.

Such was the world in which Socrates began to teach. The poets and their interpreters still claimed a divine inspiration as the warrant for the truth of their works. Ordinary men believed, if not in all the mythology of the old Olympic religion, at least in a world of supernatural powers that spoke to men by means of rites which made men blessed. Eternal things could be seen, things that satisfied men's craving for perfection and for union with a world larger than themselves. Concerning the physical world, to be sure, the wisest men differed, and their opinions involved them in absurd contradictions. In matters of conduct, however, it was possible to learn enough to be a good artisan, a good soldier, a good citizen; and there were clever foreigners to teach them how to speak well in the courts and to explain the old literature to them. In human affairs all was relative; but even what was accepted as ordained by convention was often valuable in practice; those who did not choose to obey it were deterred by no dictate of an absolute right or wrong. For every man, his own perception was the most positive thing that existed.[1]

It is worth while to pause here in our survey, before we consider the attempt of Socrates and his followers to bring order into this confusion. For the world of to-day, though immeasurably further advanced in many branches of science than it was in the day of Socrates, shows some of the same signs of confusion. We are still confronted, on the one hand, by the claims of ecclesiastical bodies that rest their case on authority and on supernatural revelations which they are unwilling to bring to the bar of reason or experience, and on the other hand by those who can reckon with nothing in the universe except the organization of matter as it is at present understood. We hear men argue that we are made wholly by heredity and environment, so that we are personally responsible for nothing; yet it is often the same people who argue that the standards imposed by others (presumably also the products of their heredity and environment) are artificial and therefore wrong. We have not yet discovered a happy reconciliation between excessive unity and excessive multiplicity, between mind and matter, between man the animal and man the thinker, between man the thinker and man the visionary. Our problem is after all not so different from that of Socrates and his followers. Like him, we need to understand better to what extent man really deserves to be called "the measure of all things," and above all to know more fully what we mean by "man." We pass, then, from science and scientific conjecture to the main problem of humanism.

[1] This paragraph is taken from my "Plato's View of Poetry," in *Harvard Studies in Classical Philology*, vol. xxix, 1918, p. 12.

3. THE LAW OF MAN

We have already [1] had occasion to consider the task that Socrates and his successors took upon themselves, so far as it concerns the relation of the individual to society; and we found that they were able to form a fairly consistent theory of this relationship and of the sort of behavior that it demands without going outside of human experience. For the Greeks ethics was almost always more closely associated with politics than with supernatural religion. We are now concerned, however, not merely with the question of conduct but with the question of what we should believe about the inner nature of things, how far we can know it, and what effect this knowledge will have on our lives. For that Plato recognized that our conception of truth has an important bearing on conduct we noticed when we saw that the guardians in his state need a special training in philosophy. [2] How this conception took form is our next concern.

The work that Socrates set before himself was to find in this world of flux and confusion certain permanent principles. It is customary to emphasize the scepticism of Socrates, the man who knew only that he knew nothing. Yet it is not likely that Socrates would have undertaken poverty, ridicule, and death simply to convince Athens of his ignorance. He clearly distinguished between the subjects in which sure knowledge cannot be found and those in which we can know something. He had nothing but ridicule for those contemporaries who speculated about the physical universe and its laws; they not only were ignorant of human affairs, but were vainly trying to learn what man can never learn. Speculation about it led to the most inconsistent ex-

[1] Pp. 164 ff. [2] Pp. 171, 175 ff.

planations, and in the end had no practical application. He himself, however, discoursed on human affairs, trying to define such moral qualities as piety, impiety, nobility, baseness, and the like. And in the definition of these qualities, he was always using an inductive method and citing analogies drawn from those practical arts in which, for ordinary purposes, no one could doubt that something fixed could be found. For him the type of all knowledge was that possessed by the artisan, who knows how to apply special knowledge to appropriate ends. Indeed, his ideal of knowledge is not really that of science but that of art; and this conception tinges not only his ethical notions but even his idea of creation as teleological. For example, his interpretation of the Delphic inscription, "Know thyself," might almost be paraphrased as: "Know what thou canst do for the service of mankind." He was in fact always trying to find the peculiar capabilities of his associates for special purposes; hence the virtues are different kinds of knowledge. And his whole account of the physical universe is directed toward showing that it is designed for the satisfaction of man's needs.

So far Socrates answered the doubters of his own time. It is possible, he asserted, by looking into the mind of man to find and by rational discourse to fix principles of conduct. Yet there is another side of his creed. Xenophon tells us that Socrates advised a resort to divination in those affairs whose termination is doubtful, but not in those in which the result is the necessary consequence of certain acts; it was in accordance with this view that Socrates would depend at times not on the exercise of reason but on a god-given voice, whose promptings were never reducible to the form of connected reasoning. It was for this reason, too, that he observed the law of the city in matters of religion and obeyed divine injunctions. Throughout all his restless life, a life

that combined the ardor of the prophet with the ironical
common sense of the man of affairs, Socrates maintained
these two aspects. To him, a life that did not examine rationally the ethical concepts that guided it was no life at all;
on the other hand, he did not give up a faith in powers and
motives that transcend reason.[1]

Such was the twofold philosophical heritage of Plato from
Socrates. But it was not his only heritage. Even before he
knew Socrates, he had tried his hand at poetry, and had been
the pupil of the Heracleitean philosopher, Cratylus. After
the death of Socrates, during his travels in southern Italy,
he came to know something of the thought both of the
subtle logician Parmenides and of the Pythagorean communities, with their insistence on mathematical reasoning and
on an ascetic life and an imagery that have much in common
with the teaching of the Orphics. All these, and much more,
went into the growth of Plato's mature philosophy; and he
tried to do justice to them all. Not that he merely wove
them into a composite structure, a crazy-quilt of dogma;
the harmony of Plato's thought is not so much the unity of a
perfect scheme as it is the balance of a personality who was
singularly capable of realizing the claims of various kinds of
beliefs and perplexities which must confront all thinkers.
Who to-day can profess to have settled for all time the relations of the conflicting principles that Plato attempted to
harmonize? Plato's value is greater than that of a system-
maker; it is the value of an eloquent spokesman of man's
perpetual and obstinate questionings and of a noble and
patient effort to harmonize at least some of these voices.
We must reckon, too, with the dramatic form of practically
all the dialogues, which allowed Plato scope for a good deal

[1] The foregoing two paragraphs are taken, with slight changes, from my
" Plato's View of Poetry," pp. 13 f.

of comedy,[1] and which allowed him to be now the dogmatist, now frankly the inquirer or even the baffled novice, trimming his sails to the wind of argument. Nor is it always possible to divide Plato's writings sharply into sections and categories, and distinguish poetry and sober reasoning, metaphysics and ethics, comedy and fact.

When Plato was a very young man, he was an adherent of the view of Heracleitus. But he found that if everything changes and nothing abides, there can be no such thing as knowledge; for no sooner has one made a statement about anything than it changes and vanishes, and the statement is untrue. Even the testimony of the senses is relative to the individual and the occasion, and gives no basis for knowledge that is absolute and eternal. This, indeed, was the contention of the followers of Protagoras, who therefore denied the possibility of absolute knowledge. Plato was not to be so easily thwarted. He merely argued that if there is such a thing as knowledge that is not merely relative, it must be of something different from the world of sensible phenomena about which, as all admitted, there were only fleeting perceptions and opinions. Now Socrates had shown that in spite of the changeableness of physical things the various moral qualities have a permanent value and meaning. Plato therefore supposed first these moral concepts, and then other concepts and relations, to have a real and permanent existence. Borrowing from the terminology of the semi-mathematical thinkers of days just before his own, he called them Ideas, or Forms.[2] This, then, is the origin of what is known as Plato's Theory of Ideas. Though individual men

[1] Cf. my "The Spirit of Comedy in Plato," in *Harvard Studies in Classical Philology*, vol. xxxi, 1920.

[2] The Greek word *idea* means a form; a kindred word, *eidos*, meaning shape or nature, had been freely used by the physicians and physicists of Ionia.

alter their characters or die, the essential character of goodness, justice, courage, and beauty are unchanging. In the
Platonizing language of St. Paul, "the things which are seen
are temporal; but the things which are not seen are eternal." [1] The Ideas, then, though unseen, are more real than
the objects which our eyes and ears give us. The Theory of
Ideas is only a postulate, an hypothesis, more or less
tested; indeed, Plato sometimes refers to it as such. Nevertheless, this appeal to permanent objects of thought is the
only possible alternative to that denial of all real knowledge
which is implied in a Heracleitean philosophy. It is a practical postulate of the reason; if there is knowledge, there
must be ideas. So far, Plato is not at all dogmatic, and differs not greatly from Protagoras and his modern followers,
Pragmatists, "Humanists," [2] and the like, who call attention to the purely relative and hypothetical character of
reasoning; concepts are convenient practical assumptions,
valid so long as they "work," but devoid of absolute validity. At times Plato would almost agree with them, except
that whereas Protagoras and the Pragmatists would test
their assumptions by constant reference to "the facts,"
that is, to the flux, the world of sensations in which knowledge can be only relative, Plato would test his assumptions
by constant reference to their mutual coherence.[3] Man, if
not the measure, is at least the measurer of all things, and he
measures them by the use of Ideas and classifications and
mathematical concepts. And the Ideas are not necessarily
dead yard-sticks; they are actually the cause of life, change,
and motion in the otherwise inert flux, as Plato shows in the

[1] II Cor. IV, 18.

[2] By this term is meant F. C. S. Schiller and those who follow him.

[3] Cf. C. P. Parker, "Plato and Protagoras," in *Harvard Essays on
Classical Subjects*.

"Sophist." [1] And yet, though Plato knows that the Ideas are an hypothesis, he is unwilling to relinquish the possibility of absolute knowledge. So he clings to his hypothesis, never attempting to demonstrate it,—for in truth there can be no demonstration of it further than to show what happens when it is given up,—and even tending to forget that it is only an hypothesis. He hopes by the rational criticism of the Ideas to arrive at a supreme principle, the Idea of the Good, which is to be the independent source and the cause of all things. This, if anything, is the absolute, by reference to which all else is to be justified, and the existence of which Plato ardently defends, although he can describe it only indirectly and by analogies; he can, for example, compare it with the sun, which is the source of motion and light upon this earth. But though, like the sailor's horizon that always lies before one, it is a goal of the imagination that cannot in practice be wholly reached or even described, it serves Plato's purpose as a standard for comparison with the Ideas that are ranged below it. [2]

These Ideas, in turn, not only provided a refuge from the logical nihilism of the philosophy of the flux but gave a firm basis for an answer to those who regarded morality as merely conventional, nature the result of chance and force, art and literature only technical skill in tickling the fancies of an ignorant people by specious emotional and rhetorical appeals. The Ideas, Plato could argue, being eternal, supply the stepping-stones of thought, the guiding principles of action, the end toward which Nature herself strives, the types which the artist and the poet, though working in the world of flux, should try to embody in their statues and

[1] Plato revised, though he did not change, his Theory in several of his later dialogues, in order to gain more varied functions for the Ideas.

[2] Cf. "Plato's View of Poetry," pp. 41–50.

poems and speeches. Just how to explain the relation of the world of flux to the world of Ideas, Plato finds difficult; and he has recourse to figurative language. A beautiful statue is not the same thing as the Idea of Beauty; but it is possible to say that it "participates in" Beauty, or "has a share" of it or "communion with" it, or again that it "resembles" or "imitates" Beauty, or that Beauty "is present with" the statue, or "takes possession" of it. Such are some of Plato's phrases for the paradoxical relation of the One and the Many, the Idea and the Particular. We have a similar difficulty in stating the relation of God to the universe; is He transcendent or immanent? In the one case, we are in danger of too great separation between creator and created; in the other case we are apt to end in pantheism. Plato was quite aware of the difficulty, and devoted a great dialogue, the "Parmenides," to a careful analysis of the difficulties that confront the Theory of Ideas. But he no more rejected his Theory than a Christian is willing to give up the idea of a God who is "in" the universe and who is yet not identical with the universe. Nor is the difficulty limited to theology. What do we mean by saying that an object "is" beautiful, or that Socrates "is" a man? Obviously the relation implied by the word "is" does not amount to identity, but rather to predication or inclusion within a class of beautiful objects or within a class of men. "Class" is only a variation of Plato's term Idea; and "predication" is not a more enlightening term than "participation." By using only figurative language Plato preserves the perpetual paradox, and so suggests that his Ideas are both immanent and transcendent: as immanent, they give form to the world; as transcendent, they preserve their character as objects of thought.

How then are the Ideas to be known by men? Fortunately their participation in the world of flux brings them within our ken, and Plato believes in a sequence of education from the most illusory deceptions of the flux to the utmost concentration of abstract thought in the contemplation of the Idea of the Good. The training of the guardians in the "Republic" in fact requires this progressive initiation into thought ever more abstract. Like the other citizens of the state, they are to train their minds by familiarity with good literature; but those few who are capable of hard thought are to proceed to science and philosophy. In the famous simile of the Divided Line, Plato sets forth the relation of the objects of knowledge according to their degree of reality and therefore of intelligibility, from shadows to solid objects, from objects to Ideas, from Ideas considered as hypotheses to the hierarchy of Ideas rationally explained by the Idea of the Good. Each part of the scale has its counterpart in the type of ignorance or opinion or knowledge of which it is susceptible. And in order to suggest the more vividly that education is not an external process but a turning of the mind's eye toward the brightness of the truth, Plato expounds the Parable of the Cave. Of the prisoners who are confined in a subterranean cave, unable to see anything but the shadows cast by puppets carried past a fire behind them, one is fortunate enough to be set free, and to make the ascent to the outer world; there he realizes the unsubstantiality of all that he has been accustomed to consider real, and he learns, at first painfully, to behold and to recognize the objects about him, last of all the sun, the author and illuminator of all. Then he returns to the cave, in order to enlighten his fellows, if they will listen to him. Such is the mission of the teacher who tries to turn the eyes of his pupils toward the Idea of the Good, the sun in the intellectual world; this task Plato thought more likely to be accomplished by the force of personality and the living, spoken word than by dead writings. From the flux to the changeless, from the senses to thought, by the aid of the various sciences and mathematics and pure logic, such is the "upward course" by which Plato hoped to lead those who would follow.

The Theory of Ideas, which arises from the desire to emerge from the flux, is not merely a logical doctrine. As the bacchanal had believed that it was possible for the soul to be set free from the body and become one with the god Dionysus, as the Orphic and the Eleusinian mysteries had taught that through initiation and an ascetic life it was possible to leave behind this mortal flesh and to win immortality for the soul, so Plato held that the true business of philosophy is to win an escape from the bonds of the flesh and to seek union with the eternal goodness of the universe; and this was possible, he held, because the rational part of man is of the same substance as the Ideas. Accordingly, the Ideas are the object not merely of logical approach but of immediate mystical intuition; and Plato's thought is permeated with the very language of the mysteries. In the "Phædo" he speaks, as the Orphics did, of the body as the sepulchre of the soul; the soul must purge itself of the evil taint of the body, and its passions and emotions, even as it is destined to free itself from the body at death, and by climbing from the seen to the unseen to reach the realm of pure Ideas. Thus philosophy is a rehearsal of death; for the death of the body means the life of the soul. So St. Paul, thinking of the body, exhorts men to "die daily." The language of Plato's "Symposium" is even more striking. The subject of the dialogue is the nature of love; and the drift of the discussion has brought out its kinship with beauty and its craving to have something more perfect than itself, and to give birth to something that shall endure. Socrates recounts the discourse of a wise woman, Diotima, who has told him of the initiation and the mystical revelation that lies before the ideal lover; he begins with the love of a single beautiful body, and should thus beget beautiful thoughts; then perceiving that the beauty in any body is akin to that in other bodies, and that their beauty is one, he should be a lover of all beautiful bodies. Next he should realize the superiority of the beauty that resides in souls, and should proceed to the contemplation of the beauty that is to be found in practices and laws, and hence to think little of bodily beauty. He will then approach the sciences and contemplate their beauty, till drawing near to the vast sea of beauty he gazes upon it and begets a host of fair thoughts in his love of wisdom, and at last he beholds a single science, namely, that of beauty. The scholar in love who has reached this point then suddenly catches sight of a wondrous beauty, the goal of all his toils, a beauty that is eternal, absolute, and unchanging. It cannot be represented to sense or stated in terms of intellect. It is absolute, and the source of the changing beauties of other things. This is the goal toward which tends the right love of beautiful things, rising as by the steps of a ladder from the love of particular beauties, through fair practices and fair sciences to the science of beauty itself, which ends in the knowledge of the essence of beauty.[1]

Again in the "Phædrus," speaking of the divine sort of madness that leads to love and other kinds of mystical experience, Plato describes the human soul as a charioteer with a pair of ill-matched, winged horses that soar with difficulty to the vault of Heaven, beyond which lies a vision of absolute reality that defies description. It is without color or form, and is intangible; it is visible only to the intelligence that is at the helm of the soul, and with it true knowl-

[1] The foregoing sentences are taken from "Plato's View of Poetry," p. 21; most of the next paragraph is from the same essay, p. 58.

edge is concerned. On this feeds the divine intelligence, and
the intelligence of every soul that is capable of receiving its
proper food. It beholds perfect justice, temperance, and
knowledge, not under the form of generation or of relation,
but in existence absolute. But most souls have difficulty in
beholding true being, because their steeds are unruly.
Many fail, and feed on opinion instead. So with broken
wings they drop to earth, and are born as men. Those souls
that have seen most of truth pass into the body of a philosopher or of a lover of beauty or of some other musical
and loving nature. Plato presently explains in purely logical
terms the meaning of this vision, and shows that it is symbolic of man's power of seeing a One and a Many in Nature.
The same goal, then, may be described now in sober terms
as the Idea of the Good and now in the glowing language of
poetry and the mysteries as transcendent beauty. Logic
and mystical intuition may culminate in the same experience, the contemplation of an absolute; there is no conflict
between the testimony of science and that of poetry and
religion. Not all poetry and not all religion, and, we might
add, not all science will lead to the heavenly vision; and
Plato has severe censure for the scientists whose interest is
wholly practical, for the charlatans in religion, for the poets
who are content to remain in the world of flux. But we are
concerned as much with possibilities as with current "facts":
and we have here an account of human experience that sets
a value on two commonly opposed tendencies, so far as they
converge toward a single end. Science is of value as it shows
the operation of a single principle in diverse ways; poetry is
of value as it embodies in sensible images the world of Ideas,
so that the mind is led from what is here and now toward
what is eternal. Indeed, the goal of pure science has been
such a unification; and poets of many ages have tried, more

or less consciously, to do something more than express a concrete fact.[1]

Having passed by bold strides of the imagination to the conception of the absolute, Plato is tempted from time to time to descend into the flux and to imagine how the Ideas shape existence. Here, though he has an ideal for science, he cannot pretend to speak scientifically, partly because the flux, being material, is imperfect and incapable of exact treatment. So Plato deals much in myths by which he can suggest in a shadowy fashion the most plausible account that occurs to him. The "Timæus" is his most striking attempt to give a poetical version of the origin of the universe. The creation means the introduction of reason into matter, in accordance with the divine model;[2] but to save the divine Creator from the responsibility of having brought into being an imperfect world, — for imperfect it must be by reason of the matter with which it is compounded, — Plato tells us that the Highest God, who is the personification of the Idea of the Good, first made lesser gods, who in turn created the inferior parts of the universe; God then sowed the immortal part of men's souls in their bodies, and left them a mixture of mortality and immortality. The dialogue is full of scientific and semi-scientific doctrines freely plundered from Empedocles and the Pythagoreans, and of conjectures about the natural world that have sometimes proved strangely near the truth. The conception of a "world-soul," not identical with the Godhead but its expression, acting as a mediator between God and the created world, was destined to influence Christian conceptions.[3]

[1] Cf. pp. 121 ff.

[2] *Tim.* 29e: "God made the world because he was free from all jealousy and desired to share his own perfection as widely as possible." Cf. "God so loved the world that He gave His only begotten Son," etc.

[3] Cf. pp. 269 f.

Not only in the "Timæus" but in several other dialogues Plato uses a myth to set forth imaginatively his conception of the dignity and the immortality of the soul. This does not imply any lack of a belief on his part that immortality is a demonstrable fact; indeed, he many times argues that the ability of man to apprehend the Ideas, truths independent of time and the flux, proves that some part of him is akin to the eternal existences, and must therefore have had a previous existence and must survive when it is severed from the body, whether it passes, as some held, into successive bodies, or whether it returns to its maker.[1] These arguments vary in kind, and vary greatly in validity; and Plato clearly feels that he is dealing with a matter that calls for the language of poetry. So in the myths of the "Gorgias," the "Republic," the "Phædo," and the "Phædrus" he suggests the sort of career that awaits the soul in another life, dwelling on the solemn consequences of moral choices in this life. Here again, as in the mysteries, the result is not so much definite information as "a certain frame of mind";[2] and whether or not immortality can be logically demonstrated, it is, like the Idea of the Good, at least an hypothesis that lends coherence

[1] There is a close resemblance to Plato's thought in Wordsworth's lines (from the "Ode on the Intimations of Immortality from Recollections of Early Childhood"):

> "Our birth is but a sleep and a forgetting:
> The Soul that rises with us, our Life's Star,
>   Hath had elsewhere its setting,
>   And cometh from afar:
>   Not in entire forgetfulness,
>   And not in utter nakedness,
> But trailing clouds of glory do we come,
>   From God, who is our home."

But the rest of the stanza is not Platonic, in its suggestion that as life advances our hope of recovering the earlier "glory" fades away.

[2] Cf. p. 232.

and meaning to all that we know, and the myths express its value.

At the foundation of Plato's philosophy, then, we find the same opposition that met us when we dealt with his political thought. There it was the discrepancy between "ideals" and "the facts"; here it is between "Ideas" and the world of flux. The trouble, one may say, is that Plato is not content to admit that Ideas are only convenient creations of the imagination; he will have it that they are entities more real than the things of sense. In another form we meet the same obstacle in Plato's distrust of the body, in that "other-worldliness" that we associate with some phases of Christianity. In art it is responsible for Plato's lack of "direct-ness," his prepossession with universals. Now to dispose of a large matter very briefly, we may admit that Plato has a seriousness that disposes him to take no chances with the flux and all that it means. He would rather go to the ex-treme of intellectualism, if need be, for that at least would explain something. Yet Plato is no intellectualist: his nature is too many-sided for that. He is half the apostle of reason, half the mystic poet; and if now one interest, now another forges ahead, shutting out at times the world that we some-how feel to be of some worth, we can perhaps forgive his ardor, by remembering the confusion that existed before Plato, and the confusion that still exists if we try to dispense with the assumption that there are firm standards of com-parison worth our struggle.

There is little of the poet and mystic in Aristotle. As we saw when we considered his political and ethical theory, he was disposed to be chary of visions and to reckon as much as possible with everyday facts.[1] The same sober attitude con-fronts us everywhere in his philosophy. He severely criti-

[1] Pp. 181 ff.

cizes Plato's Theory of Ideas for its tendency to separate
Ideas from the flux so far that they provide an explanation
neither of things and their changeability nor of our ability to
know things. This danger Plato had fully recognized, and he
had tried to give such an account of the Ideas as would
leave them both immanent and transcendent.[1] Paradoxical
they remained; and Aristotle sought a more satisfactory account. He argued that the universal element that is necessary for real knowledge must be *in* the individual object, not
anything separable from it; it is the form that matter takes
on itself. So whereas Plato had held that we can understand
the individual only by reference to the universal Idea, Aristotle's aim was to understand reality by observing the embodiment of universals in the individual. For Aristotle,
reality is thus neither substance alone nor form alone, but
the union of the two. Furthermore, he held that this reality
is capable of taking on a greater or a less degree of form, and
so mere undeveloped potentialities may progressively find
realization. This conception, which accounts for change, reminds one of the theory of evolution; it holds that entities,
beginning with mere capacities, gradually unfold these
capacities and realize their full and perfect natures, which in
a sense are logically prior to their imperfect states. This
ascending scale of development is explained by four kinds of
causation: the material cause, the substance of which a thing
is created; the efficient cause that calls it into being; the
formal cause that expresses its true nature; and the final
cause that is its goal. For example, one may say that a ship
is built of wood (the material cause) by the labor of car-
penters (the efficient cause) in accordance with the plans of
the naval architect (the formal cause) in order that it may
sail the Atlantic Ocean (the final cause). To tell what a

[2] P. 249 f.

thing is, then, would be not merely to name the substance of which it is composed, but to state the nature of its functions and the end that it is tending to realize. The application of these distinctions to a man or to a political institution is obvious; we are not what we appear to be at the moment, but what our whole nature shows that we may some day become. Man, for example, shares with the beasts much of his nature; he differs from them by the possession of reason and a degree of self-control that constitute his immortality and his point of contact with God. But Aristotle succeeds better than Plato in accounting for human action and the use of the will without splitting up the personality into separate faculties. Most beings, however, cannot wholly control themselves and realize their proper ends, since the material cause is an eternal impediment to the full working of the formal and the final causes; only one being is practically, if not quite, free from such limitations, and that is God, the unmoved mover of all things, the creative reason who acts on the world as the beloved acts on the lover. This is practically monotheism. Up to this point Aristotle has kept the development of all creation continuous; but here there is undeniably a leap from matter controlled however completely by form to pure form engaged in absolute thought. The leap is no less significant than Plato's tendency to sever the Ideas from the world of sense. It is the dualistic tendency that is apt to occur in any conception of God. Except by the denial of matter, or by the denial of spirit, there is no escape from the frank acceptance of the paradox.

In his description of the methods of reasoning, Aristotle shows the same concern for the individual "fact" that he shows elsewhere. He recognizes, as Plato recognizes, that there can be no thought without universals (Ideas, or forms, or general propositions); but since he holds that these exist

only as they are embodied in particulars, he finds that the
task of logic is to mediate between the higher and the lower
degrees of universality, bringing the particulars under their
appropriate universal or category.[1] Each science, then, has
the duty of discovering by the use of the senses its material and of noting the peculiar modes of relationship by
which its members are grouped under larger classifications.
Though Aristotle was interested in every kind of knowledge, his genius, unlike that of Plato, whose philosophy had
tended to become mathematical, was especially at home in
those biological sciences in which this process of classification is essential.

Classification without previous observation is worse than
useless. Aristotle himself was usually cautious; and his
encyclopædic investigations into natural history and politics
and literature show a fair balance between this necessary
preliminary and the speculation to which it led. His followers, captivated by the possibilities of his technical terms,
often forgot the preliminary process, and elaborated his
philosophy into a self-contained structure. During the
Middle Ages the Christian "Schoolmen" availed themselves
of Aristotle's technique to explain Christian theology, and
no science was conceivable that was not supported by Aristotle's authority. So it was possible for Bacon to attack
Aristotle, the defender of experimental methods, as one "who
corrupted natural philosophy by his logic, fashioning the
world out of categories. . . . He did not consult experience,
as he should have done, in order to do the framing of his
decisions and axioms; but having first determined the ques-

---

[1] The typical form of reasoning that Aristotle originated, the syllogism, is
still a convenient test for the validity of statements, since it brings them into
relation with larger universals. Thus, "Socrates is mortal" is true only if we
already know both that "Socrates is a man" and that "All men are mortal."
But the syllogism does not contribute to the acquisition of new knowledge.

tion according to his will, he then resorts to experience, and bending her into conformity with his placets, leads her about like a captive in a procession." [1] Even if Bacon here overstates the case with regard to Aristotle himself, it is true that the achievements of ancient science during the Alexandrian Age [2] were made possible only by the methods of observation, and that when these methods were very largely given up, scientific discovery was retarded for more than a thousand years.

For thinking men, the philosophies of Plato and Aristotle went far to explain their relation to the universe and therefore the basis of their standards of conduct. But not many men could hope to follow these philosophers in their more abstract thought. And since both the old religion and the guidance of the decaying city-state were no longer strong, ordinary men tried to find new support for their way of living. It was the Stoics, the teachers of the "Porch," who for a long time offered the most satisfying support. [3] Not at all original in their conception of the external universe, — for here they borrowed from the materialism of Heracleitus, with the pantheistic conception of universal reason in the form of fire, and presently lost interest in physical speculation, — they did succeed in arousing men to a sense of personal moral responsibility in matters of conduct. The Cynics before them had insisted on the absolute and irreconcilable opposition between right and wrong, and had held that the individual by avoiding the allurements of pleasure and by pursuing only virtue could find happiness. In their contempt for ordinary comforts and acts, the Cynics went to absurd lengths; the story of Diogenes and his tub is a well-known example. The Stoics accepted the absolute distinc-

[1] *Novum Organum*, I, 63.
[2] Cf. p. 236.
[3] For the political bearing of the Stoic teaching, cf. p. 190.

tion between right and wrong, and the dependence of
happiness on individual virtue, rather than on social conditions; but they avoided the extreme phases of the Cynic
creed. The ideal philosopher was therefore no mere logician
but the completely virtuous man; ethics, and especially the
practical application of ethics, was almost the whole of
philosophy. The Stoic philosophy spread rapidly and became a cosmopolitan creed; it found a particularly favorable
environment at Rome, where fortitude and the schooling of
the will was a national tradition. But as it was popularized
the Stoic doctrine lost some of its original severity; it no
longer held that men are either wholly good or wholly bad,
and taught that a moral progress is possible. The problem
of life therefore became one of finding what things were hu-
manly capable of achievement, of adapting oneself to conditions that could not be altered, of submitting to adversity.
The man who can hold himself superior to the passions is so
far independent, because his will is free, bound only by reason; he cannot change Nature, but he can build his life in
accordance with what he knows of the working of Nature.
And when he has done his utmost he can rest content; there
is nothing good or evil except what one makes of one's opportunities. All externals are merely the rules of the game;
the excellence of the game depends on the players. Hence
what superficially appears to be evil is often merely the
necessary condition of the existence of something good,
some discipline of the character. Finally, the cosmopolitan
nature of the Stoic philosophy, which dealt with the rationality of all men and their relation not to particular states
but to the universe, made for the notion of the brotherhood
and equality of man, even of slaves and kings.[1]

[1] A principle recognized by the Roman lawyers who identified the law of
Nature with the *ius gentium*, the law found to be common to all men, and distinguished from merely conventional laws. Cf. p. 190.

The value of Stoicism, then, though it rested on a reasoned conception of the universe, lay precisely in its practical
applicability to the life of average educated men.[1] Men's
circumstances vary greatly; but in the common necessity
of meeting circumstances and of schooling their wills to accord with the universal reason they are alike. Stoicism aims
high, but it does not refuse to see in the lives of those who
live nobly such examples of wisdom as deserve emulation.
In its insistence on the duty of the individual to work out his
own destiny, the Stoic philosophy seems almost to be committed to a purely human account of things, and to leave no
room for any supernatural power, or at most to end in
pantheism. Nevertheless the Stoics did at times think of the
all-pervasive reason as a personal God, to be addressed with
hymns:

> Most glorious of immortals, many-named, powerful over all,
> Zeus, thou author of all nature, guiding all with law,
> Hail to thee.[2]

The Epicureans, like the Stoics, were practical in their
aim, but emphasized the possibility of gaining happiness by
prudence, rather than of schooling the will.[3] Epicureanism,
which should not be superficially set down as the philosophy
of libertines, works well in times of prosperity; in adversity,
it has little to offer. Like Stoicism, it rests on a materialistic
view of the universe, but professes ignorance of any divinity,
and has no conception of a governing principle for man's life

[1] As G. Murray remarks: "Stoicism, like Christianity, was primarily a
religion for the oppressed, a religion of defence and defiance; but, like Christianity, it had the requisite power of adaptation." And Professor Murray
refers to "two quite different types of Stoics — one who defies the world and
one who works with the world; and, as in Christianity, both types are equally
orthodox." *The Stoic Philosophy*, pp. 89, 99.

[2] Cleanthes, "Hymn to Zeus."

[3] Cf. p. 190.

outside of his own sagacity. Epicureanism gradually lost ground; for one thing, it was too passive a philosophy for men of action.

In the tendency of even the Stoics to turn to a personal God we find striking testimony to the fact that few men can find permanent satisfaction in a life governed by abstract reason alone. Most men crave an outlet for their emotional capacities, for their love of definite appeals to their senses, for their interest in persons and places and stories to which associations are apt to cling, above all for their feeling that the power that guides all things cares for them as individuals even if they are weak and imperfect. No religion that is to be lasting or that is to appeal to widely differing kinds of men can afford to neglect this fact. So the history of religious life in the Greek world during the centuries just before and just after the Christian era is largely the history of successive revivals of mystical schools of thought and of invasions by various Oriental religions that, like the Orphic religion, promised happiness and salvation to their initiates.

The Neopythagoreans, and the Jewish thinkers of Alexandria who borrowed from the Platonic philosophy, and the Neoplatonists, in their several ways, all show the tendency of Plato to emphasize the opposition of flesh and spirit, and taught the importance of asceticism that leads to saintliness. They held that God is so far above the world that it is necessary to conceive of other powers to mediate or to intercede between God and the world and to carry out God's will.[1] Yet in spite of this common tendency to think of God as utterly transcendent, even beyond all knowledge, they satis-

---

[1] These the Judæo-Alexandrian Philo called "powers," or "forms," or "the word" (*logos*), with far-reaching consequences in Christian thought (cf. pp. 269 f.); the Neoplatonists spoke of "emanations" of a transcendent God, namely "intelligence," the "world-soul," and "matter," thus avoiding the attribution of evil (matter) directly to God.

fied their craving for knowledge of God by their faith in the possibility of a direct, mystical revelation of him, to be won by an ascetic life that culminates in the ecstasy of a beatific vision and of union with God. All these tendencies remind one of the earlier mysteries and of that side of Plato's teaching that recognized the value of intuition; they do not reckon much with his logical, scientific bent. They are in fact akin to such mediæval mystics as St. Teresa, and to many of the theosophic movements of our day; like them, they satisfied many natural cravings, and used much of the language of philosophy and science without being able to give a wholly rational account of themselves. Their influence on Christian thought was important.

Even these movements required of their adherents, if not high intellectual attainments, at least a high degree of morality and self-denial. But other cults from the near East spread through the Empire of Alexander, and followed the course of Roman arms and the dispersion of slaves throughout the farthest parts of the Roman world; and these cults, too, offered salvation. From Egypt came the worship of Isis and the divinities associated with her; from Asia Minor that of the Great Mother, Cybele; from Persia the cult of Mithras. Like the Greek mysteries and the later mystical philosophies, these oriental religions taught the importance both of initiation and of an ascetic life lived in the service of a god; they recognized no social caste save the various grades of initiation, and even afforded a brotherhood of the faithful; they satisfied men's desire for a personal deity, the subject of ancient legends; and they suggested by their ritual, however crudely, that the worshipper might be born into a new life and might hope for an immediate contact with divine beings. Particularly the worship of Mithras, because of its strong insistence on the eternal struggle between right and wrong, and its powerful appeal to the imagination by myth and architecture and rites of cleansing and sacred feasts, found a response among the Romans; and during the second and third centuries it was the most formidable rival of Christianity.

Among the other oriental religions that had spread in the western world was Judaism. Although it made few converts among Gentiles, its chief characteristics were becoming familiar outside of Judæa; and when Christianity made an independent claim for consideration, Christianity, too, was at first regarded as merely another oriental mystery, with rites of initiation and offers of salvation and a personal founder, whose story, indeed, dated from far less remote times than did the myths of the other religions. Its relation to the Greek world we shall presently consider.

Apart from Christianity, there were many signs of a growing conviction among the Greeks that a dependence on a purely human reason and the exercise of the will is insufficient. Not only Christians but non-Christians also tended more and more to withdraw from politics and the evils of the world, and to seek sanctity in monastic seclusion, as Plato's ideal philosopher would have preferred, but was not to be permitted, to do. The recourse to reason was replaced not only by oriental mysteries but by the recrudescence of many old superstitions which had been long neglected. Magic and astrology, the worship of Fate or of Fortune, a new invasion of the old Olympian gods,[1] the deification of the sun and other heavenly bodies, which even Plato and Aristotle and the Stoics had occasionally tolerated,—such were some

---

[1] Especially during the determined pagan revivals of the second and the fourth centuries A.D. How much nobility of thought could be read into the old religion and its mythology is surprising. Cf. G. Murray, "The Last Protest," in *Four Stages of Greek Religion*.

of the signs of a loss of faith in normal human nature and its possibilities. On the other hand, the failure of democratic institutions and the growth of monarchy had called attention to the fundamental differences between man and man, and had made possible a partial obliteration of the distinction, always emphasized by the rationalists of the Great Age, between man and god. Great kings, like Alexander, and great benefactors of humanity were worshipped as gods; and as men came to depend more and more on such persons for their material well-being, they found in them the sure help for which they had often looked to the older gods in vain. Even a Roman emperor whose character was not wholly admirable might seem, by reason of his power, a god on earth. Philanthropy was coming to be regarded as an attribute of divinity.[1] And amid all this confusion of conflicting beliefs and claims, many thinkers were inclined to see simply the varied manifestations, the symbols, of a single God who appeared in different ways to men of different tongues and of different characters.

4. The Greeks and Christianity

Christianity generally presents itself to us as a fixed institution, so that it is sometimes hard for us to remember that, like other religions, it grew out of a peculiar background, was influenced by its environment, and developed not only in accordance with its own nature but in accordance with external conditions. Christianity has profoundly changed the world, but it has also been changed by the character of the human beings with whom it has come into contact. Certainly we find at the heart of Christianity an historical fact,

---

[1] Whenever Augustus was described by his contemporaries as divine, it was because of his services to man, as R. S. Conway has well pointed out.

a living personality, that has given it a peculiar appeal and power; but even our knowledge of the life and personality of Jesus is limited, to an extent that would have appeared incredible a few generations ago, by the character and the conceptions of the earliest witnesses. Not only do many of the books of the New Testament represent the tradition of a somewhat later period than was formerly believed to be the case, but they show signs of having been composed by men who had not the modern idea of historical accuracy and whose minds were often influenced by Hebrew ideas and prophecies and by Greek philosophical ideas. Furthermore, this tradition was itself greatly changed during the early centuries of Christianity, as the need for interpretation and for harmony of thought and action was felt to be necessary; here again Greek thought had a great share, and the influence of the Roman gift for organization was felt. The change can be conveniently measured by noting the difference between the simple ethical teaching of the Sermon on the Mount and the subtle metaphysical dogmas of the Nicene Creed, or again the powerful organization of the mediæval church.

Many circumstances favored the spread of Christianity, when once it had appeared. The eastern Mediterranean was united by the Greek language and Greek modes of thought; under the efficient rule of the Roman Empire the whole Mediterranean enjoyed an unprecedented state of peace. Travel was becoming safer, and many of the earlier barriers set up by social distinctions and by national feeling had fallen before a wave of cosmopolitan feeling. Even in the realm of religion Christianity found the favoring atmosphere of a moral reformation. Judaism had for centuries struggled to uphold monotheism and the goodness of God. Stoicism was bidding men to follow God and to obey an absolute moral law, in terms that often remind one of Christian sermons, even though its sanction was the law of the orderly universe, rather than the will of a loving Father. The mystical religions and philosophies had accustomed the minds of men to the possibility of a direct, personal vision of divinity and of constant communion with God, symbolized by ritual acts. Nevertheless, there was in the world much religious unrest, much unsatisfied longing for positive experience and truth.

In its earliest phase, Christianity was a sect consisting of those Jews who had been won by the noble personality of Jesus and by his teaching about a kingdom of penitent and righteous men and women governed not merely by the Law of the Old Testament but by the love of God and of each other. This teaching was phrased generally in the poetic language of parables and exhortations that were, and are still, natural to the people of Syria, rather than in philosophical terms. Jesus himself laid little stress on his mission as the long-expected Messiah of the Jews; yet it was naturally in this light that his early followers especially regarded him. So, too, the familiar conceptions of Hebrew prophecy influenced not only their interpretation of the crucifixion as vicarious suffering but their understanding of his relation to God.

When Christianity was taken to the Gentiles, notably by St. Paul, it no longer remained a Jewish sect, but learned to speak the language of Greek thought and became a universal religion. For men without personal knowledge of Jesus, it was necessary to set forth the claims of Christianity in terms that were within their ken; and to Greeks Christianity must be presented as a philosophy and a mystery. Faith in the Jewish sense, trust in a personal friend, gradually came to mean faith in the Greek sense, belief in a dogma.

St. Paul, though not a systematic philosopher, was acquainted both with Jewish thought and with Judæo-Hellenic philosophy.[1] In language which often sounds strangely like an echo of that of the Orphics and of Plato,[2] he preached the opposition of flesh and spirit, of the seen and the unseen, and of the need of such personal acceptance of the death and resurrection of Jesus as would enable men by the mortification of the flesh to die to their lower selves and rise to newness of life with the risen Christ; this is the work of the divine Spirit or law that dwells in men.

The writer of the fourth Gospel, unlike the authors of the other three (the "Synoptic") Gospels, was interested not so much in setting forth the tradition of Christians toward the end of the first century with regard to the life of Jesus as in presenting an interpretation of his significance. This interpretation he phrased in the language of contemporary Judæo-Hellenic thought. "In the beginning was the Word (*Logos*), and the Word was with God, and the Word was God. . . . And the Word became flesh and dwelt among us."[3] As Heracleitus had used the conception of a *Logos*, a fixed principle, to govern the world of flux; as Plato had upheld the paradox of Ideas at once transcendent and immanent, and had speculated on the existence of a "World Soul," the expression of the Godhead;[4] as Philo had spoken of an intermediary *Logos*, or Word, between God and the world, expressing his will;[5] so the writer of the fourth Gospel explained the revelation of God in the person of Christ as the

---

[1] Cf. p. 263.

[2] See the passages from the Pauline epistles expressing Platonic conceptions quoted by J. Adam, "Religious Teachers of Greece," pp. 359 f.; 381 f.; 385 f.; 412 f.; 433; 436 ff.; 450. Plato's conception of the immanence of the Idea of the Good has helped to form St. Paul's doctrine of the indwelling Christ, or Holy Spirit.

[3] John I, 1, 14.   [4] Cf. p. 254.   [5] Cf. p. 263.

Logos, or Word, who was paradoxically both God and the manifestation of God in human form. In this emphasis on the incarnation of the *Logos*, he went far beyond the earlier thinkers, whose *Logos* was apt to be an abstract principle useful in explaining the processes of creation; here the *Logos* is a concrete personality, whose historical appearance is defended against possible doubters, and knowledge of whom, and faith in whom, accepted as an inward personal experience, are held to be an all-sufficient means both of beholding God and of attaining a new and spiritual life. Though much of the language of the fourth gospel, like that of the Pauline epistles, has a Platonic coloring, there is nothing in Plato, unless it be in the myths of Plato, quite so insistent on intimate personal experience, and especially on the mutual love of God and man.[1]

By the time, then, that those books were written which were later selected from a much larger literature and grouped together as the New Testament, Christianity had been restated in terms that could appeal to Greek thinkers as on the whole familiar. It follows that its subsequent history was bound to be somewhat influenced by the character of Greek thought. Not only must Christianity defend itself against the attacks of its pagan rivals with arguments that they could recognize as valid, but as it now included Greeks its inner development must naturally show the impress of its

---

[1] Cf. John III, 16: "For God so loved the world that He gave His only begotten Son that whosoever believeth in Him should not perish but have everlasting life"; XV, 12: "This is my command, that ye love one another as I have loved you." In the God of Plato love is not even so important an element as in the Prime Mover of Aristotle, which moves all things as the beloved moves the lover. (Met. 7, 1072a28; cf. p. 258.) That is perhaps part of the general Greek tradition that exalted vision above emotion; they would have regarded as a violent metaphor Dante's fine closing line, "The love that moves the sun and the other stars." See, too, Francis Thompson's poem, "The Hound of Heaven."

members. A large part of what is often held to be of the
essence of Christianity is the result of this unfolding of the
original germ as it was nourished by the soil of Greece; for
practically all our knowledge of early Christianity comes from
Greek writers who were in the full tide of the Greek tradition.

Two phases of this development are of especial importance. In the first place, those Christian writers, known as
the "Apologists," who sought to explain their religion to
pagans elaborated their faith into a universal system of
philosophy. Although they continued, of course, to stress
the historical facts of Christianity, they presented them as
only the culmination of a continuous series of revelations on
the part of God, who had spoken not merely through the
prophets of the Old Testament but through the philosophers
of Greece as well. If the Greek philosophers had attained to
only a partial degree of truth, it was because their human
minds and weak wills were unable to cope with eternal matters without this culminating revelation. Thus the apologists attempted to set forth an all-embracing system of
philosophy, using such a dualistic opposition of creator and
world as could be easily deduced from Plato, and such an
account of a mediating *Logos*, the incarnate expression of
God, as could be adapted from Philo; and, like the Stoics
and other pagan sects, they sought by an ascetic life to gain
moral perfection and a vision of God. Even Justin Martyr
reminds one more of the teaching of Plato than of the New
Testament; and he frankly writes: "We teach the same as
the Greeks, though we alone are hated for what we teach."

Other attempts to interpret Christianity in Greek terms
were made by the various early thinkers who are known as
the "Gnostics." [1] They were the heirs not only of the mys-

[1] Because they emphasized the importance of knowledge through direct
revelation.

teries, Greek and Oriental, that sought to give a direct vision
of divinity, but of the various religious philosophies that
tried to bridge the gap between God and the world by mythological schemes of emanations, angels, æons, and all manner of abstractions. Christ was apt to be explained as one of
these beings, and his life to be accounted for allegorically;
and the sacraments of baptism, the Lord's Supper, and
anointing with oil were regarded as mysteries that led by a
magical power to knowledge and salvation. Indeed, some of
the Gnostics practised all sorts of crude magic. Because of
this tendency to pervert the normal course both of Christianity and of Greek thought, the Gnostics had to be re-
pressed; yet they left a permanent mark on Christianity.

During the latter part of the second century and the
following century Christianity was further developed in
accordance with Greek methods of thought. It felt the
effect of the Greek tendency to give allegorical interpreta-
tions to sacred or important writings, and turned its attention to the development of a more subtle theology. More
subtle it had to be, for such men as Origen now attempted to
explain the relation of divine goodness to human sinfulness,
of divine omnipotence to man's freedom to act, of God to
the *Logos*. It is hardly too much to say that his account is
as much in the Greek as in the purely Christian tradition.
For example, the explanation of freedom of the will rests on
a Platonic psychology and cosmology; God, though omnipotent, allows men free choice; through the predominance of
their lower natures, they choose ill, and so fall from perfection into various forms. Other speculations of this period are
about the nature of the *Logos*. There was general agreement that Jesus is the *Logos*; the statement of Irenæus is
typical: "No one can know the Father except by the Word
of God, that is, by the Son revealing Him; nor can any one

know the Son except by the good pleasure of the Father."
But the relation of son to father was recognized as meta-
phorical, and was varied by other metaphors,—the leafing
of a plant, the flowing of water, the radiation of light. And
already the danger was felt of lapsing from monotheism into
ditheism or tritheism (for the importance attached to the
Holy Spirit, which was a conception not unknown to Greek
thought, was growing). It became necessary again to call in
Greek metaphysics to solve the problem to which Greek
metaphysics had largely given rise. Unfortunately, the
various Greek (and later the Latin) words that were used,
corresponding to the conception of substance, essence, or
nature, had come to have different meanings for various
schools of thinkers; accordingly the question of the relation
that exists between God the Creator and the *Logos*, or
Christ, was apt to be confused by men arguing at cross-
purposes. As Athanasius well remarked, "They seemed to
be ignorant of the fact that when we deal with words that
require some training to understand, different people may
take them in senses not only differing but absolutely opposed to each other." To meet this danger, there arose even
in early Christianity a tendency to formulate and to develop
creeds which should define the common ground of agreement of all who claimed to be Christians; and these are still
used by most Christians. Yet they did not end dispute.
When theology had to learn to speak in Latin for the benefit
of western Europe, the constitution of the Trinity was
described in terms of "persons." For those who remembered
the ordinary meaning of *persona*, the mask through which
the Roman actor spoke, the term was illuminating, for it
suggested metaphorically the varied manifestations through
which a single God speaks; but for those who thought of a
persona as an absolutely distinct personality, the term was a

stumbling-block, and led to something very much like tritheism. The difficulty persists to-day.

The attempt to reduce Christianity to the form of a Greek philosophy had unexpected results. The earliest Christians, who had been mainly simple men of little education or position, had been united by their common devotion to their master, and by their determination to live an upright life. All tests for admission to Christian communities were tests of conduct, not of belief; indeed the only sense in which the word "belief" could be used was not acquiescence in a creed but active faith in a personality. Now that Christianity had clothed itself in Greek garments, tests became intellectual, and it was not always possible to distinguish between questions that involved matters of historical record and matters of a purely speculative character. It became the custom to settle theological disputes by the vote of a majority of those present at a church council; and these decisions even came to be enforced by the Roman state. Those minorities or individuals who persisted in clinging to their own views were stamped with the name of "heretic."[1] Accordingly the view of a majority at a given time, influenced by the prevailing philosophy of the day, and now defined, was regarded as final, without appeal either to a more primitive faith or to later developments;[2] and dissent from such a view sometimes led to persecution. Doctrine had become more important than conduct;[3] it seemed as if Hellenism had absorbed Christianity, rather than that Christianity had borrowed from Greece. And this inter-

[1] From the Greek verb meaning "to choose for oneself."

[2] An interesting illustration of this is the word "dogma," first used by early Greek philosophers to mean their personal opinions, the ideas that seemed plausible to them; later, as they acquired a following, a "dogma" was held to be absolutely true because it had been formulated by a given thinker, and because a number of followers concurred in believing it.

[3] Cf. pp. 277 f.

pretation of Christianity, further explained in terms of Aristotelian metaphysics, after Aristotle's influence had increased, is the basis not only of mediæval Christianity (represented by the wonderfully symmetrical system of Aquinas and Dante) but of the modern Church of Rome.

If Christianity as a whole had urged its claims only as a consistent theology, or even as a noble ethical system, it might have fared with the masses not very differently from the Stoic sect or from those Christian denominations that appeal to a small but enlightened class. What saved Christianity was, first, the personality of its founder, and, secondly, the fervent and growing faith of its believers in the efficacy of certain ritual acts to give them immediate communion with God, and so to win salvation and immortality. All the pagan mystical religions could point to a sovereign lord, — a Demeter or a Mithras or an Isis; Christianity could point to a far nobler Lord and Master. The pagan mysteries gave even their humblest initiates a dramatic or sacramental approach to lasting things; and Christians soon found it possible by perpetuating among themselves two experiences in the life of their Lord, the Baptism and the Last Supper, to satisfy their longings for personal union with him. For a theology or even an ethical code, not many are willing to become martyrs; but for a personal master with whom they have shared a sacred experience men have been and always will be ready to suffer hardships without limit. As a mystery, then, a cult for initiates, Christianity presented a triumphant appeal throughout the Greek and Roman world; indeed it was so presented by St. Paul to the Corinthians: "Behold, I shew you a mystery; we shall not all sleep, but we shall all be changed." [1]

[1] I Cor. XV, 51. The whole chapter deals with various phases of the resurrection. In reading the word "mystery," we must, of course, take it in its

Naturally, therefore, the conception of the Christian sacraments was colored by the character of the Greek mysteries. Although Jesus did not himself require baptism as a condition of discipleship, as early as the Apostolic Age it became customary for converts to the new religion to be informally baptized; [1] and although the Jews had ceremonial washings, the Christian institution of baptism, though derived from them and similar to the baptism of John the Baptist, came to have less in common with them than with the pagan initiatory rites. Baptism was now interpreted not merely as symbolic of the cleansing of a penitent but as the repetition by the initiate of the death and resurrection of his Lord, and as attended by the gift of the divine Spirit,[2] or even as exorcizing evil spirits. It was no longer the immediate consequence of conversion, nor was it openly performed by any believer; it was postponed till the candidate had been prepared, often till late in life, so that Christians were divided into two classes, the initiated and the uninitiated; and it was performed only by priests, and on special occasions, such as Easter Eve, with the pageantry of a darkened chamber into which dazzling lights were suddenly introduced, as in the pagan mysteries. The very language used of the mysteries, its ritual, and its hierophants, was now often used by Christians of their rite of initiation.[3] Instead of being a purely personal act, baptism

original sense, applied to a definite type of religion. The notion of secrecy, obscurity, difficulty of comprehension is only secondary.

[1] Cf. Acts VIII, 36: "They came unto a certain water; and the eunuch said, See, here is water; what doth hinder me to be baptized?" The evidence for the points discussed above may be found in *The Beginnings of Christianity*, ed. by F. Jackson and K. Lake, Part I, vol. i, pp. 334 ff.

[2] This is the Pauline interpretation.

[3] Cf. the terms applied to baptism quoted by E. Hatch, *The Influence of Greek Ideas and Usages on the Christian Church* (8th edition), pp. 295 f. and 303 ff.

had become a social institution; as in the mysteries, the initiates were taught a secret formula or pass-word, and the rite itself began to be performed in such secrecy as was characteristic of the mysteries.[1] In other words, the Christian Church was now a secret group of initiates; and the initiation was a supernatural, almost a magical rite.

The Lord's Supper was also transformed under the influence of Greek traditions. At first apparently a memorial act that frequently ended the common meal of Christians, it was soon set apart as a special and awe-inspiring rite, reserved for those alone who had been baptized, and administered only by the priesthood. Here again the language of the mysteries was often employed to describe the Christian ritual;[2] and under its influence the rite was often conceived of not merely as a symbol of the Passion of Jesus and of the worshipper's share in this experience, but, like the sacramental meal of the mysteries, as a miracle enacted before their very eyes, through participation in which salvation was assured.

The earliest Christians were closely associated in communities that insisted on high moral qualifications, and that felt strongly their difference from non-Christians; they, the elect, were set apart from the rest of the world. But by the end of the second century Christians had come to recognize differences among themselves; some still regarded Christianity as essentially a matter of morality; others were more

---

[1] Infant baptism, a comparatively late institution, rests on a still different theory; the child, who is incapable of himself undertaking responsibilities, is accepted as a member of the body of Christians through the pledges of others; and since he is too young to have moral responsibility, the devil, the world, and the flesh that are supposed to be foresworn are not personal sin but the old Adam, "original sin."

[2] Cf. the account of the Eucharist given by Dionysius Areopagiticus, quoted by Hatch, pp. 303 ff.

interested in theology; some held that the Church included only those whose characters were without blemish; others argued that it included not merely the righteous, but also those of less spiritual attainments. As these differences became more apparent, there arose an inner circle of Christians who tried to uphold the earlier ideal of perfecting character, and who expressed their struggle in an ascetic life. Although there were ascetic sects among the Jews, asceticism was not characteristic of Judaism; and the earliest phase of Christianity, with its doctrine of social regeneration, had little of the ascetic. But many Christians now began, like pagan ascetics, to try to set the spirit free from the body by abstinence from certain kinds of food and by celibacy, and by the almost ostentatious simplicity of dress that characterized the Stoic and Cynic philosophers. Some of them went so far as to forego any attempt to reform human society, and withdrew from society, either alone or in small communities, to live a life of contemplation and of communion with God.[1] The ideal reminds one of Plato's and Aristotle's ideals for the philosopher,[2] which undoubtedly were largely responsible for it. The effect on the larger Christian community of the withdrawal of so many of its holiest members was unfortunate: the bond of union among the remaining members was less their zeal for a better moral life than their acquiescence in a theology, and their morality tended to become the average pagan morality of the day. Indeed so significant and influential a writer as St. Ambrose draws not so much from Christian thought as from the Stoic doctrines that he takes from Cicero. His book "is Stoical not only in concep-

[1] In western Europe, monasticism was more apt, in later times, to lead to unselfish devotion to human needs; in eastern Europe were more generally found solitary eremites (the word, and its doublet, "hermits," signifies "deserted") or anchorites ("withdrawers") who altogether left the world.

[2] Pp. 176 f., 258.

tion but also in detail. It makes virtue the highest good. It makes the hope of the life to come a subsidiary and not a primary motive. Its ideal of life is happiness; it holds that a happy life is life according to nature, that it is realized by virtue, and that it is capable of being realized here on earth. Its virtues are the ancient virtues of wisdom and justice, courage and temperance." [1]

The growth of distinctions within the body of Christians was hastened also by other causes. As the belief in the extraordinary efficacy of the sacraments gained ground, it was natural that the early, indiscriminate administration of them should give place to the administration of them by men of especial purity of character; the earlier, secular presbyters ("elders") became priests. The growth of the churches and the acquisition of property made further ecclesiastical organization advantageous; the "overseers" acquired the dignity of bishops. [2] Unlike the priests of the Jewish and of the Greek religions, who were concerned almost wholly with ceremonial acts, the Christian priests acquired also the authority, denied to laymen, of pronouncing on matters of doctrine; they were the spiritual heirs not only of earlier types of priests but of Greek philosophers and rhetoricians and of Jewish rabbis, who taught and preached. For it was believed that these functions could be legitimately exercised only by those who, by the "laying on of hands" in an unbroken sequence, had acquired especial gifts of the Spirit. Thus ordinary laymen came to look for guidance to ecclesiastics, and found their chief aid and comfort in the elaborate ritual, enriched with many kinds of artistic appeal to the senses, that Christianity was developing. This ritual

[1] Hatch, p. 169.

[2] "Priest" is a doublet of "presbyter"; and "bishop" (*episkopos*) means "overseer."

embodied both many of the fundamental traits of Christianity and some of the characteristic elements of the pagan mysteries; and even pagan gods and their shrines and cults were often absorbed under a slightly altered guise.[1]

In many and often in devious ways, then, the religious and philosophic experience of the Greeks helped to mould the course of Christianity, sometimes helpfully, sometimes perhaps to its disadvantage. In suggesting ways in which mystical experience of God could bring the worshipper into a state of blessedness, in the stress that it laid on sacraments, and above all in its insistence that religious experience must be not the contradiction but the culmination of other forms of experience, so that a true philosophy must reckon with them all, the truth of prose as well as the truth of poetry, Greek thought afforded to Christianity incalculable sources of strength. Yet its monotheism had been less secure than that of the Jews, its ethical systems had been more self-regarding than social, and it lacked the supreme advantage of a person, not mythical but historical, who could claim the loyalty of all classes of men. The absence in pagan experience of such a figure, human and yet the expression of the divine, led too often, despite the native optimism of the average Greek and the fortitude of the Greek philosopher, to pessimism. Average human nature, even character ennobled by the reason, failed to give the sense of a newness of life that might be felt by even the humblest Christian.[2] On the

[1] Cf. p. 234; and B. Schmitt, cited by A. Fairbanks, *Greek Religion*, p. 286.

[2] Cf. S. H. Butcher, "The Melancholy of the Greeks," in *Some Aspects of the Greek Genius*. For an instance of the failure of pagan humanism to give satisfaction to even an enlightened Roman, see the letters to and from Cicero on the death of his daughter. Cicero wrote arguments for the immortality of the soul; yet by this loss he is quite unnerved, and thinks not of a surviving personality but of the dissolution of all things. For Stoics and for

whole, during the course of centuries, historic Christianity
has not erred with the pagan humanist in trusting too much
to unassisted human nature; it has at times gone to the
other extreme and appealed to a belief in supernatural
forces which it not only could not explain,—if that were all,
there would be little to blame,—but which was plainly at
variance with the testimony of sound reason and sound
science. And Christian theology has sometimes seemed to
fall into the same error that it inherited from one phase of
Greek philosophy, — the notion that religious experience,
being different from other forms of experience, can safely
ignore them and proceed to formulate a self-contained and
consistent metaphysical theory whose inner consistency is
the sufficient proof of its validity. Sometimes an excessive
devotion to doctrine or to ritual or to ecclesiastical organization has been the result; sometimes faith, sometimes works,
have received men's exclusive attention. Like all venerable
institutions with an ancient heritage, Christianity, though
at first a revolutionary faith, has become on the whole conservative, and has been slow to recognize new types of experience and the thought of individuals outside the fold.
Finally, the negative ascetic tendency that was, after all,
only one phase of Greek life, has in some cases been developed without regard for the equally characteristic Greek
quality of moderation, or for the more positive Christian
virtues; not all ascetics have had the charity of St. Francis of
Assisi. All these criticisms may be included in the single
statement that the Church, consisting of human beings,
though of human beings bent on the noblest of all pursuits,

Romans generally the personality was so closely bound up with material conditions that permanence and immortality were conceivable only as conditions
or institutions (the state or the family) visibly survived. It was otherwise
with Platonism, which upheld immortality and inspired belief in a Heavenly
City. Butcher's essay gives only a hint of this side of the case (p. 176).

has shown evidences of those natural limitations of which human beings can only slowly and imperfectly divest themselves.

We have seen that at every stage of religion there is a tendency for men to conceive of a supreme being somehow in their own image, or at least in terms of their own experience. The ultimate conceptions and foundations of existence have always been objects of intuition, not of demonstration, however much they may be brought logically into relation with the rest of experience. For the Greek the supreme end beyond which he could not appeal was justice, whose majesty he perceived in the natural law that unifies all physical phenomena, and in the ordinances of a stable polity, and in the processes of the artist and the philosopher. For him the part was to be explained by reference to the whole, and the whole was not greatly concerned about the parts. His God was a just God, but was generally as cold and unsympathetic a being as abstractions are apt to be. The best hope that he could offer an unfortunate or a sinful man who was in distress was that by the transmigration of souls he might in a new existence choose a better lot. For the Jew the supreme object of intuition was a Father who loved his children, who was forever revealing on historic occasions the signs of his interest and mercy, and who was ready to forgive penitent sinners. The Christian believed not merely that "underneath are the everlasting arms" but that a supreme revelation of divine love had been vouchsafed in the person of Jesus, and found an all-sufficient release from suffering in the promise, "Come unto me, all ye that labor and are heavy laden, and I will give you rest." Yet difficulties remained. How could a good God tolerate evil? Was he powerless to prevent it? Why were the righteous allowed to suffer, and the sinners to prosper? Was mere repentance enough to satisfy a just God? In the attempt to solve such questions Christians have often borrowed from the thought of the Greeks. Justice does not mean an account closed in this life but a spiritual satisfaction of the largest sort. In order to preserve the moral economy of the universe, it has often been supposed that divine justice was satisfied, once and for all, by a divine sacrifice in the fact of the crucifixion. But in the end the reconciliation of justice and mercy, like a mother's love, remains a paradox and a mystery.[1]

Men's religious differences consist far less of small points of doctrine that could be reconciled by argument than of fundamental assumptions that rest on temperament and on early environment. Some men are born mystics, others are logicians; some delight in ritual, others in philanthropy; there are individualists as well as traditionalists. It is almost impossible, perhaps not even desirable, to make them see eye to eye; on some matters, wise men will argue not in order to convince, but only for the exhilaration of argument. In fact, there is no single valid form of religious experience; reason and intuition must both have play, and religious truth is the result of an experience that moves between these two poles, clarifying and deepening the life now by one and now by the other means. Probably a single, universal religion should not be expected to emerge before men's natures have more in common. Yet a far greater degree of coöperation or even of union among Christians of different kinds is by no means impossible. For example, the useless competition in the country and in small towns between churches that differ only as to trifling matters of dogma or of ritual can be, and often is, ended by federation. Many of these differences arose in the past from a failure to see Christianity

[1] As St. Paul knew; cf. Romans, chaps. ix ff.

as an historical development, growing from a vital seed and gaining nourishment from many sources. Sometimes the nourishment proved dangerous. The draughts of Greek metaphysics, for example, that tended to fix Christianity in dogmas and creeds which could not deal with new experience, have not been an unmixed blessing. But that is no reason for avoiding metaphysics; it is rather a reason for finding a truer and more inclusive metaphysics, for men cannot avoid having opinions till they lose all their sense of wonder.

Our study of the Greek's relation to the universe began with the childhood of the race; it kept pace with their advance in knowledge and in character; it has found its consummation, so far as religion is concerned, in Christianity. A better developed historical sense will tell us what in Christianity is essential and what is accidental; it will also show how far the contributions of Greek experience have been valuable, and to what extent they may be further developed. For Christianity itself cannot help developing as men's needs and powers continue to grow. It may even absorb something from the profound experience of the Orient. We may well agree with the open-minded attitude of John Robinson. "For he was very confident," we are told that he said in his farewell address to the Pilgrims, "the Lord had more truth and light yet to break forth out of his holy Word."

CHAPTER VIII

THE MEANING OF HUMANISM

MANY times in the discussion of the experience of the Greeks we have made use of the word "humanism," which seemed especially fitted to express their characteristic qualities. But the word has gathered much dust during its long history, and men may well differ in their understanding of it. Is humanity opposed to divinity, or is human nature opposed to animal nature? Says Macbeth:

> I dare do all that may become a man;
> Who dares do more is none.

And Lady Macbeth taunts him:

> What beast was 't then
> That made you break this enterprise to me?
> When you durst do it, then you were a man,
> And, to be more than what you were, you would
> Be so much more the man.

Is humanism, then, the same thing as humanitarianism? Or is it courage? Is it opposed to strict standards, as we seem to imply when we say, "Oh, do be human!" or when we sigh, "Human, all too human"? Or is it identical with a thorough knowledge of Greek and Latin Literature? Or, again, is it a conglomerate of all these? One who aspires to the name of humanist should at least know what he means by the term, and what right he has to his interpretation of it.

Any definition of humanism must begin with some recognition of the place of man in his environment. The Jews, it has been truly remarked, fixed their gaze so steadily on the conception of deity that their ideas about human nature and relationships were far less fully developed.[1] Though they asked the question, "What is Man, that Thou art mindful of him," it was rather the Greeks than the Jews who sought most for the answer. The Greeks of the Homeric poems clearly distinguished between gods and men, however much like men their gods might be; and always in later times voices were lifted in warning against ambition that exceeds mortal limits. So Pindar writes: "Strive not to be a Zeus. . . . Mortal aims befit mortal men."[2] In a more reflective age than Homer's, mythology tended to give place to speculation. Pythagoras, we are told, distinguished men as intermediate between God and the "other animals." And while physicists investigated the laws of nature, man became the subject of a separate investigation on the part of the Sophists and of Socrates and his followers. The Delphic oracle had enjoined self-knowledge; but what was the nature of the self? What laws governed human nature? Was man an animal a little higher than the beasts, to be described, classified, and dismissed, or was he capable of development into something still higher? And if he was capable of development, what was to be the standard of measurement?

The answer of the typical Greek was apt to emphasize the value of intelligence, which could make the most of a difficult world, of shrewdness and curiosity, rather than of moral qualities. Of the poet Theognis, even Xenophon thought that he was "concerned with nothing else but virtue and wickedness, and that his poetry is a treatise on man, just as if a horse-fancier should write a treatise on horses."[3] Yet

[1] R. W. Livingstone, *The Greek Genius and its Meaning to Us*, p. 138.

[2] But see the fine rebuke to this attitude in Aristotle (Eth. Nic. X, 7, 8); man should exercise his noblest, most divine part, the intelligence, and should thus "put on immortality."

[3] Xenophon, quoted by Stobæus, Flor. 88, 14.

the whole tone of Theognis is worldly-wise, if not cynical. In reading Herodotus, one is conscious of a mind that has more of curiosity than of sympathy; he has the inquisitiveness of the character in Terence who is responsible for the much-quoted (and somewhat misunderstood) remark, "Humani nil a me alienum puto"; but he is a thorough Greek in his assumption of superiority over barbarians, which is based largely on the intellect. Of his contemporaries, few condescended so far as Euripides to dignify average men and women; and Euripides alone gains Mrs. Browning's epithet, "the human." Aristophanes appreciates the sturdy peasant; but his conservatism has no toleration for the peasant who meddles with the affairs of his betters. Although Athens is now a political democracy, in literature the aristocratic ideal is still strong. Even the great chorus in the "Antigone" of Sophocles that recounts the wonders of earth and its crowning wonder, man, makes more of the strength and skill of man that conquers nature than of any unselfish intelligence or of the satisfaction of human fellowship.[1] Of the notion of a better world, or of progress, or of improvement in human nature there was among most Greeks before the fourth century hardly a trace; the Golden Age was always seen in the past.

Naturally enough it is in Plato, in whom apparent opposites are often fused, that we find the first important solution of our problem. Plato distrusts the average man, whose natural instincts are no sound basis for conduct. But in the gradual ascendency of man's rational nature over his instincts he finds the grounds of his hope for a better type of man. Yet the solution of Plato and even that of Aristotle tend to limit the possibility of dignity and happiness to a small fragment of humanity, since few men have the brains

[1] Ant. 332 ff.; so too, on the whole, Lucretius V, 925–1457.

to achieve real progress from the Platonic or Aristotelian point of view. Unless we are ready to deny to all but the lucky few any great intrinsic worth or any power of progress except what outward advantages they can borrow from others, we must grant with the Stoic and with the Christian the value of all men of good will. But we may still be wise if, with Plato and Aristotle, we recognize degrees of human values that depend at least in part on intellectual gifts. The sinner may be of great value because of his capacity for repentance, but till he does repent he is still a sinner with all his mischief-making powers; the cretin remains a cretin until his thyroid gland has been properly fed; the Latin has greater capacities than the Esquimau. Whatever the humanist may prove to be, he will face the facts and will not claim for man either more or less than his due.

The ordinary Greek of the fifth century or of the fourth century was perhaps not fully conscious that he was some day to serve as the type of the humanist, any more than he was conscious of being an ancient; it is we who view him from our vantage-ground and see to what a large extent he made himself the measure of all things. And this he did partly because his literature, in which splendid types of humanity were set forth, and his religion, which was largely anthropomorphic, developed sooner and more rapidly than his science and his philosophy. This was fortunate, I think; but it was fortunate only because the Greek was himself instinctively a sane and sociable sort of creature. The result was that when science and philosophy came into being they were developed chiefly as phases of humanism, interested in ethics and politics and the satisfaction of man's curiosity, giving a rational basis for what instinct had often surmised; only metaphysics, as it came to be divorced alike from daily life and from science, turning hypothesis into dogma and dogma into propaganda, entered into a perilous alliance with Christian theology, and became one of the chief sources of schism, inquisition, and persecution. *Tantum religio potuit suadere malorum.* True religion, meanwhile,— the religion based both on everyday experience and on those rarer experiences that so far transcend our usual sources of knowledge that we agree to call them divine,— true religion found nothing to lose and much to gain by an alliance with true humanism,— the humanism that proves all things and holds fast to that which is good. There is not so much difference, after all, between Socrates, the apostle of reason who nevertheless heard a divine voice, and St. Francis of Assisi, and John Woolman. And if the claim of Christianity to an exclusive loyalty seems at first to prevent any effective coöperation with a humanism that recognizes only different levels of human experience, a common ground may yet be found in the catholicity of the humanist who can easily recognize as valid the claim of all that is most vital in Christianity, even if some Christians could easily dispense with much that the humanist holds dear.

For the ancient Greek,— to attempt a generalization,— humanism meant the attempt to train himself in accordance with the types of character with which his history and his literature made him familiar; to recognize in physical forces nothing more than the theatre for the human drama, and in supernatural powers nothing alien to his own methods of thought and his own moral standards. In a word, he either was himself the measure of all things, or else,— and here I am thinking chiefly of Plato and his followers,— he felt that by self-discipline he could create within himself a microcosm that corresponded to the divine order outside him which he held to be independent and absolute. In either case, man was at the centre of his experience, as, indeed, he must always be; only it was a profound and original achievement on the part of the Greek that recognized this truth.

Our acquaintance with Greek humanism was for centuries at second hand, through the medium of the literature of Rome, the proud city that took captive Greece and was herself overcome by the culture of Greece.[1] It is the custom to say that Latin literature is only an imitation of Greek literature; and I need add nothing to give greater currency to the saying. It is true that Latin literature has not the originality of Greek; nor did it ever pretend to such originality. Roman poets used to boast of their borrowings from Greece. But we have already seen that convention and imitation are an incident, and a highly useful incident, in all art;[2] the only question is how the thing is done. Virgil plundered Homer and Hesiod and Theocritus, and was not the less Virgil. He realized the difficulty of his feat; and we are told that he said that it is easier to steal the club of Hercules than to appropriate to one's own context a line of Homer,— as any one might prove to his own satisfaction by trying it. The challenge is still open. The glory of the literature of Rome is that it knew how to absorb from Greece what it wished,— myth or verse-form or tenet,— without in the least ceasing to be the literature of Rome. The reason for this, I suspect, is not that Rome assumed Greek culture like borrowed plumage while keeping all the while her own body of faith. The real reason, I think, is that at bottom the faith of the Roman, like that of the Greek, is humanism; when he borrows most from the Greek, it is to enable him to express more imaginatively and more eloquently the faith that is already in him. For an example, Horace will do as well as another. He is a Hellenist, even a

---

[1] Græcia capta ferum victorem cepit. Horace, Epistles II, 1. 156 f.

[2] So "the man who plants cabbages imitates, too."

plagiarist, if we insist; yet when he is most himself he is most Roman, when he tells of ancient piety and of Regulus, and when he asks, "Of what avail are mere laws without men's characters?" [1] Horace's question, however, prompted by patriotic misgivings, really goes back in substance to the remark of Aristotle: "Law has no power to command obedience except that of habit." [2] If the foundation of law on the character of a people strikes us as a commonplace, it is only because we have been habituated to our legacy from Greece and Rome; there are despotisms even to-day where it is not a commonplace.

The Roman, trained to revere the *mores* of his fathers and to strive to emulate the great exemplars of national virtues, was at first suspicious of Greek culture. It was new-fangled, frivolous, apt to unsettle men's ideas, and to breed the dilettante and the voluptuary. In some cases, to be sure, the results of the introduction of Greek culture confirmed this suspicion. But on the whole the story of Roman education from the days of the Scipionic Circle well into the Empire was largely that of successful adaptation of Greek ideas to the needs of disciplined Romans.[3] Greece could teach Rome little of thrift and loyalty to kin and country; but she could do much to clarify the Roman's ideas and to show him the value of beauty. In this twofold

---

[1] Quid leges sine moribus vanæ proficiunt? Odes III, 24, 35. There is an echo of this in the possibly satirical intent of Tacitus in remarking of the Germans, "among them good character is of more avail than are good laws elsewhere." Germania, 19. In his sorrow over the degeneracy of Rome, Tacitus perhaps idealizes here too much the noble savage of the German forest.

[2] ὁ ... νόμος ἰσχὺν οὐδεμίαν ἔχει πρὸς τὸ πείθεσθαι παρὰ τὸ ἔθος Pol. 2, 1269a20. ἔθος and *mores* both emphasize the importance of habit in the formation of character.

[3] Cf. W. W. Fowler, *Social Life at Rome in the Age of Cicero*, pp. 103–121, 168–203.

way, in the stress of practical life and in the hours of relaxation, she fostered what was best in Rome. Cicero did not overstate the case in his famous digression on poetry in the Speech for Archias: "The study of letters sharpens the minds of young men and charms old men; in times of prosperity it is a distinction, in times of misfortune it holds out a refuge and a consolation; it is a delight to us when we are at home, and is no impediment to us when abroad; it passes the night with us, and accompanies us on our travels and our sojourns in the country." Indeed Cicero himself might well serve as our best champion and exemplar of Roman *humanitas*. Drawn by circumstances and by ambition into a political career which must by all outward standards be judged a failure, yet which set forth most eloquently for all time the conservative republican ideal, in his leisure and in the days of political impotence and of personal grief he found consolation in literature. And here, though devoid of creative ability, Cicero contrived by means of Greek formulæ to set forth the principles of propriety in conduct, in expression, and in belief. Nothing is more valuable in his writings, as nothing is more characteristic, than his conception of the ideal orator. Against the growing tendency to think of oratory as a matter of mere verbal technique, Cicero holds that the true orator must speak from the fullness of a complete education. "Wisdom without eloquence," he says, "is of little use to a state, while eloquence without wisdom is often positively harmful, and never of any value." [1] And the *De Oratore* is throughout a defense of humanism and of all-round training for the career of oratory.

We need not limit ourselves to Cicero, if we wish examples of Roman humanism. I have spoken of Virgil, who knew how to fuse Arcadia and Sicily with Mantua, Hesiod with

[1] *De Inventione*, I, 1.

Lucretius, Greek epic with Roman saga; to whom the *fatum Romanum* and the human hearts of Dido and Turnus alike were known. I have spoken of Horace, that winsome champion of opposing causes who has something for every one; humble in origin, yet the associate of the most distinguished men; soldier under Brutus and court poet under Augustus; lover both of society and of seclusion; sensitive to all that is attractive, but slave to no desire; bachelor and poet of love; master of lyric and of pedestrian verse; mingler of Epicureanism and Stoicism. His is no colorless average of qualities, but the gaiety that has reckoned with sadness and the simplicity that scorns wealth not through ignorance of it but because it knows all too well what wealth means.

But it would be idle to begin a list of Roman humanists; we should have to include too many names. We should find Christian writers, devoted to the pagans, compounding with their consciences: St. Jerome, pricked by the taunt, "Ciceronianus es, non Christianus"; St. Augustine converted to "philosophy," by which he means Christianity, by the reading of Cicero's *Hortensius*,[1] and like Clement of Alexandria and Lactantius and Ambrose and many another, pleading for Cicero and for pagan letters generally as part of a Christian education; Prudentius writing hymns in Virgilian and Horatian measures; Boethius gathering up the garments of Plato and Aristotle and wearing them so much as one to the manner born that some have failed to see the Christian beneath them. The monasteries of the Middle Ages at their best found the basis of education in pagan culture; at their worst they handed on the knowledge of humanism to better days. The roots of the *trivium*[2] and the *quadrivium*[3] of the Middle Ages go back to Plato's scheme of education. The

---

[1] Conf. III, 4. [2] Grammar, Logic, and Rhetoric.
[3] Music, Arithmetic, Geometry, and Astronomy.

universities more boldly found a large place within their walls for the study of the Classics, and gradually turned from the service of the church to the service of the world outside as well. Even in earlier days, however, humanism was in complete accord with the purpose of the universities; the motto of Bishop William of Wykeham, "Manners Makyth Man," is still borne by his two foundations, Winchester College and New College, Oxford. At the Scotch universities the chairs of "Humanity" are still held by the professors of Latin; and the undergraduate training in Classics at Oxford culminates in the study of philosophy and ancient history, still known as Literæ Humaniores. Particularly in English and American schools and universities the academic ideal has always included the all-round social development of the student; the purpose has been by tolerating or even by encouraging athletics and other kinds of association to produce not merely students but men.

Not all humanism, of course, has been confined to formal education. When Italy and then northern Europe rediscovered the classical literatures and found that life had once been lived, on the whole successfully, in a world that knew nothing of monastery and cathedral, the classical humanities were naturally thought of by many as the antithesis of the study of divinity, and humanism came almost to mean a revival of paganism. For some humanists of this period asceticism and theology (both of which owed much to Platonism) gave way to the cultivation of all that was appealing in the present, together with the flesh-pots of this pleasant world. They knew late Greek literature better than classical Greek literature, and they knew Latin better than Greek.[1] Some of them, in their zest for living and their

[1] Cf. S. L. Wolff, "The Greek Gift to Civilization," reprinted by L. Cooper in *The Greek Genius and its Influence*, pp. 218 ff.

joy at versatile mastery of many arts, forgot that the older, pagan humanists had subjected themselves, so far as they were able, to laws hardly less stringent than those of the Christian Church; and of these their supposed heirs knew nothing. Benvenuto Cellini, fascinating personality though he was, is not a figure that we should wish to duplicate many times.

It would not be fair to blame true humanism for the aberrations of some of its sons; and at its best it has many aspects. Petrarch in solitude and Lorenzo in his court and his Academy were also in the humanistic tradition. And this is not the place to attempt, even in summary, to enumerate the results of the classical influence in European letters and thought. Our obvious debts have been chronicled often enough. We need only read Milton for an example of a profound assimilation of divers classical elements,— Homer and Euripides, Virgil and Ovid, Plato and Theocritus and Horace. Or, for wit and familiarity with ancient writers and a shallow philosophy that pretends to the name of humanism, we may read Alexander Pope. In these men we have the true humanism and the tinsel. Or follow the course of Platonism outside of technical philosophy; we shall meet it, of course, in the New Testament and in the dogmas of the early Church; it envelopes the Dream of Scipio and the revelation of Anchises to Æneas; it is in St. Augustine's City of God and in all the countless Utopias that men have ever dreamed of; it speaks in Dante and in Spenser and in Milton and in a host of minor poets in Italy and France and England in the sixteenth and the seventeenth centuries. Sidney speaks, to confound the deaf who will not understand Plato; "and that the poet hath the Idea is manifest." Wordsworth and Coleridge and Shelley in their own experience bear testimony to the truth of Platonism, the "love of the unseen and eternal

cherished by one who rejoices in the seen and temporal." [1]
One might almost say that most of all great poetry is some-
how, consciously or unconsciously, Platonic; one might
argue that much of modern drama and the dependent arts
that depict character are largely indebted to Plato's followers Aristotle and Theophrastus for their conceptions of
normal and of abnormal human nature.[2] And if we go on to
include our debts to the ancients in the other arts and in
philosophy, religion, law, and science, — fields of activity
that are indispensable to one another, — it is easy to understand why "the humanities" have seemed to include almost
the whole of human experience.

Of course we know that not every one to-day accepts such
an ideal. And I think that those who quarrel with it do so
generally on one of two large and plausible grounds. Either
they are opposed to humanism as such,— this attack is
usually launched in the name of some conception of science,
— or else they admit the claims of humanism, but object to
limiting it to classical studies. Since each of these attacks is
neither wholly justified nor wholly without reason, they
deserve consideration.

Let us first meet the frank opponent of humanism. "In
earlier days," we can imagine him saying, "there was perhaps a good case for the Classics when they contained almost all that was known. But how can they expect to hold
their own in the face of the developments of modern science?

[1] J. A. Stewart, "Platonism in English Literature," in G. S. Gordon,
English Literature and the Classics, p. 30.

[2] Cf. G. S. Gordon, *op. cit.*, "Theophrastus and his Imitators"; and L.
Cooper, *The Greek Genius and its Influence*, pp. 11 f. Addison is a good
example of the humanist, both in the interests that he derives from classical
authors and in his outlook on contemporary life. He quotes and translates,
as the motto for one of his papers, a phrase of Martial: hominem mea pagina
sapit — "humanity is the predominant flavor of my book."

Classical literature is always emphasizing the importance of man, even of the individual man and his powers; but we have learned how infinitely small is man's place in the universe, and how little he can do to change the course of events. Indeed, since science tends to reduce everything to a chain of causes and effects and to the slow and inevitable evolution of types, and since Nature shows no sentiment or favoritism toward any of her children, is it not nobler to admit our weakness, and to find what consolation we can in our increasing knowledge of the processes of nature and in such practical uses of this knowledge as mechanical inventions give us?"

If I were to venture a reply in the name of humanism, I should resist the temptation to convict the scientist of plagiarizing from Lucretius, and should answer to this effect. The humanist has learned from the Greeks to revere the disinterested seeker for scientific truth. He rejoices with the scientist as more and more is learned of natural processes. But he has also learned from the Greeks, and he notices that modern scientists agree, that, even apart from matters of observation, into which the judgment often enters, there is still in science a vast deal, perhaps even an increasing amount, of hypothesis with regard to ultimate principles, so that man remains the measure of all things. And, in particular, although Nature has no favorites, and as willingly lets die a genius as an idiot, we do not. Man's place in the universe may be small, but we prize the more the Shakspere or the Newton who makes that place desirable and valuable to us. Man is an animal in the evolutionary sequence; but unlike all other animals he can make use of the past experience of the race, and he can, within limits, act with a view to results in the future. He is partly, but not wholly, as some of our novelists would have us believe, the resultant of past conditions and psychological complexes; but he can also act as a personality, as a living individual. It is sheer assumption to hold otherwise; to argue for example, from sequences of physical causation (which are, by the way, only inferences) that the will is merely the sum of physical impressions. All the relevant evidence, that is to say, our own experience, tells another story; our action is at least part of the time governed by ideas; it is "awareness," as well as "behavior." And this belief is enough for humanism. Ancient literature is founded on this conviction: that man is engaged in a precarious struggle against nature; that he can command nature by obeying her; and that by understanding himself he can govern himself. The struggle is so precarious that the Greek sometimes thought of the opposition as a thwarting fate or destiny. But he was not often a fatalist. He was not carried automatically on the tide of events either toward a better or toward a worse state; the issue rested on his will. However much, even in the drama, the individual seemed to be in the clutches of circumstance, there were always august moments when he could, with greater or with less realization of the consequences, choose his course and set in motion the wheels of events.[1] Humanism, therefore, has always held that it matters how we choose; and it matters now rather more than less, in the day of mechanical inventions; if we do not master them, they will master us. Textile mills and poison gas are not things to play with. And in our world events seldom happen; men are responsible for them. Furthermore, there is no possibility of predicting scientifically how men will act, because we cannot analyze their information and their emotions and their desires as the chemist can analyze his samples; even in psychoanalysis there is always an imponderable residuum. All

[1] Cf. p. 197, n. 2.

that we can do is to cultivate by our acquaintance with human experience, past and present, the power of judging human motives; even then it is largely guess-work. This is the more important since we are scientists or lawyers or business men only eight hours a day for perhaps about forty years, whereas we are men and members of families, and citizens for, we may hope, twenty-four hours a day and for threescore years and ten.

So far I have been reasoning with the scientist, hoping that in his studies he will not relegate man to a subdivision of the animal kingdom, but will consent to include his science as a part, and a most valuable part, of the programme of humanism.[1] Yet even if I have in any degree convinced him, I have still to turn to those who believe in recognizing human values, but who begrudge classical studies any privileged position.

It is true that in Modern History and Government and Economics and in Modern Literature there are subjects of immense importance, which are often called the "New Humanities." They have the power and the charm that always attach to the things that lie close at hand and that seem to express our own lives. I am far from having any quarrel with them; but I am sorry for any one who thinks that they are the sum total of humanism. For one thing, they lack

[1] For an eloquent plea for harmony between science and humanism from the pen of a distinguished physician, see the late Sir William Osler's address as President of the (English) Classical Association, 1919 (published in the Proceedings of the Classical Association, vol. xvi; also reprinted separately under the title, *The Old Humanities and the New Science*). It ends with a quotation from Hippocrates: "' Where there is the love of man (philanthropia) there is also the love of the craft (of medicine).' Memorable sentence indeed! in which for the first time was coined the magic word *philanthropy*, and conveying the subtle suggestion that perhaps in this combination the longings of humanity may find their solution, and Wisdom — philosophia — at last be justified of her children."

context and perspective and the discipline that comes only with the comparison of institutions and ideas as they have existed in widely differing periods and environments. Then, too, they are apt to be too highly specialized or subdivided; they describe conditions or experiences within too limited an area. Economics is severed from Government, and Government from Ethics; and all these are distinct from "mere literature." I feel a more wholesome attitude in Plato's "Republic," in which all elements are fused, and the contact with actuality is not divorced from that preoccupation with the ideal that is of the essence of poetry. The real error of the New Humanists is their assumption that History or Government or Economics or even the novel must be either a science, dealing with isolated facts and with eventualities that can be predicted, or else the gossamer of whim and fancy. But life is neither of these. It is the interplay of wills that have come to hold certain things dear and that will struggle for them; and history, like literature, is not a science but an art of understanding the present through the past.[1] For, strictly speaking, there is no present known to us by anything else than immediate experience. Apart from this, all that we know is the more or the less remote past; and the humanist in his attempt to understand the present will go back into the past as far as he continues to find significant experience. And since history is an art, the historian and the economist and the statesman need to know both the motives of men as they see them and the larger world of men whose motives have happily been recorded in the past. Their task is one of intimate understanding and sympathy;

[1] Perhaps Godwin and Comte and others who have dreamed of a scientific perfecting of society did not reckon enough with the obstinacy of human nature, which has far more in common with the active, artistic, selective temperament than with the engineering sciences.

and it happens that few disciplines could be devised that more completely test all the powers of sympathy and understanding than artistic translation from a foreign language. That is the best reason for making one's own translations rather than using another's. In any case the value of the "New Humanities" depends very largely on the extent to which they fall into their place as a phase of humanism.

The churchman will approve of the humanist's insistence on values and standards and his refusal to regard himself as wholly immersed in the flux of mechanical causality and of unconscious evolution. But he may grieve that the humanist is not more ready to assent to fixed standards outside his own experience. And here I think the humanist will agree that standards should by all means be as objective as possible. He will find much that is beautiful and something that is disappointing in the prayer of Socrates:[1] "O beloved Pan and other gods here present, grant me to become fair within. Let my outward possessions be such as are favorable to my inward life. May I think the wise man rich. Give me so much gold as only the temperate man can bear or carry." He will find in this prayer an exquisite sense of justice and of resignation; but he will find it hard to explain how its author could have become the martyr that he was with nothing more ardent in his nature than the philosophic temper. Perhaps in some rare cases that is enough, and even the golden mean has its heroes and martyrs. But most men, if their loyalty is not to flag, need faith in a personal Lord; and the ardor that says, "Thy will be done" is not exactly the same as the sense of justice. The humanist will welcome religious convictions as a precious part of human experience. He will not on that account forget that religious experience has had its vicissitudes, or that the conception of God and

[1] *Phædrus*, 279b.

of the will of God has varied with the passing of time. He may find it hard, without a close scrutiny of special circumstances, to discover a content for the will of God or for the Golden Rule. He may welcome a kindred spirit in the writer of the curious "Saying of Jesus," lately discovered: "The kingdom of heaven is within you; and whoever shall know himself shall find it. (Strive therefore?) to know yourselves, and ye shall be aware that ye are the sons of the (almighty?) Father." [1] And this he will feel to be akin to Benjamin Franklin's "project of arriving at moral perfection" and his desire to "conquer all that either natural inclination, custom, or company might lead [him] into," and his attempt to ground the virtues on a wholly secular basis: "vicious actions," he says, "are not hurtful because they are forbidden, but forbidden because they are hurtful, the nature of man alone considered." [2] The definition would doubtless satisfy Aristotle, but probably not St. Paul. It must be the task of the humanist to mediate between churchman and pagan, and to discover the proper relation between man's highest experience, his religious intuitions, and all the other elements in his experience. In this task the humanist will play the rôle of the sympathetic historian, studying the characteristic conditions and types of religious experience, distinguishing so far as possible the accidental from the permanent and historical fact from poetry. He will remember that humanism without mysticism has usually ended in pessimism, but that mysticism uncriticized always becomes fanatical. He will not forget that in humanizing the world the chief force has been historical Christianity and in particular the virtues that on the whole are most characteristically Christian,—faith and humility. Perhaps he will recall the words

---

[1] Quoted by J. Adam, *The Religious Teachers of Greece*, p. 341.
[2] "Autobiography."

of William James: "There is a state of mind, known to religious men, but to no others, in which the will to assert ourselves and hold our own has been displaced by a willingness to close our mouths and be as nothing in the floods and waterspouts of God. In this state of mind, what we most dreaded has become the habitation of our safety, and the hour of our moral death has turned into our spiritual birthday."[1] This may seem a paradox; but it is a paradox that experience verifies. Surely the humanist, if he understands his Plato, believes that it is necessary to lose one's life in order to save it, and that the deepest things in life must always be expressed in the form of poetry. So the humanist will not, I think, explain away religion; he will rather try to understand its meaning and its value and to use its experience. And in doing so he will necessarily trace in its history a certain progress.

Progress is a surprisingly modern conception.[2] The Greeks thought of succeeding ages, usually going from better to worse, or of cycles, perhaps with their own political revolutions in mind. But they did not believe in "one far-off, divine event to which the whole creation moves"; nor did they believe that progress leads to perfection. And as things were, they held that few men could be long or greatly happy. Christianity brought the conception of a divine kingdom gradually to be realized and of human blessings more widely diffused. During the Middle Ages, despite the great work done by and through the Church, the notion,

---

[1] *The Varieties of Religious Experience*, p. 47.

[2] Cf. *Progress and History*, edited by F. S. Marvin, Oxford, 1916: esp. the introductory essay, by the editor, on "The Idea of Progress"; "Progress as an Ideal of Action," by J. A. Smith; and "Progress and Hellenism," by F. M. Stawell. See also J. B. Bury, *The Greek Historians*, Lect. VIII; and his *The Idea of Progress*, Macmillan, 1920; and W. R. Inge, *The Idea of Progress*, Oxford, 1920.

largely due to Platonism and disseminated through Christianity, that this world is evil, led to intense preoccupation with the saving of souls for the next world and to the neglect of glaring abuses; and feudalism, though better than utter lawlessness, was a form of tyranny. With the Renaissance came a new interest in the delights and the possibilities of this world and a feeling that they should be shared as widely as possible. Especially was this the case as science unfolded its story and man's active powers seemed to be enhanced. So Descartes hoped that science would make us the masters of nature not solely for pleasure, but principally for the "preservation and improvement of health which is both the foundation of all other goods and the means of strengthening the spirit itself." [1] The voice of Turgot is typical of the hope of eighteenth-century thinkers: "The total mass of the human race marches continually, though sometimes slowly, towards an ever-increasing perfection." Evolutionary doctrines seemed to support these hopes, and even where religious motives no longer operated, humanitarianism was strong. For the love of God was substituted the love of man; and for faith, good works. There is to-day no word that calls forth so quick a response from the average man as the word "progress."

In the notion of progress dangers undoubtedly lurk. Men have sometimes thought that because God has planned everything, man need or can do nothing; or that evolution or mechanical necessity will inevitably take its course, so that there is no field left for us. The effect on the will is devastating; incentive is wholly removed, yet any sort of action can be condoned. Predestination or evolution or economic law, if elevated into an omnipotent abstraction, deprives progress of all moral significance for man. Against this notion the

[1] Discours de la Méthode.

humanist of course protests that real human progress is the result of intelligent and purposive human action. Things that we value do not, as a rule, just happen. We note conditions and currents, and undertake to help or to deflect the stream, or even to resist it, for not all change is necessarily for the better. If we find that scientific discoveries and inventions accelerate the diffusion of the things that we value, so much the better; yet we must not forget that shrapnel is no respecter of persons, and that the printing-press can turn out bad books as rapidly as good books. The direction of events still depends on man's judgment.

Progress is, in a sense, a fact, which can be measured by reference to fairly stable ideals. In another sense, progress is only an ideal, a sense of direction. Why should we ever hope to reach the end of the road? Well, as a matter of fact we do not hope personally to reach it. Yet we are not satisfied unless we cling to the road and make some headway on it. And as to our power of making headway we learn much, both positively and negatively, from science; we learn what is perhaps even more to the point from human history in its largest sense. "The ideal of Progress which we present to ourselves is and must be one which is partly determined or limited by past achievement and partly enlarged by the study of what powers higher than our own have accomplished and are accomplishing. The formation of it must move constantly between a respect for what has been achieved and a worship, so to speak, for what is far better than anything that has yet been or become fact, and therefore incumbent or imperative on us." [1]

We have noticed that there is a general tendency for human experience to be secularized; for religious motives to give place, for example, to humanitarianism. But humani-

[1] J. A. Smith, *op. cit.*, p. 309.

tarianism is not identical with religion, or even an adequate substitute for religion. Not that religion does not ordinarily stimulate humanitarian enterprises, or that humanism has not fostered them. The Greeks were instinctively quick to feel pity and tenderness toward the young and the weak, and felt a difference between themselves and barbarians on this score: there were some things that no Greek would do. This ideal, enlarged by other humane and liberal qualities and inculcated by education, became by the fourth century a conception of man as such. "What a fine thing is man," says Menander, "when he *is* man." [1] And for a more modern version of the whole idea, let us hear Chaucer: "Pitie renneth sone in gentil herte." Yes, in well-bred minds the humane sentiments are indeed instinctive. But they are apt to remain at the level of instincts, if they have no contact with religion. What if I do not happen to feel pity when I should? What if the Athenians had not repented of their cruel decision to put to death the Mitylenæans just in time to save them? [2] What of the fact that under great excitement they *did* carry out their cruel design against the Melians? Instinctive humanitarianism, even rational humanitarianism, does not seem to be proof against sudden reverses. Well, it may be said, neither is religion; do we not know of persecutions and inquisitions carried on deliberately and in the name of religion? Certainly, and I have no defense for them, except that they were carried on under a perverted conception of religion which it is the business of humanism to correct. Nevertheless the prevailing influence of religion has been on the side of humanitarianism, since religion has given to secular moral progress the sanction of

[1] Cf. C. B. Gulick, "Notions of Humanity among the Greeks," in *Harvard Essays on Classical Subjects.*

[2] *Ibid.*, pp. 47 f.

deep personal conviction that comes from permanent and transcendent experience. Secular humanitarianism will find itself losing headway if it loses the momentum of centuries of religious sanction. However irrational it may seem, with most men the conviction "I know that God wills this" is a stronger motive than "I feel this" or even than "I see the logic of this." Our conception of the nature of God may change, and may even depend very considerably on our feelings and our logic; but it is not wholly composed of these, and religion is not likely to be wholly resolved into a form of hallucination.

On the other hand we must guard against the notion that humanitarianism is the whole of humanism.[1] Of the nobility of humanitarianism there can be no question; it tries to extend as widely as possible the peculiar opportunities that we ascribe to man as man, recognizing no distinctions of wealth or race or age or sex, and feeling a particular tenderness for the young, the weak, and the suffering. It is opposed to privilege and vested interest, to war and violence. In many ways it seems to be a practical manifestation of the essence of Christianity. Yet in many practical phases it is contrary to the soundest principles of humanism. Religion agrees with humanism that in the world of heartless physical fact, which recognizes no values, man's action must be based on a recognition or a creation of values. But Christianity by holding that we are all brothers, as the sons of God, has encouraged humanitarians to regard all men as of absolutely equal value. Humanism has been more anxious to insist on different values. Though we are all human beings and should treat each other with elementary consideration and respect, we do differ greatly in our powers, physical, intellectual, and moral. Racial differences must be faced; men and

[1] For an ancient protest against this identification, cf. A. Gellius, XIII, 16.

women are not identical in their capacities; and individuals vary enormously in their inheritance and in what they have made of themselves. To take a trivial instance, the indiscriminate use of such words as "lady" and "gentleman," — words which, all snobbishness aside, should convey a notion of real personal distinction,— not only confers no compliment on the undeserving recipient but destroys all meaning in the terms themselves. This is, as I have said, a trivial instance; but the humanitarian would like to obliterate differences as far as possible. Up to an uncertain point we all sympathize with him; then doubts occur. How far is it wise to educate all men alike? Shall we adopt the slogan, "One man, one vote, one job, one college degree," and scale everything to the level of the average man,— supposing that we can find him? But what right have we to take this hypothetical average man as our standard, rather than the exceptional man? Are we wise to tax the thrifty farmer for the support of institutions for the feeble-minded, and to allow the feeble-minded to multiply faster than his intellectual superiors? [1] Is the state necessarily right in all its actions? It needs no Carlyle or Nietzsche to proclaim the value of the individual, of the great and exceptional man. [2] We need go no further than Plato, whose ideal is not democratic but aristocratic, and not aristocratic for the benefit of the aristocrat alone, but for the good of everybody. It is interesting to compare the attitude of Saint-Simon, a humanitarian and a socialist, if ever there was one. Here is his motive: "The whole of society ought to strive towards the amelioration of the moral and physical existence of the poorest class; so-

[1] As is now the case. Cf. the article on Eugenics in Encyclopædia Britannica, 12th edition: and W. R. Inge, in *Edinburgh Review*, July, 1922.

[2] Cf. Nietzsche, "We Philologists": "How can one praise and glorify a nation as a whole? Even among the Greeks, it was the individuals that counted. . . . The object of mankind should lie in its highest individuals."

ciety ought to organize itself in the way best adapted for attaining this end." Yet Saint-Simon ends in an autocratic organization, with a social hierarchy based on men's capacities. But ideal aristocracy and ideal democracy meet when real distinctions are recognized for what they are worth, no more and no less, and "a man's a man for a' that." The difficulty is not one of theory but of practice; it is hard to reconcile the welfare of the whole of society with that of all its members, who do not always at any given moment fit into the artistic scheme so neatly as Plato would like.

In our attempt to discover the meaning of humanism we have found that it bears a very close relation to Greek and Roman culture. Nevertheless we have from time to time entertained the suspicion that there may be humanists quite outside the classical tradition. These are not humanists by education or by imitation, but humanists by luck or by the grace of God. They are more Greek than the deliberate imitators of the Greeks; for instead of reading about the Greeks they have lived their own experience, and their experience has sometimes been strangely like that of the Greeks. I have cited Benjamin Franklin; I might cite Abraham Lincoln, who derives little directly from Greek sources, and stands on his own feet. We must recognize a genuine type of character and attitude that seems almost spontaneously to show a humanistic bent. I, for one, should not dream of valuing these sturdy natural saplings less than the carefully grafted and pruned scions of Greek stock. If an American can instinctively act true to the underlying conditions of human life, adjusting the rights of work and leisure, of the one and the many, of change and permanence, of matter and mind, of reason and intuition, without realizing that he is treading on an ancient and a well-worn road, marked with signposts,— yes, and strewn with the bones of unhappy wayfarers,— I can only bless him for his innocence and wish him good luck. He is a nobler and a rarer creature than the humanist whose humanism is contained not under his own skin but within bindings of calf-skin. Rarer, I fear, he will be, because he is only the product of lucky chance. If one takes a chance of being "naturally Greek," one takes a considerable chance of being natural, but not Greek. That is why classical studies are still no roundabout course but actually a short cut. To the student of Greek letters we may say, as the younger Pliny wrote to his friend who was going out to govern the province of Achaia, *Cogita te missum . . . ad homines maxime homines.* For, indeed, no men have been more broadly human than the Greeks. To them most of the fundamental phases of human experience were known. We know more of many things than they did; we do not know a great deal more about the art of living. We know more of science, for example; yet much of what we think we know will be out of date in fifty years. Human nature has changed very little during the past three thousand years, the only part of human history that we really know; compared with the age of the universe, the period that includes Homer and ourselves is hardly a point of time. The span of our life is all too short a time in which to master the art of living, and every child begins at the beginning. Nature has allowed the growth of his body to recapitulate, in general, the evolution of human kind from lower forms; if man chooses, he can also to a large extent recapitulate with his unfolding mind and will the course of man's experience in the art of living. Thus he neither has to pass through the painfully slow development of all his ancestors, nor can he at once begin where his father left off; but he lives rapidly and intensely by his power of sympathy and understanding, and, it may be, finally adds a trifle from his own experience to the total of human experience.

Many who grant the value of ancient experience are impatient at the long years that have to be spent in order to know it even superficially; especially they are sceptical about the need of translating the very words of ancient authors. Why can we not as profitably read their words in a translation, or become acquainted with their subject-matter in works by modern authors? Certainly only a minority can hope to read Greek and Latin fluently; and certainly, too, it will always be important that modern thinkers interpret ancient experience, which is not always easy to understand or to appreciate. But we know men and their works only by living long with them and entering into their minds; and those who have more than average ability will wish to understand literature as fully as they can. Although the writings of some authors lose little by being translated into another language, there are others in which thought and forms are so intimately wedded that they can never be adequately translated. There are words that carry a train of associations which must be lost in another language; for words, unlike coins, are not provided with equivalents at accepted rates of exchange; they mean what men intend them to mean. Especially where human interests and values are involved translation aims not at mathematical equivalence but at sympathy and judgment. How can we translate ὕβρις or ἱμερόφωνος or *humanitas* or *pius*? Such words are not mere words, but are part and parcel of the life that they express. That is why the art of translation, real translation, is no negligible part of a humanistic training; it requires the utmost degree of sympathy and tact. Above all, great poetry cannot be really translated; like painting or any creative art, it is alive and speaks for itself, and it resents the liberties that the translator must take. There is a story that on a certain occasion, when Beethoven had played a new and unfamiliar sonata, a member of his audience, being puzzled by it, asked what it meant. Beethoven immediately played the sonata over again. "That," he said, "is what it means."

The humanist is willing to be patient. He is not over-ready for dogma and propaganda. He wants to know the facts, and he is willing to interpret them as far as he can; but he knows that in many matters there is room for more than one point of view. Martin Luther thought that his appeal to the Bible provided a final tribunal for all religious disputes; but the Bible has been interpreted so variously as to afford an apparent basis for very different sects. Of the historians Mitford and Grote, ostensibly dealing with the same body of materials, one wrote, as I have remarked, a Tory history of Greece, the other a eulogy of Greek democracy. During the Great War, Prussian and British classical scholars did not have the same outlook on life. Humanism must include something more than a set of data; it must include the power of interpretation and sympathy, and it must include tolerance. It seems to be by no means clear that men grow more like each other as they are more educated; and for the sake of the interest that comes from personality this is not to be regretted. We agree upon certain facts; we vary in the values that we set upon them. But humanistic education ought, if it is worth anything, to teach men their common inheritance and common standards of valuation at least so far that their differences will not prove wasteful or destructive; and it ought then to leave them to develop their personalities in their several ways.

In his attitude toward nature Socrates was a humanist: "The fields and the woods," he says, "have nothing to teach me; I learn my lessons from men." But this is incomplete humanism, like that of Samuel Johnson, who wrote in his Journal, of the Scotch Highlands, "Before me were high hills which by hindering the eye from ranging forced the mind to find entertainment for itself." Wordsworth wrote of his visit to these same Highlands, thirty years later, that his object was

> To cull contentment upon wildest shores
> And luxuries extract from bleakest moors.[1]

This is a truer type of humanism, based on a saner view of man's place in nature. Wordsworth, to be sure, sometimes fell into extravagances.

> One impulse from a vernal wood
> May teach you more of man,
> Of moral evil and of good,
> Than all the sages can.

To be brutally frank, the wood teaches nothing, though one may moralize quite profitably about it, if one does not trust too much to "one impulse." For an antidote let us take a remark by Viscount Grey, from a speech "in which he said that the love and appreciation and study of birds was something fresher and brighter than the second-hand interests and conventional amusements in which so many in this day try to live; that the pleasure of seeing and listening to them was purer and more lasting than any pleasures of excitement, and, in the long run, ' happier than personal success.' " [2] That, I take it, is genuine humanism, in which poet and scientist, Virgil and Lucretius, could well agree.

[1] The passage from Johnson and the first one by Wordsworth are quoted by E. S. Roscoe, "Johnson and Wordsworth in the Highlands," in *North American Review*, Nov., 1921.

[2] W. H. Hudson, *Birds and Man* (Duckworth, 1915), p. 33.

And here we come to the end of our inquiry into the meaning of humanism. It has seemed that humanism has a paradoxical aspect. Yes; humanism is a paradox, because life is a paradox. Man is an animal, yet he can govern his life partly in accordance with what he holds to be valuable; he lives in the present, yet he knows only the past. He has to reconcile his own will with that of others, the experience of science with the experience of religion. So humanism, which is nothing more or less than man's attempt to cope with all the conflicting currents of his experience, has to be as conservative as the facts and as radical as man's needs. Modern philosophers have often attempted elaborate schemes that should include and harmonize all forms of knowledge and activity. Among them, if I may speak boldly, I find Spencer and Comte one-sided; they have not sufficiently distinguished the spheres of scientific knowledge and of feeling and of creative energy. Spencer's scheme explains at once too little and too much; it accounts for all that it can on a single hypothesis, and then lumps together the misfits under the term "the Unknowable." Hegel's organization is too Procrustean, and leaves little room for future developments; one is suspicious of a scheme that shows all the pieces neatly in place with nothing left over. Bergson and James have brought us back to a sense of growth and of the infinite multiplicity of life; but they often leave us adrift in a fog without stars or compass. Among recent thinkers I find most help in Benedetto Croce, a mind aware of the long development of the past, conscious both of unity and of variety, both of fact and of value, and tracing in history the unfolding of a creative mind whose work is never finished and in which individuals participate.[1]

[1] The best introduction to Croce for the reader who knows no Italian is H. W. Carr, *The Philosophy of Benedetto Croce*. There are also translations of some of his works.

The work of the philosopher is not always easy to follow even when it is sound. Character and taste come not from precept alone, but by familiarity with example. For most of us the crowning experience in life is not pure thought but contact with personality. The Word must be made flesh, or we cannot know it. For most of us this means the experience of poetry, that by showing us the seen reminds us of the unseen; of love, that is always between possession and non-possession of the beloved; of religion, that ushers us into the immediate presence of a person. What humanism can do is to survey the paths that men have trod and are still treading, and to help them as wisely as it may to walk in the paths that will most surely lead them toward the light.

LIST OF BOOKS

LIST OF BOOKS

THESE lists are far from exhaustive. Preference is given to works that are easily accessible, and, of these, to books that are readable and intelligible to readers who are not expert classical scholars. In the arrangement of the individual lists an attempt has been made to place first the more general and popular works and those that deal with the phases of each subject that come chronologically first, and to pass from them to more specialized works; but it has not been possible to follow this principle consistently. Parts of some of the works included in the general list are cited again under special subjects; and other works are cited in footnotes to the text.

I. GENERAL

Dickinson, G. L. *The Greek View of Life*. Twelfth edition. Methuen, 1919.

Livingstone, R. W., editor. *The Legacy of Greece*. Oxford Univ. Press, 1921.

—— *The Greek Genius and its Meaning to Us*. Oxford Univ. Press, 1912.

Cooper, L., editor. *The Greek Genius and its Influence*. Yale Univ. Press, 1917.

Stobart, J. C. *The Glory that was Greece*. Sidgwick and Jackson, 1911.

Butcher, S. H. *Some Aspects of the Greek Genius*. Third edition. Macmillan, 1904.

—— *Harvard Lectures on Greek Subjects*. Macmillan, 1904.

Hardie, W. R. *Lectures on Classical Subjects*. Macmillan, 1903.

Abbott, E., editor. *Hellenica*. Rivingtons, 1880.

Smyth, H. W., editor. *Harvard Essays on Classical Subjects*. Houghton Mifflin Co., 1912.

Symonds, J. A. *Studies of the Greek Poets*. American edition, two vols. in one. Harpers. N.d.

Mahaffy, J. P. *Social Life in Greece*. Macmillan, 1890.

—— *What Have the Greeks Done for Modern Civilization?* Putnam's, 1909.

Translations of Greek authors generally; see the Loeb Series (Greek and English on opposite pages. Putnam's), and the list in Dickinson.

II. THE BACKGROUND OF GREEK LIFE: GEOGRAPHY

Zimmern, A. E. *The Greek Commonwealth*. Second edition. Oxford Univ. Press, 1915. Pp. 13–51.

Gulick, C. B. *The Life of the Ancient Greeks*. Appleton, 1907. Chapters 1 and 2.

Myres, J. L. *Greek Lands and the Greek People*. Oxford Univ. Press, 1910. Pp. 12–32.

Stobart, J. C. *The Glory that was Greece*. Sidgwick and Jackson, 1911. Pp. 3–11 (also reprinted in Cooper, *The Greek Genius*, etc.).

Allinson, F. G. and A. C. E. *Greek Lands and Letters*. Houghton Mifflin Co., 1909. (Pp. 12–31 are reprinted in Cooper).

Gardner, W. A. *In Greece with the Classics*. Little, Brown, 1908.

Newman, J. H. (Passages from Historical Sketches, reprinted in Cooper.)

Tozer, H. F. *Lectures on the Geography of Greece*. Murray, 1873.

Wordsworth, C. *Greece: Pictorial, Descriptive, and Historical*. Edited by H. F. Tozer. Murray, 1882.

Frazer, J. G. *Studies in Greek Scenery, Legend, and History*. Macmillan, 1919.

Felton, C. C. *Greece, Ancient and Modern*. Eighth edition. Houghton Mifflin Co., 1889.

Mahaffy, J. P. *Rambles and Studies in Greece*. Third edition. Macmillan, 1887.

Symonds, J. A. *Sketches and Studies in Italy and Greece*. Smith, Elder, 1898.

Fulleylove, J. *Greece*. (Illustrations in color by Fulleylove, text by J. A. M'Clymont.) A. and C. Black, 1906.

Ferriman, Z. D. *Greece and the Greeks*. J. Pott, 1910.

Rodd, J. R. *Customs and Lore of Modern Greece*. Stott, 1892.

Bædeker's Greece.

Articles on Greece (Geography and History) in Encyclopædia Britannica, eleventh and twelfth editions.

III. THE GREEKS IN HISTORY

Myres, J. L. *The Dawn of History.* (In Home University Library.) Holt, 1911.

Baikie, J. *The Sea Kings of Crete.* A. and C. Black, 1910.

Fowler, H. N., and Wheeler, J. R. *Handbook of Greek Archæology.* American Book Co., 1909.

Murray, G. *The Rise of the Greek Epic.* Second edition. Oxford Univ. Press, 1911.

Heath, R. M. *Achilles.* (Newdigate Prize Poem.) Blackwell, Oxford, 1911.

Bury, J. B. *History of Greece to the Death of Alexander the Great.* Macmillan, 1920.

Botsford, G. W. *Hellenic History.* Macmillan, 1923.

Grote, G. *History of Greece.* Various editions, Murray; also in Everyman's Library, Dutton; also abridged and revised edition (by J. M. Mitchell and M. O. B. Caspari), Routledge, 1907.

Holm, A. *History of Greece.* English translation. Macmillan, 1902–09.

Thomson, J. A. K. *Greeks and Barbarians.* Macmillan, 1921.

Ferguson, W. S. *Greek Imperialism.* Houghton Mifflin Co., 1913.

—— *Hellenistic Athens.* Macmillan, 1911.

Wheeler, B. I. *Alexander the Great.* Putnam's, 1900.

Finlay, G. *History of Greece.* Edited by H. F. Tozer. Oxford Univ. Press, 1877. (For the later periods.)

Articles on Modern Greek History in Encyclopædia Britannica. Eleventh and twelfth editions.

Davis, W. S. *Readings in Ancient History: Greece.* Allyn and Bacon, 1912.

Translations of:

Homer —

    Iliad, by Lang, Leaf, and Myers. Macmillan, 1911.

    Odyssey, by Butcher and Lang. Macmillan, 1912.

    —— by G. H. Palmer. Houghton Mifflin, rev. ed., 1921.

    Herodotus, by G. Rawlinson, in Everyman's Library. Dutton, 1910.

    Thucydides, by B. Jowett. Oxford Univ. Press, 1881; or by R. Crawley, in Everyman's Library. Dutton, n. d.

    Plutarch, by J. Dryden and others, revised by A. H. Clough, in Everyman's Library. Dutton, 1912.

IV. DAILY LIFE

Gulick, C. B. *The Life of the Ancient Greeks*. Appleton, 1907.

Mahaffy, J. P. *Social Life in Greece*. Macmillan, 1890.

Tucker, T. G. *Life in Ancient Athens*. Macmillan, 1906.

Zimmern, A. E. *The Greek Commonwealth*. Second edition. Oxford Univ. Press. Part III.

Gardiner, E. N. *Greek Athletic Sports and Festivals*. Macmillan, 1910.

Van Hook, L. R. "Was Athens in the Age of Pericles Aristocratic?" In *Classical Journal*, XIV, 8 (May, 1919).

Fiske, J. "Athenian and American Life." In *The Unseen World*. Houghton Mifflin Co., 1902.

Davis, W. S. *A Day in Old Athens*. Allyn and Bacon.

V. THE FINDING OF BEAUTY

1. ART AND LIFE

Dickinson, G. L. *The Greek View of Life*. Twelfth edition. Methuen, 1919. Chapter IV.

Haigh, A. E. Three passages from *The Attic Theatre*, reprinted under the title "The Attic Audience," in L. Cooper, *The Greek Genius and its Influence*. Yale Univ. Press, 1917.

Butcher, S. H. "The Written and the Spoken Word." In *Some Aspects of the Greek Genius*. Third edition. Macmillan, 1904.

—— "Art and Inspiration in Greek Poetry." In *Harvard Lectures on Greek Subjects*. Macmillan, 1904.

2. DIRECTNESS AND IDEALISM

Livingstone, R. W. "The Note of Directness." In *The Greek Genius and its Meaning to Us*. Oxford Univ. Press, 1912.

—— "Greek Literature." In *The Legacy of Greece*. Oxford Univ. Press, 1921.

Symonds, J. A. "Realism and Idealism." In *Essays, Speculative and Suggestive*. Third edition. Scribners, 1907.

Butcher, S. H. "The Dawn of Romanticism in Greek Poetry." In *Some Aspects of the Greek Genius*.

Stewart, J. A. *Plato's Doctrine of Ideas*. Oxford Univ. Press, 1909. Part II.

Butcher, S. H. *Aristotle's Theory of Poetry and Fine Art*, with a critical text and translation of the *Poetics*. Macmillan, 1902.

Greene, W. C. "Plato's View of Poetry." In *Harvard Studies in Classical Philology*, Vol. XXIX, 1918.

Cowl, R. P. *The Theory of Poetry in England*. Macmillan, 1914.

3. CONVENTION AND ORIGINALITY

Smyth, H. W. "Aspects of Greek Conservatism." In *Harvard Studies in Classical Philology*, Vol. XVII, 1906.

Harrison, J. E. *Ancient Art and Ritual*. (In Home University Library.) Holt, 1913.

Symonds, J. A. *Studies of the Greek Poets*. American edition, two vols. in one. Harpers. N.d.

Gardner, P. *The Principles of Greek Art*. Macmillan, 1914.

Butcher, S. H. "Sophocles" (pp. 104–132 of *Some Aspects*, etc.).

Leach, A. "Fatalism of the Greeks." In *American Journal of Philology*, Vol. XXXVI, 373–401; reprinted, with changes, in Cooper, under the title, "Fate and Free Will in Greek Literature."

Symonds, J. A. "On the Application of Evolutionary Principles to Art and Literature." In *Essays, Speculative and Suggestive*.

Lowes, J. L. *Convention and Revolt in Poetry*. Houghton Mifflin Co., 1919.

VI. INDIVIDUAL AND SOCIETY

Dickinson, G. L. *The Greek View of Life*. Twelfth edition. Methuen, 1919. Chapters III and IV.

Fowler, W. *The City State of the Greeks and Romans*. Macmillan, 1893.

Butcher, S. H. "The Greek Idea of the State." In *Some Aspects of the Greek Genius*. Third edition. Macmillan, 1904.

Adam, A. M. *Plato, Moral and Political Ideals*. Cambridge Univ. Press, 1913.

Nettleship, R. L. *Lectures on the Republic of Plato*. Macmillan, 1910.

—— "The Theory of Education in Plato's Republic." In *Hellenica*. Edited by E. Abbott. Rivingtons, 1880.

Bradley, A. C. "Aristotle's Conception of the State." In *Hellenica*.

Barker, E. *The Political Thought of Plato and Aristotle*. Putnam's, 1906.

—— *Greek Political Theory: Plato and His Predecessors*. Methuen, 1918.

Willoughby, W. *The Political Theories of the Ancient World*. Longmans, Green, 1903.

Bosanquet, B. *The Philosophical Theory of the State.* Second edition. Macmillan, 1910.

Seeley, Sir J. R. *Introduction to Political Science.* Macmillan, 1908.

Bagehot, W. *Physics and Politics.* Appleton, 1902.

Bosanquet, B., and others. "The Place of Experts in a Democracy." In *Proceedings of the Aristotelian Society,* 1909.

Bryce, Viscount. *Modern Democracies.* Macmillan, 1921.

VII. MAN AND THE UNIVERSE

1. MAN AND GOD

Dickinson, G. L. *The Greek View of Life.* Twelfth edition. Methuen, 1919. Chapter I.

Gayley, C. M. *The Classic Myths in English Literature and in Art.* Revised edition. Ginn, 1911.

Fiske, J. *Myths and Mythmakers.* Houghton Mifflin Co., 1902.

Lang, A. *Myth, Ritual, and Religion.* Longmans, 1906.

—— Article, "Mythology," in Encyclopædia Britannica.

Fairbanks, A. *A Handbook of Greek Religion.* American Book Co., 1910.

Harrison, J. E. *The Religion of Ancient Greece.* Constable, 1913.

—— *Prolegomena to the Study of the Greek Religion.* Cambridge Univ. Press, 1903.

Cornford, F. M. *From Religion to Philosophy.* Arnold, 1912.

Jevons, F. B. *Comparative Religion.* Putnam's, 1913.

Reinach, S. *Orpheus, a General History of Religions.* English translation. Putnam's, 1909.

Moore, G. F. *History of Religions.* Scribners, 1916–19.

Burnet, J. *Early Greek Philosophy.* Third edition. A. and C. Black, 1920.

Moore, C. H. *The Religious Thought of the Greeks, from Homer to the Triumph of Christianity.* Harvard Univ. Press, 1916.

Murray, G. *Four Stages of Greek Religion.* Columbia Univ. Press, 1912.

Adam, J. *The Religious Teachers of Greece.* Aberdeen Univ., 1909.

Campbell, L. *Religion in Greek Literature.* Longmans, Green, 1898.

Myers, F. W. H. "Greek Oracles." In *Hellenica.* Edited by E. Abbott. Rivingtons, 1880.

Smyth, H. W. "Greek Conceptions of Immortality from Homer to Plato." In *Harvard Essays on Classical Subjects.* Houghton Mifflin Co., 1012.

2. THE LAW OF THINGS

Benn, A. W. *The Greek Philosophers*. Second edition. Smith, Elder, 1914. Chapters I–III.

Burnet, J. *Greek Philosophy: Thales to Plato*. Macmillan, 1914. Introduction and Chapters I–VI.

Heath, Sir T. L. "Mathematics and Astronomy." In *The Legacy of Greece*. Edited by R. W. Livingstone. Oxford Univ. Press, 1921.

Thompson, D. W. "Natural Science." In *The Legacy of Greece*.

Singer, C. "Biology" and "Medicine." In *The Legacy of Greece*.

3. THE LAW OF MAN

Benn, A. W. *The Greek Philosophers*. Chapters IV–XIV.

Taylor, A. E. *Plato*. Constable, 1911.

Pater, W. *Plato and Platonism*. Macmillan, 1894.

Shorey, P. *The Unity of Plato's Thought*. Univ. of Chicago Press, 1903.

Nettleship, R. L. *Lectures on the Republic of Plato*. Macmillan, 1910.

Schiller, F. C. S. *Plato or Protagoras?* Blackwell, Oxford, 1908.

Parker, C. P. "Plato and Pragmatism." In *Harvard-Essays on Classical Subjects*. Houghton Mifflin Co., 1912.

Taylor, A. E. *Aristotle*. T. C. and E. C. Jack, 1919.

Moore, C. H. *The Religious Thought of the Greeks*. Harvard Univ. Press, 1916.

—— "Greek and Roman Ascetic Tendencies." In *Harvard Essays on Classical Subjects*.

Adam, J. *The Religious Teachers of Greece*. Aberdeen Univ., 1909.

Smyth, H. W. *Greek Conceptions of Immortality*. In *Harvard Essays on Classical Subjects*.

Murray, G. "The Stoic Philosophy." In *Tradition and Progress*. Houghton Mifflin Co., 1922. Also published separately, Putnam's, 1915.

4. THE GREEKS AND CHRISTIANITY

Fairbanks, A. *A Handbook of Greek Religion*. American Book Co., 1910. Pp. 288–293.

Temple, W. *Plato and Christianity*. Macmillan, 1906.

Adam, J. *The Religious Teachers of Greece*. Aberdeen Univ., 1909.

Moore, C. H. *The Religious Thought of the Greeks*. Harvard Univ. Press, 1916.

Hatch, E. *The Influence of Greek Ideas and Usages upon the Christian Church*. Eighth edition. Williams and Norgate, 1901.

Foakes-Jackson, F. J., and Lake, K. *The Beginnings of Christianity*. Part I, Vol. I. Macmillan, 1920.

VIII. THE MEANING OF HUMANISM

Cooper, L. *The Greek Genius and its Influence.* Yale Univ. Press, 1917. The Introduction.

Butcher, S. H. "What We Owe to Greece," and "The Unity of Learning." In *Some Aspects of the Greek Genius.* Third edition. Macmillan, 1904.

Mahaffy, J. P. *What Have the Greeks Done for Modern Civilization?* Putnam's, 1909.

Murray, G. "Greece and the Progress of Man." (Chapter I, pp. 21–49) of *The Rise of the Greek Epic.* Second edition. Oxford Univ. Press, 1911.

—— *Tradition and Progress.* Houghton Mifflin Co., 1922. Especially "Religio Grammatici," and "Literature as Revelation."

—— "The Value of Greece to the Future of the World." In *The Legacy of Greece.* Edited by R. W. Livingstone. Oxford Univ. Press, 1921.

Livingstone, R. W. "The Note of Humanism." In *The Greek Genius and its Meaning to Us.* Oxford Univ. Press, 1912.

Fowler, W. *Social Life at Rome in the Age of Cicero.* Macmillan, 1909. Pp. 103–121, 168–203.

Rand, E. K. "The Classics in European Education." In *Latin and Greek in American Education.* Edited by F. W. Kelsey. Macmillan, 1911. Also reprinted in Cooper.

Symonds, J. A. *The Renaissance in Italy: The Age of the Despots.* Scribners, 1906. Chapter I.

Gordon, G. S., editor. *English Literature and the Classics.* Oxford Univ. Press, 1912.

Tucker, T. G. *The Foreign Debt of English Literature.* Bell, 1907.

Murray, G. "What English Poetry May Still Learn from Greek." In *Essays and Studies by Members of the English Association,* Vol. III. Edited by W. P. Ker. Oxford Univ. Press, 1912.

Proceedings of the Classical Association of England and Wales. Presidential Addresses:

      Sir W. Osler (1919). *The Old Humanities and the New Science.*

      G. Murray (1918). *Religio Grammatici.* (Also published in *Tradition and Progress.*)

      Viscount Bryce (1917). *The Worth of Ancient Literature for the Modern World.*

Marvin, F. S., editor. *Progress and History.* Oxford Univ. Press, 1916.

Symonds, J. A. "The Philosophy of Evolution." In *Essays, Speculative and Suggestive.* Third edition. Scribners, 1907.

INDEX

INDEX